The Chinese Fashion Industry

Dress, Body, Culture

Series Editor: **Joanne B. Eicher,** *Regents' Professor, University of Minnesota*

Advisory Board:
Ruth Barnes, *Ashmolean Museum, University of Oxford*
James Hall, *University of Illinois at Chicago*
Ted Polhemus, *Curator, "Street Style" Exhibition, Victoria and Albert Museum*
Griselda Pollock, *University of Leeds*
Valerie Steele, *The Museum at the Fashion Institute of Technology*
Lou Taylor, *University of Brighton*
John Wright, *University of Minnesota*

Books in this provocative series seek to articulate the connections between culture and dress, which is defined here in its broadest possible sense as any modification or supplement to the body. Interdisciplinary in approach, the series highlights the dialogue between identity and dress, cosmetics, coiffure and body alterations as manifested in practices as varied as plastic surgery, tattooing, and ritual scarification. The series aims, in particular, to analyze the meaning of dress in relation to popular culture and gender issues and will include works grounded in anthropology, sociology, history, art history, literature, and folklore.

ISSN: 1360–466X

Previously Published in the Series

Helen Bradley Foster, *"New Raiments of Self": African American Clothing in the Antebellum South*
Claudine Griggs, *S/he: Changing Sex and Changing Clothes*
Michaele Thurgood Haynes, *Dressing Up Debutantes: Pageantry and Glitz in Texas*
Anne Brydon and Sandra Niessen, *Consuming Fashion: Adorning the Transnational Body*
Dani Cavallaro and Alexandra Warwick, *Fashioning the Frame: Boundaries, Dress and the Body*
Judith Perani and Norma H. Wolff, *Cloth, Dress and Art Patronage in Africa*
Linda B. Arthur, *Religion, Dress and the Body*
Paul Jobling, *Fashion Spreads: Word and Image in Fashion Photography*
Fadwa El Guindi, *Veil: Modesty, Privacy and Resistance*
Thomas S. Abler, *Hinterland Warriors and Military Dress: European Empires and Exotic Uniforms*
Linda Welters, *Folk Dress in Europe and Anatolia: Beliefs about Protection and Fertility*
Kim K. P. Johnson and Sharron J. Lennon, *Appearance and Power*
Barbara Burman, *The Culture of Sewing*
Annette Lynch, *Dress, Gender and Cultural Change*
Antonia Young, *Women Who Become Men*
David Muggleton, *Inside Subculture: The Postmodern Meaning of Style*
Nicola White, *Reconstructing Italian Fashion: America and the Development of the Italian Fashion Industry*
Brian J. McVeigh, *Wearing Ideology: The Uniformity of Self-Presentation in Japan*
Shaun Cole, *Don We Now Our Gay Apparel: Gay Men's Dress in the Twentieth Century*
Kate Ince, *Orlan: Millennial Female*
Nicola White and Ian Griffiths, *The Fashion Business: Theory, Practice, Image*
Ali Guy, Eileen Green and Maura Banim, *Through the Wardrobe: Women's Relationships with Their Clothes*
Linda B. Arthur, *Undressing Religion: Commitment and Conversion from a Cross-Cultural Perspective*
William J. F. Keenan, *Dressed to Impress: Looking the Part*
Joanne Entwistle and Elizabeth Wilson, *Body Dressing*
Leigh Summers, *Bound to Please: A History of the Victorian Corset*
Paul Hodkinson, *Goth: Identity, Style and Subculture*
Leslie W. Rabine, *The Global Circulation of African Fashion*
Michael Carter, *Fashion Classics from Carlyle to Barthes*
Sandra Niessen, Ann Marie Leshkowich and Carla Jones, *Re-Orienting Fashion: The Globalization of Asian Dress*
Kim K. P. Johnson, Susan J. Torntore and Joanne B. Eicher, *Fashion Foundations: Early Writings on Fashion and Dress*
Helen Bradley Foster and Donald Clay Johnson, *Wedding Dress Across Cultures*
Eugenia Paulicelli, *Fashion under Fascism: Beyond the Black Shirt*
Charlotte Suthrell, *Unzipping Gender: Sex, Cross-Dressing and Culture*
Irene Guenther, *Nazi Chic? Fashioning Women in the Third Reich*
Yuniya Kawamura, *The Japanese Revolution in Paris Fashion*
Patricia Calefato, *The Clothed Body*
Ruth Barcan, *Nudity: A Cultural Anatomy*
Samantha Holland, *Alternative Femininities: Body, Age and Identity*
Alexandra Palmer and Hazel Clark, *Old Clothes, New Looks: Second Hand Fashion*
Yuniya Kawamura, *Fashion-ology: An Introduction to Fashion Studies*
Regina A. Root, *The Latin American Fashion Reader*
Linda Welters and Patricia A. Cunningham, *Twentieth-Century American Fashion*
Jennifer Craik, *Uniforms Exposed: From Conformity to Transgression*
Alison L. Goodrum, *The National Fabric: Fashion, Britishness, Globalization*
Annette Lynch and Mitchell D. Strauss, *Changing Fashion: A Critical Introduction to Trend Analysis and Meaning*
Catherine M. Roach, *Stripping, Sex and Popular Culture*
Marybeth C. Stalp, *Quilting: The Fabric of Everyday Life*
Jonathan S. Marion, *Ballroom: Culture and Costume in Competitive Dance*
Dunja Brill, *Goth Culture: Gender, Sexuality and Style*
Joanne Entwistle, *The Aesthetic Economy of Fashion: Markets and Value in Clothing and Modelling*
Juanjuan Wu, *Chinese Fashion: From Mao to Now*
Brent Luvaas, *DIY Style: Fashion, Music and Global Cultures*

The Chinese Fashion Industry

An Ethnographic Approach

Jianhua Zhao

B L O O M S B U R Y

LONDON · NEW DELHI · NEW YORK · SYDNEY

Bloomsbury Academic
An imprint of Bloomsbury Publishing Plc

50 Bedford Square
London
WC1B 3DP
UK

175 Fifth Avenue
New York
NY 10010
USA

www.bloomsbury.com

First published 2013

British Library Cataloguing-in-Publication Data
A catalogue record for this book is available from the British Library.

ISBN	978 1 84788 936 2 (Cloth)
	978 1 84788 935 5 (Paper)
e-ISBN	978 1 84788 938 6 (epub)
	978 0 85785 302 8 (ePDF)

Library of Congress Cataloging-in-Publication Data

Zhao, Jianhua.
The Chinese fashion industry : an ethnographic approach / Jianhua Zhao.
p. cm. — (Dress, body, culture)
Includes bibliographical references and index.
ISBN 978-1-84788-935-5 (alk. paper) — ISBN 978-1-84788-936-2
(alk. paper) — ISBN 978-1-84788-938-6 (alk. paper) —
ISBN 978-0-85785-302-8 (alk. paper)   1. Clothing trade—China.
2. Fashion design—China.   3. Fashion merchandising—China.
4. China—Economic conditions.   5. China–Social conditions.   I. Title.
HD9940.C62Z54 2013
338.4'76870951—dc23   2012033165

Typeset by Apex CoVantage, LLC
Printed and bound in the UK

Contents

List of Illustrations

To Xiao Yin, Sophy, and Evelyn Zhao

Acknowledgements

This book reflects an intellectual journey that spans roughly a decade. In the course of this journey, I have accumulated many intellectual and personal debts, without which this book would not have seen the light of day.

During the field research for this book, which was mostly conducted in 2004 and followed by several visits from 2009 to 2011, I benefited from numerous professionals in the Chinese fashion industry who kindly shared their insights and experiences with me. In order to protect their identities, I used pseudonyms in the book for all my interlocutors, except Mr. Chen Yifei, who passed away in 2005. I want to express my sincere gratitude for their help, along with the assistance of many other individuals who facilitated my field research in important ways. They introduced me to their friends and colleagues, opened doors for me to otherwise exclusive social circles and events, allowed me to shadow them on trips to factories and shopping malls, or shared with me their photographs. In alphabetical order of their last names, these individuals include Bao Mingxin , Anthony Bednall, Bian Xiangyang, Christopher Brennan, Chen Hua, Chen Yifei, Chen Yiming, Mark Cheung, Ding Xiaowen, Kenneth Fong, Gu Qingliang, Ge Xinhong, Jiang Huifen, Liu Canming, Liu Hejia, Liu Qing, Liu Ting, Liu Xiaogang, Ma Renhe, Miao Hongbing, Pan Kunrou, Qing Xiaoping, Song Xiaoxian, Su Jing, Tan Zhijia, Tian Zhanguo, Wang Guoqing, Wang Meng, Wang Xinyuan, Wang Tonghui, Wang Yiyang, Wei Lin, Wei Zengqiang, Wu Haiyan, Wu Minshan, Wu Xuekai, Xia Qihong, Xiao Nan, Xu Mifang, Xu Ye, Xuan Yanni, Yang Bo, Marjorie Yang, Yang Yixiong, Ye Yin, Yu Xinlian, Yu Ying, Zhang Li, Zhang Luyin, Zhou Hong, Zhang Zhifeng, and Zoe Zheng. Together, they made my field stay in China not just an enlightening experience, but also that much more fun. I truly regret any omissions due to the lapse of my memory.

The writing of this book began as a doctoral dissertation, the completion of which was peppered with the advice and suggestions of my doctoral committee at the University of Pittsburgh, including Professors Joseph Alter, Nicole Constable, Evelyn Rawski, Harry Sanabria, and Andrew Strathern. Drs. Alter, Constable, Sanabria, and Strathern provided important inputs on relevant anthropological theories and studies that informed this book. Dr. Rawski, as an East Asian historian with incredibly diverse interests, was especially helpful with historical and current sources on Chinese clothing. My mentor,

Dr. Nicole Constable, has been there for me every step of the way. She oversaw the initial project design, corresponded with me during my field research, read and edited various drafts of the dissertation, and offered ample suggestions each time. For this project and the entire duration of my graduate study, I have benefitted from her penetrating insights, fine editorial skills, warm friendship, professionalism, wisdom, and patience. Being born and raised in China, my completion of the dissertation and graduate school in Pittsburgh was not just an intellectual journey, but also a personal one. A French–Canadian anthropologist, David Guilbault, a friend who brought me to anthropology when I was an undergraduate student assisting him with his field research in China, once told me that learning a foreign culture was like being born again. Through the completion of this book and especially my years in graduate school, I came to fully appreciate Mr. Guilbault's analogy as I experienced intellectual growth and simultaneously learned the American way of life. For that, I want to sincerely thank Nicole and all the professors and friends at Pitt who made this life-altering experience a memorable and enjoyable one.

Several institutions and funding agencies provided financial support for this project at various stages, for which I am grateful. An exploratory field trip to China was supported by the Department of Anthropology at the University of Pittsburgh in 2002. My year-long field research in 2004 was funded by the Wenner-Gren Foundation. The writing of my dissertation, on which this book is based, was supported by the Provost Development Fund at the University of Pittsburgh and the Chiang Ching-kuo Foundation for International Scholarly Exchange. My follow-up research from 2009 to 2011 was supported by internal grants of the Department of Anthropology and the University of Louisville. A subvention fund from the University of Louisville also helped defray the cost of producing the index and the editing of some images.

I would like to express my appreciation for the editors and the production team at Berg Publishers for their hard work to bring the book into publication. Joanne Eicher, Series Editor of Dress, Body, and Culture, was the first to see the value of the book in dress studies. Her vast contribution to dress studies has always been a source of inspiration for me. Anna Wright, Senior Commissioning Editor at Berg, oversaw this book project. She has given great attention to this project and helped, among many things, with choosing a stunning cover design for this book. I would also like to thank three anonymous reviewers for Berg. Their comments and suggestions (as well as the suggestions of my doctoral committee) have made this book better. However, should there be any errors in the contents of the book, I am solely responsible. My research assistant, Brittany Saltsman, helped with creating the bibliography using End-Note. Victor Simon provided help with some editing of the photographs used in the book.

Finally, my heartfelt thanks go to my family. During the research and writing of this book, my two daughters, Sophy and Evelyn, were born. I am sorry for all the time I spent away from them on this project. In the meantime, my wife, Xiao Yin, had to do more than her share of the household chores and caring for our little ones. But her support went far beyond the family and emotional level; her numerous conversations with me on the topic of Chinese clothing have been the driving force for writing this book from the very beginning. She was also my first reader and editor of early drafts. To her and our lovely daughters, I dedicate this book.

Introduction

TWO VIGNETTES

On a sultry summer day in Beijing in 2002, I was riding a taxi to a department store near Wangfujing. The store sold traditional Chinesestyle clothing, in which I was interested as part of my research on Chinese clothing styles. Suddenly, the taxi driver, a man in his forties, started yelling, "*Ji* (hooker)! *Ji*! [That] must be a *ji*." Guided by his angry finger, I saw a tall slender young Chinese woman wearing a glaringly red backless silk halter-top secured with only two strings in the back, marching confidently down the street. I couldn't help but be wowed by the young woman's attire, though not in the same manner as the taxi driver, whose visceral reaction left no doubt of what he thought of the wearer's sense of morality and modesty in her choice of fashion style.

The style of clothing that the woman was wearing in fact has a name; it is called the *dudou* (literally meaning stomach cover) in Chinese, and it was traditionally an undergarment made of a piece of red cloth. As an undergarment, it functioned as a protective cover from the cold for the chest and navel. Because it is typically red, traditional folk beliefs say it has the power to ward off evil spirits.[1] But wearing the *dudou* as outerwear outdoors was unheard of and even unthinkable, either in imperial China (before 1912) or during the Maoist period (1949–78). As a matter of fact, only a little over two decades ago, the fashion scene in China was largely dominated by the nearly ubiquitous unisex Mao style *zhongshanzhuang* (also known as the Mao suit). As an American-trained anthropologist who had a research interest in Chinese clothing, this incident was revealing, pardon the pun, of the conflict between modern fashion and traditional attitudes toward clothing. As a native-born Chinese, I was caught up in the conflicting attitudes and was very much taken aback by the bold appearance of the *dudou* as a fashion item, even though I had previous learned, somewhat doubtfully, from fashion magazines and news reports that wearing the *dudou* as an outer garment had recently become a fashion in urban China.

Another event during my field research was perhaps less dramatic, but equally surprising. It was during China Fashion Week in Beijing in the fall of 2004, where I accidentally met Zheng Yifan (pseudonym),[2] Chief Designer of a medium-size private company based in Dalian city. Upon learning her profession, I introduced myself as an American-trained anthropologist who was interested in Chinese clothing and fashion and requested an interview with her. She agreed to meet with me in two days in the Starbucks shop in the hotel in which China Fashion Week was held. When I went there at the scheduled time, I found Zheng Yifan was still in a meeting with her colleagues in one corner of the crowded coffee shop. I looked for seats near her so that I could wait for her to finish her meeting, but I was disappointed to find that the table next to them was occupied by a group of young, smartly dressed, Caucasian women, whom I assumed to be foreign tourists. At the same time, Yifan saw me and gestured at me to go over as one of her colleagues dragged a seat for me from another table. As I sat down, she told me that she was interviewing models for the photo shoot of her spring collection and that the interview would be soon over. For a second, I wondered who the models would be, but quickly found out as one of Yifan's colleagues called a white woman from the table next to us to come over. As it turned out, those smartly dressed young women beside us were all fashion models from East Europe. While flipping through the portfolio of the models, Yifan commented that she was not really impressed by the candidates the modeling agency selected for her and that there were many good models from Russia and East Europe who came to China to look for work these days.

My encounters with the *dudou* and Zheng Yifan's interview of East European models are some of the incidents that have stuck with me throughout my field research in China. They constantly remind me of the dramatic extent of changes that Chinese clothing and the fashion industry have undergone in the past thirty years. I still remember when I was little, a time when China was still in a shortage economy, in order to get new clothes for me, my parents had to first use government-issued coupons (*bupiao*) to buy the cloth needed, then went to a tailor with the fabric to have the clothes made. The practice of cloth rationing was not officially abandoned in China until December 1983. Back then, ready-made clothing was not widely available, and clothing styles were rather limited and largely represented by the Mao style *zhongshanzhuang*.

By contrast, China today is not only home to one of the largest clothing markets in the world, it also supplies about a quarter to one-third of all the garments sold worldwide. Clothing styles have become increasingly diverse; even vanguard styles such as the *dudou* are readily seen on the streets of urban China. Fashion design has become a prestigious profession and a domestic fashion industry has emerged and is thriving.

This book is about changes in Chinese clothing and the fashion industry, especially from the 1980s to the present, but it is also about the broad social, political, and economic changes that have taken place in contemporary China. More specifically, it addresses three major questions: How did the phenomenal changes in Chinese clothing and the fashion industry come into being? What are the implications of these changes for the professionals such as fashion designers who work in the industry? And what can these changes tell us about the macro processes of modernization and globalization in China? In this chapter, I will provide some clarification of the terminologies I use in the book. Then, I will explain my field sites and research methods, as well as why I adopt a cultural economy approach in this book. In the end, I will provide some background information of the economic reforms in the post-Mao period, which is followed by an overview of the book.

DRESS, CLOTHING, FASHION

In the English language, there are many synonyms for clothing: clothes, out-fit, garb, attire, wear, garment, apparel, costume, fashion, dress, and so on. In fact, I will be using many of these terms in different contexts throughout this book. Do I use them to refer to the same thing? Not exactly, nor do most scholars of clothing or practitioners in the industry use them interchangeably as if they mean precisely the same thing. While many scholars in the social sciences use "dress" as the most comprehensive term, as in dress studies and dress historians, practitioners in the industry generally use *clothing* or *fashion* as the most comprehensive term, which includes dress, by which they mean a type of formal wear for women.

What, then, do scholars in social sciences, especially anthropologists, mean by *dress*? Joanne Eicher and Mary Ellen Roach-Higgins give an explicit and concise definition as follows:

> [W]e have been intentionally supporting use of the word 'dress' as a comprehen-sive term to identify both direct body changes and items added to the body . . . we define dress as an assemblage of body modifications and/or supplements dis-played by a person in communicating with other human beings. (1997: 15)

According to this definition, *dress* not only includes clothing or body covering, accessories or adornments, but also bodily modification, such as tattoos, piercing, scarification, and so on.

The intellectual merit of this definition of dress cannot be understated, for Eicher and Roach-Higgins have systematically and thoroughly surveyed earlier anthropological literature and identified the pitfalls in the dichotomous treat-ment of clothing and adornments. Because of the strength of this definition, Fadwa El Guindi hails Eicher and Roach-Higgins's work as having paved the ground for the "anthropology of dress" (El Guindi 1999: 49–57). While I agree with this assessment and recognize that dress is probably the best term that captures comprehensively all body coverings, supplements, and modifications humans add onto their bodies,[3] the scope of this book is limited to one aspect of dress—It is about clothing or body covering, not so much about accessories, and not at all about bodily modification. This by no means suggests that accessories and bodily modifications are not important or should not be included in the study of dress, but is only to situate this study of Chinese clothing and fashion in the broader study of dress. In general, I use clothing, garment, and apparel interchangeably, although I tend to use garment or apparel to refer to mass-produced clothing. I also treat outfit, garb, and attire as synonyms that refer to a particular dress or style.

However, I recognize that there is an important distinction between clothing and fashion which is made clear by sociologist Yuniya Kawamura. She points out that "fashion as a concept means something more than [clothing] because it signifies additional and alluring values attached to clothing, which are enticing to consumers of 'fashion'" (Kawamura 2005:4). In addition to the extra value of fashion, the term also has the connotation of change. Kawamura writes:

> No matter which time period in history one is talking about, the definite essence of fashion is change. The fashion process explains the diversity and changes of styles. . . In some societies, where the dominant ideology is antipathetic to social change and progress, fashion cannot exist. (2005: 5)

Following Kawamura, I acknowledge that *fashion* contains elements of change whereas *clothing* does not necessarily do so. However, I do not believe ideology is the sole factor that precludes or gives rise to fashion change. For example, Aubrey Cannon's study of the North American fur trade provides clear evidence of frequent style change in beads and cloth worn by the Native Americans, a traditional society that was generally assumed not to have fashion (Cannon 1998). She points out that personal charisma, uncontrolled influx of resources, rapid population increase or decrease, political power shift, as well as industrial production and image distribution, are all factors or contexts that can give rise to emulation and differentiation in fashion. Cannon thus distinguishes the fashion process from the fashion industry: The former exists in all human societies, but the latter exists only in modern industrialized societies (Cannon 1998: 25). Despite their differences, Cannon and Kawamura would both agree that change is essential to fashion. Moreover, both Cannon's broader notion of "fashion process" and Kawamura's narrower definition of fashion are relevant to the context of China. In some historical periods such as the Maoist era, clothing styles were relatively stable, and fashion existed in the form of fashion processes that differentiated individuals or groups, similar to Cannon's findings among the Native Americans. But these fashion processes in the Maoist era were often individualized or random and not widespread or systemic enough to be conducive to the rise of the fashion industry. The latter only came into being in the reform era. Therefore, in this book I use fashion as a marked term and in the narrower sense as indicated by Kawamura, and clothing as an unmarked term that broadly includes fashion. The subject of this book, Chinese clothing and the fashion industry, is also used in this narrower sense of fashion.

FIELD SITES AND METHODOLOGY

This book is primarily based on fifteen months of field research that I conducted mostly in Shanghai and Beijing, but also in the Zhejiang and Jiangsu areas near Shanghai, from May to July in 2002 and from January to December in 2004. In the summers of 2009, 2010, and 2011, I returned to Shanghai and Zhejiang and renewed my contact with some of the people I interviewed in 2002 and 2004. I chose Shanghai as the main field site because it is the largest and arguably the most fashionable city in China. It is also the birthplace of China's textile industry, and enjoys a high concentration of fashion companies, fashion media, and colleges and universities that offer programs related to fashion. During 2004, I visited Beijing three times, mainly because it is the host city of China Fashion Week, the most important fashion event in China. While in Beijing, I also visited the headquarters of the China Fashion Association and its parent organization, the China National Textile Industry Council, where I interviewed some officials and collected some archival data. In addition, I interviewed journalists from two major newspapers in the industry and collected archival materials from *Zhongguo fushi bao* (*China Fashion Weekly*). Besides the two main sites of Shanghai and Beijing, I also took five field trips to visit factories in the Zhejiang and Jiangsu areas that manufacture garments both for domestic and international markets.

During my field research, I employed a number of research techniques. First, utilizing contacts established in 2002, I conducted participant observation at one private designer fashion company in Shanghai for over a month in 2004, which was followed by intermittent return visits throughout the year. During my field research at the company, I was given office space as a researcher. I observed the entire design process for a seasonal collection, from sketching to finished sample garments. I shadowed the chief designer to shopping malls, trade fairs, meetings with sales representatives of fabrics, and various departments within the company to ensure the design and production of the perfect products. I also interviewed executives and workers in each department of the company.

I attended over 100 fashion shows of various sorts in different venues, including shows on college campuses, internal shows inside fashion companies for their wholesale buyers (*kanhuohui*), fashion shows in shopping malls and at trade fairs, and most importantly shows during Shanghai Fashion Week and China Fashion Week. Those fashion shows not only allowed me to observe new fashion designs and trends, the overall characteristics of fashion shows in China, but also provided me the best opportunities to meet and interview fashion designers and other professionals in the industry. This leads to the third research method—interviews.

By interviews, I mean semi-structured interviews that were pre-arranged and for which I prepared an interview guide. The host designers of the fashion shows typically had time for interviews with the media after the show. During Shanghai Fashion Week in 2004, I was granted a media pass by the organizer of the event and was able to meet and interview many designers just like a fashion reporter. Because the fashion weeks attracted many fashion designers and other professionals in the industry, I was able to meet and interview many fashion designers who were in attendance at those events. I also interviewed fashion designers away from the fashion weeks, in their offices as well as outside their workplace, generally through pre-arrangement by myself or through personal friends or acquaintances. These interviews snowballed into more introductions and opportunities for interviews.

In addition to fashion designers, I also interviewed other professionals in the industry, including models, journalists, business executives, trade agents, and university professors. In total, I have conducted semi-structured interviews with about 120 professionals in China's fashion and clothing industry during my field research, but I have met and conversed informally with a much larger number of Chinese professionals in the industry. Participant observation allowed me to see firsthand how fashion was designed and produced, but the semi-structured interviews with fashion designers and other fashion professionals provided me with opportunities to gain deeper insights into their views and approaches toward their work or businesses.

Among the other fashion professionals that I interviewed were international trade agents whom I met through personal friends. I shadowed several trade agents on field trips to visit factories in Zhejiang and Jiangsu provinces to inspect the facilities, monitor the production of the garments, and audit the factories in order to ensure the factories' compliance with local labor laws and the foreign buyers' codes of conduct. During those visits, we were given tours of the entire assembly lines of the factories, the cafeterias, and the dormitories of the workers, who were predominantly migrants from poor rural areas in nearby provinces or inland China. I also gained knowledge of garment manufacturing by accompanying Professor Gu Qingliang[4] (of Donghua University) and his team to Ningbo City, Zhejiang province, in their field trip to several factories for a research project on the competitiveness of the garment industry of Ningbo city. Although I did not initiate these field trips, they allowed me to observe and meet with various groups of people who are connected to the fashion industry.

In addition to the field research, I also conducted archival research in libraries at Donghua University, Shanghai Library, Capital Library (formerly known as Beijing Library), as well as in several organizations related to the textile and clothing industry, in order to investigate the development of China's textile and clothing industries, changes in national organizations of the industries, and the evolution of clothing styles in contemporary China. I use the term archive in a broad sense, which includes internal documents I obtained from the China National Textile Industry Council and China Fashion Association, the Textile Industry Almanacs, statistical yearbooks, academic publications, and other textual documents including fashion magazines and newspapers. The archival research allowed me to gain knowledge of how China's textile and apparel industries evolved to what they are today and to sort through the changes of clothing styles in contemporary China, which I will discuss in detail in Chapters 2 and 3 respectively.

THE CULTURAL ECONOMY OF THE CHINESE FASHION INDUSTRY

Through my interactions with Chinese professors in the field of textile and clothing, it is evident that there exists a dichotomy between culture and economy in the Chinese higher education institutions of textile and garments. Take Donghua University in Shanghai (formerly known as China Textile University) for example. It has two separate schools that are relevant to my research (there are other schools and departments at the university, many of which deal with the technical aspects of textile and clothing): the School of Garments (*Fuzhuang xueyuan*) and the School of Management (*Guanli xueyuan*). The former focuses on the cultural aspects of clothing, such as art history, fashion design, and modeling, and the latter contains programs that specialize in the business aspects of clothing, including management and marketing. The two schools have separate faculty and library collections. From my interviews and interactions with faculty members from both schools, I could see clear differences in their views and approaches to clothing. In the School of Management, clothing is seen as a commodity and sometimes an image that is a part of the commodity; in the School of Garments, on the other hand, clothing is considered an artifact, a sign, or a representation, which parallels the tradition of art history, design, and ethno-historical studies of clothing (e.g., Huang and Chen 1995; Lin et al. 2000; Shen 1997; Yang 1999; Yuan 1994; Zhou and Gao 1984).[5] The differences between clothing commodity and clothing as an artifact mirror the broad perception of culture and economy as two separate and autonomous fields.[6] According to sociologist Paul du Gay (1997), the contrast between "culture" and "economy" could not be sharper. He writes:

> Certainly there is a powerful tradition of thought which holds that 'culture'—
> and this normally means 'high' culture—is an autonomous realm of existence
> dedicated to the pursuit of particular values—'art,' 'beauty,' 'authenticity' and
> 'truth'—which are the very antithesis of those assumed to hold sway in the banal
> world of the economy—the pursuit of profit, unbounded 'instrumentalism' and so
> on. (du Gay 1997: 1)

Anthropologists, however, have traditionally treated *economy* as a part of a total way of life or culture of a small-scale and relatively bounded society. Economy in this type of society amounts to the ways in which people make a living, which is integrated with other aspects of the culture. In later decades, this holistic view of culture and economy gave way to divergent approaches to culture and economy. The interpretive turn in anthropology in the 1970s has shifted the emphasis of anthropology from human behavior and social structure to symbols, meanings, and mentality. According to Clifford Geertz, a prominent advocate of interpretive anthropology, the job of an anthropologist is to conduct thick description of the local context in order to gain insights into the local knowledge of local cultural meanings (1973b: 3–30, 1983). At the same time, anthropologists who are inspired by Karl Marx adopt a political-economic approach to anthropology that focuses on various dimensions of power and inequality in human society.[7]

However, in the late 1980s and early 1990s, anthropology faced rigorous challenge and questioning from postmodernism (Marcus & Fischer 1986). Postmodernist anthropologists asked: How can anthropology, a discipline that was established on the basis of studies of small-scale and relatively bounded societies, retain its relevance in an increasingly globalized and interdependent world? And how can anthropologists reconcile the local cultural meanings learned through cultural interpretations with the external and frequently global political and economic forces that have shaped and even penetrated the life-worlds of practically every local community in the world? As Marcus and Fischer point out, in responding to the postmodernist critique, a growing number of anthropologists are trying to bring together the two previously plowed and separate furrows of interpretive anthropology and historical political economy to inform their research (1986: 44). For example, Jane Schneider (1994) shows that the changes in popularity or unpopularity of polyester in the United States were not merely a matter of consumers' preference or taste but also deeply linked to the fierce competition among global fiber manufacturers and their connections to politics.

My use of a cultural economy approach in this book reflects my intention to bring together interpretive and political economic analyses of Chinese clothing and the fashion industry. More importantly, it is based on what I have learned during my field research in China, which began at Donghua University.

The reason why I was interested in the University's School of Garment and School of Management was that they contain knowledge and information critical to my research subjects—the practitioners in China's clothing and fashion industry. Although university professors tend to maintain disciplinary boundaries, practitioners in the industry need to have the knowledge of both cultural and business aspects of clothing. I will use fashion designers to illustrate this point. During my field research, I learned that a Chinese fashion designer's responsibilities extend far beyond the processes of sketching or design. He or she would have to do market research that does not just involve leafing through fashion magazines or surfing on the internet, but also taking trips to various types of department stores or shopping malls, stores of world-leading name brands, and trade fairs. They would have to pick out the right fabrics by looking at tons of swatches or going to the fabric market, and then they may even have to negotiate with sales representatives from fabric companies. After the designs are done, they still would have to meet frequently with personnel from many other departments in order to coordinate the production process. Once the products are made, they would have to organize an internal show for wholesale buyers, provide training for the sales team, and get sales reports on a daily basis. These activities and responsibilities of a fashion designer (especially the chief designer) suggest that in order to score a market success, a fashion designer not only needs to be equipped with know-how of fashion design and a good sense of future trends in terms of color, fabrics, and styles, but he or she also needs to have a thorough knowledge of the target consumers, the production capacity of their company (or their suppliers if they outsource their production), the appropriate sales channels, and the right marketing strategies. For a fashion designer, the perfect products are the ones that are not just made with the best designs and perfect fabrics, but also made in the appropriate factories and sold in the most suitable marketplace. Making perfect products like those clearly requires interdisciplinary knowledge and skills. To understand the way in which fashion designers and other practitioners in the industry work, I have to adopt an approach that takes into consideration both the cultural and economic aspects of clothing and the fashion industry.

ECONOMIC REFORMS IN CHINA

The Third Plenum of the Eleventh Central Committee of the Chinese Communist Party (CCP) in December 1978 was a watershed event. At that meeting, the CCP, under the de facto leadership of Deng Xiaoping, decided to shift the national focus from political struggles and campaigns to economic reforms.

The economic policies adopted by the Chinese government were summarized and propagated as two broad measures (as well as slogans): implementing economic reforms domestically (*duinei gaige*) and opening up China to the world (*duiwai kaifang*). As will be discussed in detail in Chapter 2, the economic reform measures were designed to shift China from the centrally controlled planned economy (*jihua jingji*) of the radical socialist period (the Maoist era) to a market-oriented one (*shichang jingji*). The planned economy in the Maoist era was secluded from Western economies (except limited and indirect connections through Hong Kong), whereas the market-oriented economy in the reform period increasingly participates in the global economy. The goal of the reforms adopted by China was to realize the Four Modernizations (*sige xiandaihua*), including agricultural modernization, industrial modernization, modernization of national defense, and modernization of science and technology. Even though the Four Modernizations were not new inventions at the 1978 meeting, the renewed focus on them popularized the term and made modernization the rationale for the economic reforms.

Modernization was and still is hailed by the Chinese as the only route to improve the lives of the Chinese people and the status of the nation-state, but, as a theory, it has its origins in the West. The term *modernization* has been taken to mean different things, ranging from industrialization, economic development, and rationalization, to secularization (Tipps 1973). It was advocated by Western scholars, especially American scholars, to deal with "the problems of economic development, political stability, and social and cultural change" in the Third World societies in the post-World War II era (Tipps 1973: 200). Scholars of modernization suggest that developing countries must learn from the West and follow its path in order to achieve economic development because Europe and the United States have undergone a series of stages of economic growth to become developed as they are (e.g., Rostow 1960). Differently put, modernization theory postulates a unilinear evolution of human societies culminating in a mirror image of the West. As such, it has been subjected to a wide range of ideological, empirical, and methodological criticism.[8] The ideological critique of modernization theory is especially potent in pointing out that it is Western-centric and makes implicit or explicit justification of European colonialism. Subsequently, modernization theory was largely repudiated by anthropologists and other scholars in the West and it has lost its currency since the 1970s.

Why, then, was a problematic and largely repudiated theory in the West enthusiastically embraced by China? This has to do with several factors. First, China's goal of Four Modernizations was first proposed by China's paramount leaders Premier Zhou Enlai and Chairman Mao Zedong in the 1950s and 1960s.[9] Although the Cultural Revolution (1966–76) and various other political campaigns had in effect put those goals on hold, Mao and especially Zhou were not blamed by their successors for China's failure to fully carry out the agenda of the Four Modernizations in the Maoist era (1949–1978). Instead, their role in proposing the Four Modernizations lent legitimacy for their successors to embrace them as the national goals in the post-1978 reform era. Second, the evolutionary schema entailed in modernization theory is not seen as problematic by the Chinese Communist Party. In fact, it resonates with the Marxist theory of the evolution of human societies,[10] which is also unilinear and to which the Chinese Communist Party still subscribes today. Therefore, for the Chinese, it is not a problem, at least not ideologically, that they have to learn from the West for the purpose of modernizing China. Finally, modernization is not equated with Westernization by Chinese leaders. It is hard to imagine that Chinese Communist leaders like Mao or Deng would envision a completely Westernized China just by learning Western industry or science and technology. To the Chinese leaders, modernization, specifically, the Four Modernizations is merely a means to achieve a Chinese modernity, not the Westernization of China.

After over three decades of economic reforms, China today has evidently become more modernized and globalized, and it has become a major and ascending power in military, political, and economic realms in the world. As a nuclear power and a permanent member of the U.N. Security Council, China has clout on global security issues. In the past three decades, the Chinese economy has enjoyed double-digit or near double-digit growth. In 2001, China gained entry to the World Trade Organization (WTO) after years of tough negotiations with the United States and the European Union. When most major economies in the world suffered from a recession in 2009, China maintained an annual growth rate of over eight percent. In the aftermath of the global recession in 2009, the G-20 (The Group of Twenty major world economies) replaced the G-8 (The Group of Eight Industrialized Nations) as the main economic council of the world's largest economies to deal with issues pertaining to economic growth and the global finance system. As a key member of the G-20, but not of the G-8, China has obviously gained more influence in global economic affairs. In 2010, China surpassed Japan as the second largest economy in the world. It has amassed the world's largest foreign reserve, exceeding 3 trillion U.S. dollars by March 2011, thanks to the huge trade surpluses it accumulated over the years, to which Chinese export of clothing and textiles made a significant contribution.

Against the general backdrop of the rise of China, this book examines the rise of the Chinese fashion industry. It aims to demonstrate that the rise of the Chinese fashion industry not only involves economic development, but also social and political dynamics, that fashion is not just a means to a rags-to-riches style modernization, but also a medium through which a Chinese notion of modernity is articulated and contested, and that the globalization of the fashion industry is always met by various forms of localization practices and simultaneously shaped by the global political economy. In very broad terms, this book examines how changes in Chinese clothing and the fashion industry are constitutive of and constituted by the phenomenal changes China has undergone in the contemporary period.

ORGANIZATION OF THE BOOK

This book is organized into four sections: the Introduction and Conclusion are separate from the two substantive sections. Chapters 2 and 3 (Part I) outline the historical processes in which Chinese clothing and the textile industry have evolved. While I make specific arguments in Chapters 2 and 3, these chapters also serve as a general background to the rise of the Chinese fashion industry. Part II includes Chapters 4 through 7, and each chapter involves case studies of creating fashions in various ways and for different markets. Together they provide a portrayal of the various contexts in which Chinese fashion professionals deal with diverse constraints, and pursue their strategies. It is through their work that I hope to reveal the various facets of the social life of the Chinese fashion industry.

Chapter 2 examines the development of China's textile and apparel industries. In Chapter 2, I outline the major stages through which China's textile and apparel industries developed to their current scale. The goal of the chapter is two-fold: 1) to provide a general background to this book, and 2) to address the question of how the phenomenal changes in China's textile and apparel industries came into being. In answering the question, I focus on the dynamic relationship between the Chinese state and market forces. Because of the unique dynamic between the state and market, I argue that the rise of the Chinese textile and apparel industries does not represent a wave of modernization that is spread from the West to China, but developed in the Chinese political and economic context that includes, but is not limited to, China's response to globalization.

Chapter 3 examines the evolution of clothing styles in contemporary China, specifically in the four major periods: the late Qing, Republican China, the radical socialist period (1949–78), and the reform era. The nature of the changes of clothing styles in these four periods suggests that they are not the result of fashion cycles, nor merely the outcome of economic development; instead, it indicates a close association with the political and social dynamics in each of the historical periods.

Moreover, the correlation between changes in clothing styles and time paves the ground for the Chinese to construct a uniquely Chinese notion of modernity as narrated in the official representations of the sartorial evolution in contemporary China. According to this Chinese notion of modernity, China becomes modern not because of the adoption of Western styles of clothing (hence becoming more Westernized), but because clothing styles now are considered better than the ones in the past. It is in this sense that I argue that the Chinese modernity encoded in the evolution of clothing styles is a story that the Chinese tell themselves about themselves in relation to their own past rather than to others (c.f. Rofel 1999; Geertz 1973a).

Chapter 4 focuses on one particular style created for a political occasion, the *tangzhuang* jacket, which was designed by a team of designers for the heads of state attending the APEC Summit in Shanghai in 2001. Based on interviews with the designers and government officials, as well as media reports, I document and analyze the processes through which the *tangzhuang* jackets were made, the government's attempt to map specific meanings onto this style, and the controversy surrounding the name of the jacket. By juxtaposing these with an average Beijing citizen's account of her *tangzhuang*, I suggest that the diverse views of the *tangzhuang* and the eventual waning popularity of the style put the official notion of modernity (as well as tradition) to the test.

Chapter 5 examines the choices and strategies of Chinese fashion designers, specifically the choice of whether to design for the sake of art or for the market. In dealing with the divergent objectives of originality and marketability, fashion designers came up with three major approaches, and subsequently three business models: haute couture (high fashion), prêt-à-porter (high-end ready-to-wear clothing), and fast fashion. Primary case studies in this chapter include two prominent fashion designers, Ms. Ye Li and Mr. Yuan Xing, and their business models. One favors art in her design and the other emphasizes the market; one owns a design studio and the other a designer label company. This chapter provides an understanding of the rationale behind the choices and strategies of Chinese fashion designers. Building on Geertz's insights on the distinction between "authors" and "writers," I argue that the way in which Chinese fashion designers work shapes the very meaning of being a fashion designer in China.

Chapter 6 examines fashion shows in China, particularly fashion shows during China Fashion Week (CFW). Based on firsthand experience of China Fashion Week in Beijing in 2004, I argue that CFW is the objectification of the Chinese field of fashion, and as such, CFW is similar to London Fashion Week (LFW), studied by Entwistle and Rocamora (2006). By situating fashion shows and fashion week in the Chinese context, I also highlight the differences between CFW and LFW. Due to the unique characteristics of China Fashion Week, I argue that fashion shows during CFW represent a shortcut for Chinese fashion designers to advance their careers, and similarly the institution of CFW represents China's desire to jumpstart its fashion industry.

Chapter 7 investigates some of the global connections of the Chinese apparel industry, with special attention on the exportation of garments made in China to the United States. Using the example of a Steelers jersey, this chapter seeks to understand the apparent contradiction that while the Steelers jersey provides material evidence of the connection between Chinese manufacturers and U.S. consumers, the meanings of the garment constructed by the U.S. consumers are completely disconnected from the Chinese producers. In order to do so, I examine the pattern in which Chinese-made garments are exported to the United States. I argue that this pattern is characterized by the dominance of the U.S. corporate buyers over the Chinese suppliers and the privilege of the United States over China. Using the trade dispute between the United States and China in 2005 as a case study, I highlight the differences between various parties (stakeholders) and their interconnections through the garments. By applying a network analysis to the case study, this chapter provides a critique of globalization from a clothing perspective.

Chapter 8 concludes this book by highlighting the Chinese characteristics of the Chinese fashion industry. I summarize the major arguments I have made throughout the book, and I also offer some propositions for future research on Chinese clothing and the fashion industry.

PART 1

Rise of the Chinese Fashion Industry

–2–

The Growth of Chinese Textile and Apparel Industries: Is It Just an Illustration of Modernization?

INTRODUCTION

The textile and apparel industries are of vital importance to the Chinese economy, even though they are often regarded as "sunset industries" in developed countries such as the United States. These industries provide fabric and clothing to meet the basic needs of a population of 1.3 billion people, employ about 19 million workers,[1] and earn much-needed hard currencies to finance the nation's modernization projects. In 2004, for example, China exported US$97.4 billion worth of textile and apparel products, accounting for 16.4 percent of China's total export, and generated a trade surplus of US$64.9 billion, which was 2.52 times China's total trade surplus (China National Textile Industry Council 2010: 318). Without the trade surplus in textile and apparel products, China would have had an overall trade deficit in 2004. This pattern of the disproportionate contribution of textile and apparel exports to China's trade surplus began in, and has continued since 1999.[2] Given the significance of trade surplus to economic development in China,[3] the textile and apparel industries are especially important to the country's modernization efforts in the post-1978 reform era.

The importance of the Chinese textile and apparel industries is matched by their scale. China is home to the world's largest textile and apparel industries. Not only is China one of the largest clothing markets in the world, it also exports more textile and apparel products than any other country in the world. In fact, China has been the world's largest exporter of textile and apparel products since 1994. In 2008, China's textile and apparel exports accounted for 26.1 percent and 33.2 percent of the world's total textile and apparel exports respectively (WTO 2009). Contrary to the popular belief that Chinese exports are cheap, low-end products, they cover a wide range of quality and price levels, including moderately priced and high-end products. In one report, the U.S. International Trade Commission (USITC) had the following assessment of China's textile and apparel industries: "China is expected to become the 'supplier of choice' for most U.S. importers [large apparel companies and retailers] because of its ability to make almost any type of textile and apparel product at any quality level at a competitive price" (USITC 2004: xi). Amazingly, the enormous scale of the Chinese textile and apparel industries has primarily been built in a relatively short period of time, mostly since the 1980s. In fact, cloth was still rationed in China and the Chinese had to use government-issued coupons to buy cloth or clothes before 1984.[4]

The phenomenal growth of the Chinese textile and apparel industries in the past few decades raises several important questions: How did it come about? What role did the Chinese state, which adheres to a Communist ideology, play in the dramatic growth of the industries? What was the role of the market? Given the common association between the textile industry and industrialization, economic development, and modernization in many parts of the world, is the rise of the Chinese textile and apparel industries simply another illustration of economic development and modernization that has been spread from the West to China?

This chapter addresses these questions. The main goal of the chapter is to delineate the historical trajectory in which the Chinese textile and apparel industries have emerged and developed into a global powerhouse. In particular, I will examine the roles of the state and the market in the growth of the Chinese textile and apparel industries, which provides a backdrop to the rise of the Chinese fashion industry. I will explore the relationship between the development of the Chinese textile and apparel industries and narratives of modernization and globalization. I argue that the rise of the Chinese fashion industry is *not* a wave of modernization spread from the West to China, but that it developed in the context of the Chinese political economy, which includes, but is not limited to, China's response to globalization.

To chart the development of the Chinese textile and apparel industries, I rely heavily on the Chinese official numbers and narratives. My primary sources of data include the *Almanacs of China Textile Industry* (*ACTI*; Editorial Board of the Almanac of China's Textile Industry 1982–1999) and *China Textile Industry Development Report* (*CTIDR*; CNTIC 1999–2010),[5] both of which are Chinese official yearbooks of the industries. I also utilize statistics available from the World Trade Organization. Moreover, the use of statistics is informed by the knowledge I gained through interviews with national-level officials in the textile ministry, industry council, and associations;[6] the interviews help put the numbers in the Chinese context. Some explanations of the Chinese terminologies will demonstrate why that is the case.

SOME CHINESE TERMINOLOGIES

To start, the term "the textile industry," or *fangzhi gongye*, needs clarification. A book that is primarily concerned with Chinese clothing and its fashion industry has to first address the textile industry not just because the textile industry provides input for the clothing industry, but also because the "textile industry" has somewhat unique connotations in China. The English term "industry" is loosely used by the government, professionals in the trade, and scholars alike on several different levels, such as the "men's wear industry," the "garment/apparel/clothing industry," the "textile industry," and the "fashion industry." In Chinese, however, the "industry" of a particular category of clothing, such as the men's wear industry, is called a *hangye*, and industry as in the "garment industry" or the "textile industry" is called *gongye* or *chanye*. To complicate the matter even more, *fangzhi gongye* in China has broader connotation than what textile industry means in English, in the sense that it officially includes the apparel industry (*fuzhuang gongye*). For example, the current national umbrella organization of the textile and apparel industries is named the China National Textile Industry Council (CNTIC), or *zhongguo fangzhi gongye xiehui*,[7] which includes the national garment industry association and associations of specific product categories as member organizations. The predecessor of CNTIC was the former Chinese Ministry of the Textile Industry (*zhongguo fangzhi gongye bu*), which also included both the textile and apparel industries. In other words, in the eyes of the Chinese government, the textile and apparel industries are one industry, the *fangzhi gongye*, which is normally translated into English as the textile industry. To avoid confusion, I use the term "the textile and apparel industries" to refer to *fangzhi gongye* and "the textile industry" when addressing the textile sector alone. Furthermore, the textile and apparel industries in general include three sectors based on the end use: garment textiles, home textiles (home furnishing), and industrial textiles. This book is only concerned about clothing and garment textiles, which is also the largest among the three sectors, accounting for over 52 percent of all textiles in China in 2003 (Xu 2004: 174). Thus, in this chapter, the Chinese "apparel and textile industries" specifically refers to the Chinese clothing industry and the garment-textile industry.

With the parameter of the Chinese textile and apparel industries defined, I now address how the Chinese bureaucratic structure affects the statistics. For historical and bureaucratic reasons, Chinese garment manufacturers are fragmented and fall under the administration of three relevant governmental or semi-governmental industry organizations: the China National Textile Industry Council (formerly the Ministry of Chinese Textile Industry), the China National Light Industry Council (formerly the Ministry of Chinese Light Industries), and the Ministry of Commerce (formerly the Ministry of Domestic Commerce). Consequently, statistics compiled by the Textile Ministry and later the Textile Industry Council, though including the majority of Chinese garment firms, do not include those garment manufacturers that are (were) under the administration of the other two ministries or industry councils. Frequently, only firms with annual revenue of over 5 million yuan (*guimo yishang qiye* or enterprises above scale) are included in the national statistics, and those enterprises are dubbed Statistically Worthy Enterprises (SWEs). For all the above reasons, the statistics cited in this chapter are in fact official estimates rather than actual numbers. Yet, these statistics are the best estimates available and they are fairly consistent in their measurements, hence helpful in illustrating historical trends and development of the Chinese industries.

In the following sections, I will outline the major developments in the Chinese textile and apparel industries. To do so, I will divide the course of their development into three stages: infancy, development, and take-off, which roughly correspond to the late Qing and the Republican era (pre-1949), the radical socialist period in the People's Republic of China (1949–1978), and the reform era in the PRC (post-1978) respectively.

INFANCY: CHINESE TEXTILE AND APPAREL INDUSTRIES BEFORE 1949

The modern Chinese textile industry emerged when nationalist entrepreneurs and foreign capitalists set up textile mills in Shanghai and other coastal cities at the end of the nineteenth century. However, because the late Qing (1644–1911) and the Republican era (1912–1949) were riddled with wars (including civil wars and wars with European imperial powers and Japan), the Chinese textile industry did not have a stable political and social environment in which it could quickly develop during those periods. Given the social and political turmoil, it is quite an achievement that 179,000 textile firms were established in 1949 when the PRC was founded, with a combined workforce of 745,000 workers and 5 million cotton spindles and a small number of wool, bast fiber, and silk spindles.[8] Yet, about half the national production capacity was located in Shanghai, the product mix was limited to natural fibers (primarily cotton yarn and fabric), and the industry relied heavily on imports of Western equipment and raw materials. For example, all the textile equipment and 80 percent of the cotton were imported in Shanghai before 1949 (*ACTI* 1983: 7).

Compared to the textile sector, the industrialization of the apparel sector emerged even later and was much smaller in scale. Before 1949, clothing was mostly hand-made, either at home, by itinerant tailors who would visit villages in rural areas to solicit customers, or by tailors in tailor shops in urban areas. Most tailor shops would have a master tailor with a few apprentices who made clothes primarily to the orders of customers and occasionally sold some ready-made clothing on the side (similar operations still exist in urban China today but have diminished to a minimum presence).[9] For example, one of the first Chinese fashion firms, Hong Xiang Women's Fashion Company, was a high-end tailoring shop that was established in Shanghai in 1917. The founding brothers (Hong Xiang was the name of the elder brother) began their careers as apprentices to a master tailor (Tsui 2010: 11). Garment factories appeared in the Republican era; however, they were small in scale and manufactured only basic items such as shirts and undergarments. According to some sources, there were 18 shirt factories in Shanghai before the anti-Japanese war (1937–1945), employing about 200 workers, with a monthly output of just over 9,000 shirts (Huang 1994: 249).

DEVELOPMENT: CHINESE TEXTILE AND APPAREL INDUSTRIES IN PRE-1978 PEOPLE'S REPUBLIC OF CHINA

When the Communists came to power and founded the People's Republic of China in 1949, they immediately started a nationalization campaign, which was accomplished in three steps. First, they took over the *Guomindang* (or KMT) and foreign-owned textile mills and turned them into state-owned enterprises (SOEs). Then, they transformed privately owned mills into state-run enterprises and the private owners into shareholders, which was dubbed *gong si he ying* (literally meaning public–private cooperation). The government launched an active campaign, and the enterprise owners purportedly participated in the program on a voluntary basis. Whether private business owners willingly gave up their partial or complete ownership of their ventures is hard to know today, but the reality was that the private textile mills had few options but to cooperate with the government not only because of the political pressure, but also because the state took complete control of the distribution of raw materials and the final products. Textile mills could only buy cotton from and sell finished yarn and fabric to the government. It is hard to imagine that any private firms could survive without cooperating with the government in that environment. By January 1956, all private textile firms had adopted the mode of *gong si he ying* in Shanghai (*ACTI* 1983: 8). Nationwide, the second step of nationalization was completed by the end of 1956. The third step was to organize independent workers into co-ops (*hezuoshe*) and then to turn the co-ops into state-owned enterprises. This final step was completed in Shanghai (as well as nationally) in 1958. By the end of 1958, the entire textile and apparel industries (and the overall economy) became state-owned and state-run and fully integrated into a socialist planned economy.

In the planned economic system, the state was the ultimate owner and manager of the entire economy, which is sometimes compared to a huge single factory (Wu 2005: 17). Take a textile mill, for example. It would receive directives, derived from the central government's five-year plans (*wunian jihua*), as to what and how much to produce in each year, then it would buy the required amount of raw materials from another state-owned organization at a state-regulated price, and finally it would sell its products to designated state-owned organizations at a regulated price. The workers and managers/cadres of the mill were all employed by the state, and were all paid fairly equally by the type of work they performed (*tong gong tong chou*, meaning "equal work with equal pay"). Slight variations in pay did exist due to such factors as the rank or title (*zhicheng*) and the number of years of work experience (*gongling*). The mill and its workers were only responsible for production, not the sale of their products; the state would ultimately pocket the profits or underwrite the losses, which had no bearing whatsoever on the pay of the employees of the mill. Under the planned economic system, therefore, all textile mills and garment factories, which could indeed be seen as a single large factory, were merely production units, filling orders from the state. Hence, the planned economy is also called a command economy.[10]

In the early years of the PRC, the planned economy had the advantage of rapidly achieving economy of scale and of concentrating scarce resources on the most pressing needs after years of war. Despite the disruptions of the natural and man-made disasters between 1958 and 1961 and the Cultural Revolution (1966–76), the growth of the textile industry in China was impressive. In 1970, China's annual yield of cotton yarn and fabric reached 11.31 million bales and 9.15 billion meters respectively, a five-time increase from 1949. In the same year, then-Premier Zhou Enlai announced during a reception of the American journalist Edgar Snow that China's cotton yarn and fabric output had taken the first place in the world (*ACTI* 1990: 2). In addition to natural fibers, China started to develop chemical fibers vigorously in the early 1970s. By the mid-1980s, China's production capacity of chemical fibers exceeded 1 million tons, and had become one of the world's largest producers (*ACTI* 1987: 1).

Compared to the textile sector, the development of the garment sector was not nearly as impressive. Clothing continued to be made at home or by tailors, and ready-to-wear clothing (*chengyi*) was still a rarity in the late 1970s. In 1978, a total of 673 million pieces of ready-to-wear clothing were made, which came down to less than one piece per person, even before a portion of those was exported. In Shanghai in 1984, for example, about 81 million pieces of cotton-made garments were exported, which was equivalent to 17.9 percent of the total amount of cotton fabric exported in the year. For the domestic market in the same year, about 23.5 percent of the cotton fabric was made into ready-to-wear clothing, about 80 million pieces (*ACTI* 1985: 252). Evidently, both the export and domestic markets relied heavily on fibers and fabrics, rather than finished garments, in Shanghai in 1984. The Chinese garment industry only started to take off in the late 1980s and the early 1990s (see Figure 2.1). Its development was bottlenecked by, among other things, development in the upstream textile sector. The fact that textile products (including

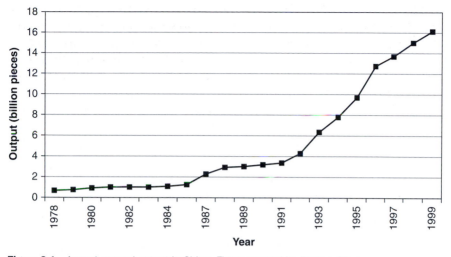

Figure 2.1   Annual apparel output in China. Figure created by Jianhua Zhao.
Source: Almanacs of Chinese Textile Industry (2000: 135).

clothing) were only purchasable with rationed cloth coupons between 1954 and 1983 indicated a shortage economy in China during that time. Under those circumstances, production—rather than consumption—of fabrics, instead of finished garments, was prioritized. The centrally controlled planned economic system before 1978 dealt with those priorities effectively and rapidly. However, there are also significant drawbacks to the planned economic system, which will be discussed in the following section.

TAKE-OFF: CHINESE TEXTILE AND APPAREL INDUSTRIES IN THE POST-1978 REFORM ERA

The planned economic system began to change when the Third Plenum of the Eleventh Central Committee was held in December 1978. This watershed meeting orchestrated economic reforms and open-door policies, which ushered China into a new era. The reform policies adopted at the meeting dramatically transformed the Chinese economy. Even though the specifics of China's economic policies today are rather different from the late 1970s and early 1980s, they are considered part of the continued and deepening economic reform process that was set forth at the meeting in 1978, and hence the post-1978 period is generally considered by China scholars as the (post-)reform era. With respect to the Chinese textile and apparel industries in particular and the Chinese economy in general, the meeting marked a gradual structural shift away from a state-controlled planned economy toward a market-based economy, and from a largely closed economy to one with increased participation in the global economy, culminating in China's accession to the World Trade Organization in 2001. In the post-1978 period, the Chinese textile and apparel industries have seen continued processes of state deregulation, market-oriented reforms, and industrial upgrading.

China's ability to implement economic reforms clearly had to do with the political environment at the time, with the death of Mao in 1976 and the ensuing ascendance of Deng Xiaoping. However, economic reforms were needed because of the intrinsic problems of a planned economic system. First, it disconnected distribution from production, and pay from performance. Hence, there was a lack of incentives and accountability for both the workers and management, which eventually led to low productivity and inefficiency, which became especially pronounced after the waning of Communist revolutionary enthusiasm in the 1970s. Second, the absolute monopoly of state-owned enterprises excluded competition, resulting in further inefficiency. Last, but not the least, the state's emphasis on production and its adoption of a rationing system depressed consumption demands. These problems became more acute when the shortage problem was solved and the socialist calling for "devoted spirit" (*fengxian jingshen*) was losing its grip on the people after Mao's death. Top government officials in the textile and apparel industries began to recognize and address those problems in the early 1980s.

At the 1982 annual National Textile Industry planning meeting, Hao Jianxiu, the model worker turned Minister said, "In the new situation, a new predicament has emerged: [the problem of] scarce commodities in the past has been solved, whereas previously popular products became surplus inventory" (*ACTI* 1983: 178). She thought that there should be a shift in emphasis from quantity to quality, and called for enterprises to study the changes in consumer demands rather than to merely produce according to the orders from the commerce department (*ACTI* 1983: 177–182). After a few years of rapid growth in the early 1980s, the problem of overcapacity in production, coupled with weak consumption, became more severe. In December 1983, the state decided to abandon the rationing system of cloth coupons once and for all. This measure temporarily mitigated the problem of overcapacity by releasing the depressed demand. At the symbolic level, it marked the end of the production-driven era and entry into a market-driven period in the Chinese textile and apparel industries.

In the early 1980s, all economic and political factors were pointed to reforms that would rectify the problems in the old planned economic system. In one speech in 1983, Wu Wenying, the new Minister of the textile industry, emphasized the terms "shifting tracks" (*zhuangui*) and "changing models" (*bianxing*). She reiterated the principle of "three shifts" (*sange zhuanyi*) proposed by her predecessor Hao Jianxiu, "to shift from the focus on speed, production, and capacity to focus on product diversification and quality, technological innovation, and profitability; and to change from a pure production model to a production and commerce model" (*ACTI* 1985: 175).[11] This might still sound like a typical Chinese political speech, more about principles and slogans (typically in the form of enumerations) than practices, but in actuality pilot reform programs were being tested in some state-owned enterprises.

In 1984, four successful measures were concluded from the pilot programs: 1) reforming the management system at the firm level and adopting a general manager responsibility system (*changzhang fuzezhi*); 2) transforming the firm from an administrative unit to a business unit, and allowing the management of the firm to make independent decisions, such as diversifying their products according to market demand and forming alliances with other firms, commerce departments, and regions; 3) breaking down the lifetime employment system or the "iron rice bowl" (*tiefanwan*) of cadres and workers, and partly adopting a contract-based employment system; and 4) reforming the old egalitarian salary system by tying bonuses and compensation to work performance (*ACTI* 1985: 188–190).

These four measures brought about two significant changes in the SOEs that were under reform. For one, those reformed firms were granted more authority by the state and were able to function as relatively independent business units rather than as de facto administrative units (*danwei*) that were extensions of the state apparatus. For the first time, a manufacturer (typically a SOE) would be allowed to decide what to produce and to cross the rigid boundary between industry and commerce, known as *gong bu jing shang* (which historically had meant that industrial units ought not to conduct commercial activities, as they derived their mandates from two separate authorities, namely the Ministry of Industry and the Ministry of Commerce). Consequently, the reformed firms were able to sell their products directly rather than through the commerce department, and shifted from a pure production model to the production and commerce model that Ministers Wu and Hao called for. The other major change was that incentives were introduced into the system as salaries and bonuses became more flexible and were tied to job performances. Not surprisingly, the overall performance of those SOEs improved, and the final report of the experiments concluded, "practice (*shijian*) proves that the reform measures bring about profits, and they are beneficial to the country, to the enterprises, and to the workers" (*ACTI* 1985: 189).

Indeed, the pilot reform programs were so successful that the central government decided to implement structural reforms at the enterprise level nationwide. It issued a strong order that unless authorized by the central government, all enterprises had to adopt the reform measures by June 1987, and that enterprises unreformed by the deadline would be dismantled (*ACTI* 1988: 178). The tough initiatives from the central government ensured that China's

SOEs shifted from administrative units to relatively independent business units, an important first step to diverge from the track of a planned economy and onto that of a market-based economy. To enhance the administrative capacity of the Ministry of the Textile Industry, the garment and silk sectors were transferred from under the administration of the Ministry of Light Industries to the Ministry of Textile Industry in 1987. Ironically, these significant market reform measures had to be carried out under the direct orders of the state, a prominent feature of a command economy.

In addition to implementing structural reforms in the SOEs, the state also started to introduce competition into the economy by allowing the establishment of enterprises with other types of ownership, primarily township and village enterprises (TVEs) and foreign-funded enterprises (FFEs). Since 1978, the TVEs took off quickly, absorbing the first wave of excessive agricultural labor freed by the household production responsibility system (*jiating lianchan chengbao zerenzhi*) adopted in rural China. The TVEs in the textile industry produced a revenue of 43.8 billion yuan in 1987, a six-time increase from that of 1983 and about 30 times the 1978 level. The growth in the apparel sector was even more remarkable. In 1987, township and village garment factories produced 1.94 billion pieces of clothing, accounting for more than half of the total national output (*ACTI* 1990: 33). In 1990, 79.1 percent of all ready-to-wear garments were manufactured by the TVEs (*ACTI* 1991). The TVEs' market share in China's garment industry peaked in 1993, totaling 5.8 billion pieces, and amounting to over 90 percent of the national output of all ready-to-wear garments in the year (*ACTI* 1994:11–2). These numbers indicate that the Chinese garment industry has been predominantly led by the market, i.e. the non-state-owned sector, since the 1990s.

The boom of TVEs in the garment industry also gradually expanded to the more capital-intensive textile industry. In 1995, there were a total of 61,783 TVEs in the textile and apparel industries, employing 5.7 million people and creating an aggregate revenue of 518.6 billion yuan (*ACTI* 1996: 221–222). The phenomenal growth and success of TVEs was partly because they started up as relatively independent business entities rather than administrative units like the SOEs, which were directly and inefficiently managed by the state. Though the name of TVEs may suggest that they may be owned by the townships or villages (i.e., as collectives), many of them were in fact private businesses carrying the politically correct name, which is called by some scholars a red hat strategy (e.g., Tsai 2002: 39). Yasheng Huang (2008) goes even further and argues that the TVEs are defined by their geographic locations rather than ownership, as Western academic literature tends to assume. Given the lack of reliable historical statistical data, we do not know for sure what the exact percentages of the truly private TVEs (with a "red hat" disguise) and the purely collectively owned TVEs were. What we do know is that the TVEs' relationship with the local village and township governments was much less rigid than the SOEs' relationship with the municipal, provincial, or central government, and that the TVEs were much more independent than the SOEs. In the late 1980s and the early 1990s, most of the TVEs were contracted out, or changed their ownership structure via privatization (usually through management buy-out), turning into joint ventures by absorbing foreign capital, merging with other domestic firms, or going public in the stock market, or through a combination of the above-mentioned approaches.

One of the well-known TVEs that changed its ownership was the Youngor Group (*Yage'r jituan*), the largest garment manufacturer in China, which had a revenue of 10.12 billion yuan in 2003. It was established in 1979 as a small township enterprise by a few returned educated youth (*zhiqing*)[12] from the countryside, who later turned it into a private business (Ren 1998). The company went public in the Shanghai Stock Exchange in 1998. Like the Youngor Group, many TVEs as well as SOEs became publicly owned corporations in the late 1990s, which made ownership types of the firms more complex statistically. In fact, the TVEs were no longer included in the statistics published in the national textile industry almanacs in 1997, which suggests that by then many of the TVEs had transformed their identities into private businesses or publically listed companies just like the Youngor Group. Nevertheless, the TVEs were one of the most dynamic players in the Chinese textile and apparel industries and contributed significantly to the growth and competitiveness of the industries in the 1980s and much of the 1990s.

Meanwhile, another type of firms also entered the competition: the foreign-funded enterprises (FFEs), including joint ventures and wholly foreign-owned firms. The growth of foreign direct investment (FDI) in China's textile and apparel industries was as impressive as the TVEs, but with a relatively later start. In the end of 1982, there were only two joint ventures in China's textile and apparel industries. The number increased to 150 in 1986, 46 of which were apparel firms (*ACTI* 1988: 26). By 1990, there were a total of 2,192 FFEs in China's textile and apparel sectors, with a cumulative investment of about US$2 billion. FDI in China picked up even greater speed in the 1990s. In the year 1991 alone, 972 new FFEs invested in China's textile and apparel industries, representing an annual increase of 44 percent (*ACTI* 1992: 14). By 1999, a cumulative total of 5,156 foreign-funded textile and apparel firms had been established in China, accounting for 28.7 percent of the national output of textile and apparel products in the same year, a close second to the state-owned sector, which accounted for 29.7 percent (*ACTI* 2000: 2).[13] In other words, the FFEs and the SOEs in the textile and apparel industries had roughly comparable capacities in 1999. However, the same could not be said about their profitability; the state-owned sector had a loss of 3.73 billion yuan in 1999, whereas the FFEs made a total profit of 55.53 billion yuan in the same year (ibid). Apparently, the state sector lost out to the non-state-owned sectors, including the TVEs and the FFEs, in a competitive market environment, which suggested that China's economic reforms in the 1980s and 1990s mainly focused on facilitating the growth of the TVEs and the FFEs (i.e., the market economy sectors), rather than on thoroughly reforming the SOEs.

In fact, after initial reforms in the 1980s, the SOEs were still operating in a primarily planned economic system. In a national textile industry planning meeting in 1982, Minister Hao Jianxiu talked about the ways to execute the State Council's reform plans within the primarily planned economic system. She quoted Chen Yun, the then Vice Premier, "'Our country has to stick to the principle of the planned economy as the basis and market adjustment as the supplement' [jihua jingji weizhu, shichang tiaojie weifu]. . .we have to realize that the planned economy is an essential characteristic of the socialist economy. . .the primary and supplementary positions [of planning and the market] should not be subverted, nor should [the two] be equally treated" (ACTI 1983: 181). The establishment of an intrinsic ideological linkage between socialism and the planned economy is derived from an orthodox Marxist belief that the economic base determines the superstructure. As the Chinese Communist Party has long subscribed to Marxism, for many senior party members fundamentally reforming the base of the socialist planned economy (i.e., the SOEs and collective enterprises) would entail endangering the superstructure of socialism. Due to the objection of the hardliners in the CCP, such as Chen Yun, further reforms of the SOEs after the early 1980s proved to be rather difficult.

It was not until Deng Xiaoping, one of the core leaders of the CCP and the architect of the 1978 reform, made his famous commentaries on the market reforms during his visits to Shanghai and the special economic zones (SEZs) in southern China in 1992 that the market mechanism (shichang jizhi) became accepted by the CCP as an essential characteristic of socialism. He stated that planning and the market were not markers of socialism or capitalism, and that there was planning in a capitalist economy just as there was market in a socialist economy. He clearly felt that the pace of reform in the country as a whole was not fast enough and remarked that "the courage [to reform] should be even greater, and the pace [of reform] should be even faster." Deng's statements essentially settled the ideological debate over where China's economic reform should be headed. His remarks on the association between the market and socialism, which were officially dubbed Deng's "South Tour Remarks" (nanxun jianghua), were widely studied by the Communist Party and broadly circulated in the state-controlled media, and later incorporated into the official Report of the 14th Party Congress in the same year. The Party Congress monumentally declared that the goal for further economic reform was to fully construct the socialist market economy, which heralded the extraordinary growth of Shanghai in the 1990s, much like the phenomenal growth of the Special Economic Zones in the 1980s.

Lauding Deng's contribution to the monumental economic reforms and the astounding growth of the Special Economic Zones in South China,[14] a popular song by the name of "Stories of the Spring" begins like this: "Year 1979 was a spring, there was an old man who stood by the South Sea of our motherland and drew a *circle*. . .Year 1992 was another spring, there was an old man who stood by the South Sea of our motherland and wrote down *poems*. . ." (emphases mine).[15] Even though the lyrics of the song were supposed to be taken figuratively, to the Chinese the message of the song was quite simple and direct: History was made by Deng (the "old man") in 1979 and 1992. Thanks to Deng's policy, Shenzhen (the "circle") was established as China's first SEZ in 1979, which turned out to be extremely successful. And again thanks to Deng's remarks (the "poems") on market mechanisms as a part of socialism in 1992, further reforms led to the dramatic growth of Shanghai, particularly the Pudong district. The miracle of Pudong, changing from rural farm lands into the "Manhattan of China" in less than a decade, was indeed the direct result of China's effort to construct the socialist market economy. Pudong today is a major financial district in Shanghai, home to the Shanghai Stock Exchange and hundreds of domestic and foreign banks, which in themselves embody the spirit of a capitalist market economy. Yet, the growth of Pudong was just as sudden and nearly as mysterious as that of Shenzhen, so much so that a Chinese professor and friend of mine jokingly expressed to me that the second part of the song should be changed into: ". . .Year 1992 was another spring, there was an old man who stood by the *East* Sea of our motherland and *drew another circle*" (emphases his). He referred to the Chinese-style market economy as a "circle economy" (*quanquan jingji*), underlining the fact that dramatic growth only came about under heavy state intervention and investment rather than being regulated by the law of supply and demand.

Deng's South Tour Remarks led to what amounted to the second wave of economic reforms, which differed from the first wave of reforms in the 1980s in that it allowed the market to play a fundamental instead of a supplemental role (as it did in the 1980s) in allocating resources. What that entailed was two trends taking place simultaneously: the continued expansion of the non-state sector (no longer with the limitation of being a secondary player to the state sector) on the one hand and further reform of the SOEs on the other hand.

Though not as ground-breaking as the initial reforms in the 1980s, the second wave of reforms was essential to the continued growth of the textile and apparel industries and the overall Chinese economy. This was so especially because top government officials conservatively tied the economy to the socialist ideology in the 1980s, which became an obstacle for further market reforms. Internationally, the second wave was a much needed assurance that China would not stall its economic reforms or go back to its old way of closing its doors to the outside world again, which some China observers speculated was happening after the state suppressed the democratic movements in 1989.[16] FDI reacted favorably to China's second wave of economic reforms, as evidenced by the previously described boom of the FFEs in the 1990s. The boom of FFEs and the continued expansion of the TVEs further strengthened the market forces in the Chinese economy. In the textile and apparel industries, the non-state sector exceeded the state sector and became the dominant player in the economy in the early 1990s. Following the shift to a market-based economy, the Chinese state disbanded the Ministry of the Textile Industry, which was the administrative organ in the planned economic system, and formed a voluntary organization—though still with strong governmental ties—of the General Textile Council (*fangzhi zhonghui*) in 1993. The organizational change was yet another indication that the state was loosening its control on the textile and apparel industries.

The other trend of the second wave economic reforms had to do with the SOEs, specifically their problems of excess capacity and unprofitability. Production capacity in itself is not necessarily a problem; it becomes a problem when there's insufficient demand and/or it is coupled with inefficiency. Take the cotton textile industry for example: in 1981, there were a total of 18.9 million spindles; ten years later, the capacity had more than doubled to 41.9 million spindles (*ACTI* 1999: 174). The dramatic increase clearly had to do not just with the SOEs, but also with the growth of the TVEs and the FFEs. In addition, the increased capacity was needed because the demand was met by the growth in the export of Chinese textiles and clothing (see Figures 2.2 and 2.3). That being said, increased export alone does not eliminate the problem of overcapacity, especially in a competitive market environment in which efficiency and productivity tend to be uneven across the firms and sectors. This was generally true in the 1980s and 1990s, during which the growth in the export of textiles and clothing correlated to the growth of the TVEs and the FFEs. The SOEs, on the other hand, were losing market shares to the FFEs and the TVEs and continued to be inefficient. Consequently, the excess capacity in the textile and apparel industries was concentrated in the SOEs, and increasingly more SOEs suffered from losses during the same period. In 1990, 37.9 percent of all state-owned textile firms and collective enterprises, known as firms "within the socialist system" (*xitongnei*),[17] were running at a loss (*ACTI* 1991: 7). In 1991, the loss increased to 41.9 percent (*ACTI* 1992: 8). In 1993, the number of SOEs and collectives at a loss further widened to 44.9 percent, and for the first time the entire state-owned sector suffered an aggregate after-tax loss of 616 million yuan (*ACTI* 1994: 1).[18] This trend continued in 1995 and peaked in 1996, when over 54 percent of all SOEs in textiles suffered

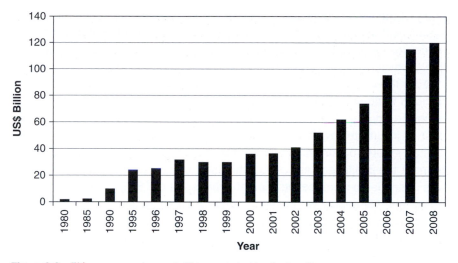

Figure 2.2 Chinese apparel export. Figure created by Jianhua Zhao.
Source: World Trade Organization (2009).

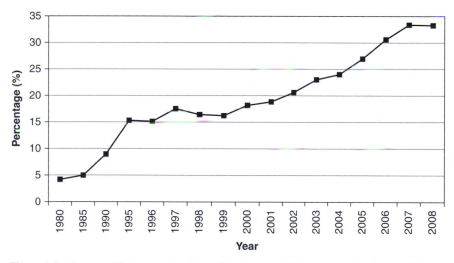

Figure 2.3 Shares of Chinese apparel export in the world. Figure created by Jianhua Zhao.
Source: World Trade Organization (2009).

losses and the entire SOE sector had a negative aggregate after-tax profit of 10.58 billion yuan (*ACTI* 1999: 346–47). This pattern of system-wide losses continued through 1999. The underwhelming performance of the socialist sector or the *xitongnei* firms, primarily the SOEs, was partly because of the excess capacity built up over the years and partly because the SOEs were ill-equipped for market competition compared to the TVEs and the FFEs. Among many of the systemic disadvantages of the SOEs is the life-time employment system with guaranteed pensions. Worse yet, an SOE could not discontinue a money-losing operation, divest any non-core assets, or declare bankruptcy by itself, which lay ultimately in the hands of its owner, the state.

After five consecutive years of system-wide losses, the central government decided to do something about the SOEs in the textile industry in 1997. The timing to address the problem also had something to do with China's prospect of joining the WTO, which entailed more severe market competition as well as greater opportunities for Chinese textile and apparel firms. For them to meet the challenges and opportunities of China's accession to the WTO, it was essential to increase the competitiveness of the SOEs. Then-Premier Zhu Rongji and his deputy Wu Bangguo outlined an aggressive plan to dismantle millions of outdated spindles, to lay off 1.2 million textile workers, and to return the textile SOEs to profitability by 2000, one year before China's scheduled admission to the WTO (*ACTI* 1999: 173–78).

In 1998, the Chinese state launched a three-year campaign of demolishing spindles (*yading*), which began in the cotton textile sector. The problem of loss plagued the SOEs in all sectors in the textile industry, but because the cotton textile sector was the largest and suffered the worst loss, it was chosen by the state to shed production capacity first, and serve as a model for the other sectors to follow. Hence, the campaign to dismantle excess spindles in the cotton textile sector was dubbed Project Breaking Point (*tupokou gongzuo*). As the ultimate owner of the SOEs, the central government took the initiative in the campaign. To better execute its policies, in March 1998, the central government reinstated the "voluntarily-based" China Textile General Council as a governmental organization and renamed it the China State Textile Industrial Bureau. One specific responsibility of the Bureau was to oversee Project Breaking Point. In addition, the central government set aside hundreds of million yuan in special funds to compensate those SOEs that had dismantled spindles, laid off workers, or gone bankrupt altogether. It also worked closely with local governments and required them to share the cost of compensation and subsidy, and tied the project to local officials' work performance. By the end of 1999, a total of 9.06 million outdated cotton spindles had been dismantled and 1.16 million textile workers had been laid off (*ACTI* 2000: 47).[19] In 2000, an additional 300,000 cotton spindles were dismantled. Following the cotton textile sector, about 280,000 wool spindles and 1 million silk spindles were dismantled in 2000. Throughout this campaign-style reform of the SOEs in the textile industry, 300 SOEs were forced to go bankrupt, more than 400 SOEs were acquired by or merged with other firms, and 45 billion yuan of bad loans were written off (CNTIC 2000/01: 14).

As the three-year campaign was completed, the China State Textile Industrial Bureau was disbanded by the central government in 2001. In its place, the China National Textile Industry Council (CNTIC) was formed on a purportedly voluntary basis, and has since been chaired by Mr. Du Yuzhou, the former Minister of the Textile Industry and Director of the disbanded China State Textile Industrial Bureau. The industry yearbook or almanacs published under the former government Ministry or Bureau were also replaced by the *China Textile Industry Development Report* (*CTIDR*), which was published by the newly founded CNTIC. Unlike the almanacs, the new *CTIDR* contains no state directives or speeches by government officials—the emblems of the command economy had apparently gone permanently, along with the governmental bureaucracy of the industries.

Upon the completion of Project Breaking Point, the SOEs in the textile sector as a whole returned to profitability in 2000, though still not as profitable or competitive as the non-state-owned sectors. In the final report of Project Breaking Point by the Textile Bureau, Premier Zhu Rongji praised the achievements of the Project and commented: "In order to face the opportunities and challenges of the accession to the WTO, the textile and apparel industries' tasks to readjust and upgrade are still very grave . . ." (*ACTI* 2000: 47). Nevertheless, the overall level of technology adopted by the SOEs has improved tremendously as a consequence of over 10 million outdated spindles being destroyed during the campaign, and the SOEs have become leaner and meaner by laying off about 1.5 million workers and severing huge sums of bad loans—shedding the baggage carried over from the socialist planned economy (the unemployment and reemployment of those workers was a related but different kind of painful adjustment). Following the completion of the campaign, the SOEs had become much more independent and better positioned than ever before to compete with non-state-owned textile firms and international competitors, poised to cash in on market opportunities to be offered by China's pending entry into the WTO.

In parallel with the growth of the Chinese textile and apparel industries, the export of Chinese textile and apparel products also has been growing consistently. To a large extent, it was the exports that fueled much of the dramatic growth in the Chinese textile and apparel industries. This was because the demands for textile and clothing from the domestic market were initially quite limited and were depressed by the rationing system; and even after cloth rationing was abandoned in 1984, the increase in domestic demand could not keep up with the pace of the increase in production capacity. In fact, an export-fueled growth strategy was by design; at two major economic meetings in 1986, the central government decided that the strategic goal of the textile and apparel industries in the twentieth century was to expand exportation of their products. Subsequently, China adopted a host of favorable policies for the exportation of textile and apparel products, including tax deductions and tax rebates (*ACTI* 1988: 2). The textile and apparel industries have since become export-oriented industries and major hard currency earners for China. It is precisely due to the heavy emphasis on exportation that Chinese textile and clothing exports, especially clothing exports, have witnessed phenomenal growth. As Figures 2.2 and 2.3 illustrate, Chinese apparel exports have seen dramatic growth since 1980, and China has become the world leader since the mid-1990s. It has become a dominant player by capturing about one-third of the world's total clothing export market in 2007 (WTO 2009).

It is also worth noting that in the overall rising trend in Chinese clothing exports, there were two growth spurts: one in the late 1980s and early 1990s and the other in the 2000s. Growth in export was somewhat flattened in the second half of the 1990s. The trend in Chinese clothing exports correlates with the pace of economic reforms in China discussed previously. One may say that the two growth spurts in exportation were simply delayed reactions to the two waves of economic reforms, but exports also had to do with external factors, among which was the Multi-Fiber Arrangement, the international trade regime that regulateed international trade in textile and clothing, which will be discussed in Chapter 7.

In summary, modern Chinese textile and apparel industries have undergone three stages: infancy, development, and take-off. In the course of these developments, two major political events in the history of the PRC have led to structural shifts in China's textile and apparel industries and the overall economy. One event was the founding of the PRC and ascension of the Chinese Communist Party to power in 1949, which resulted in the nationalization of the Chinese economy and the establishment of a centrally controlled planned economic system. The other was the Third Plenum of the Eleventh Central Committee, held in 1978, which charted a path of economic reforms toward a market-based economy. During the post-1978 reform era, there were two phases of structural adjustments for the textile and apparel industries. In the first phase, the initial reform measures transformed the SOEs from largely administrative units to relatively autonomous business units in the early 1980s, and simultaneously encouraged the growth of the non-state sectors, including the TVEs and the FFEs. In the second phase, a new wave of market reforms was implemented in the early 1990s, which facilitated a boom of the FFEs and encouraged further growth of the TVEs in the textile and apparel industries. Market reforms during this phase allowed the non-state sector in the textile and apparel industries to rise to dominance. In the meantime, the SOEs were losing market shares to the non-state sector and suffered losses. By the end of the 1990s, the SOEs were forced to downsize, sever more ties to the abating planned economic system, and further shape themselves in the image of non-state-owned enterprises in order to take advantage of the opportunities afforded by China's imminent accession to the WTO. The export of Chinese textile and clothing provides a measure that helps to illustrate the phenomenal growth of the Chinese textile and apparel industries (see Figures 2.2 and 2.3).

Next, we need to explore the implications of such extraordinary growth in the contexts of China and the global textile and apparel industries. Is the rise of the Chinese textile and apparel industries simply another illustration of economic development and modernization that has been spread from the West to China? Related to that question, what role did the Chinese state play in the dramatic growth of the industries? And what was the role of the market? The following section will address these questions.

CHINESE TEXTILE AND APPAREL INDUSTRIES, INDUSTRIAL UPGRADING, MODERNIZATION, AND GLOBALIZATION

The textile and apparel industries are frequently implicated in two related grand narratives: modernization and globalization. Their connection to modernization has to do with the fact that the industries have a relatively low threshold in terms of the requirements for technology and capital (i.e., a low barrier to entry), and the requirement for a large low-skill labor force. The textile and apparel industries are typically the "starter industries" for a newly industrializing country (NIC) that is just embarking on the path to industrialization and modernization. Their link to the globalization discourse is reflected in the fact that the textile and apparel industries are among the most globalized industries today. This is the direct result of the decades-long process of developed countries outsourcing labor-intensive manufacturing, chief among which is textile and garment manufacturing to developing countries, beginning in the late 1960s. For example, the fashion giant Liz Claiborne, Inc.,[20] was among the leaders of this trend to outsource garment manufacturing to Mexico and East Asia (Collins 2003). Today, most of the Western fashion manufacturers like Liz Claiborne only have in-house capacities for design and marketing, which are more lucrative and less labor-intensive, while outsourcing the labor intensive and low-value-added segment of production to developing countries. Consequently, the global fashion industry becomes interconnected and integrated (Chapter 7 has further discussion on this point). Because of these factors, one may say that the textile and apparel industries' connections to modernization and globalization are grounded in facts. However, it is problematic to analyze and interpret these facts in a way that naturalizes the relationship between the textile and apparel industries (including those in China) and modernization and globalization.

All too frequently, scholars of the textile and apparel industries, economists in particular, describe the development of the textile and apparel industries as a series of industrial upgrades that appears to be natural and unavoidable (e.g., Shaw et al. 1994a, 1994b; Milberg 2005). According to this narrative, it is natural for a NIC to start up its industrialization and economic growth through developing the textile and apparel industries, just as it is natural for Western countries to outsource the labor-intensive manufacturing of textile and apparel products and focus on design and marketing. The differences between the textile and apparel industries in developing countries and those in the West are explained not just as comparative advantages of each economy but naturalized as different developmental stages, with the West being in the most advanced stage. This narrative of industrial upgrading and development is consistent with the modernization theory (Rostow 1960), as both adopt a unilineal evolutionary framework: the textile and apparel industries of a country would grow from a low-tech, labor-intensive stage to an advanced, high-tech, capital-intensive stage. Other than close kinship to modernization theory, this narrative is also wrapped up in the language of globalization and international division of labor. In other words, the development of the textile and apparel industries is not just temporal—going through a series of upgrading sequentially—but also spatial, in the sense that the wave of modernization started in the West and gradually spread to developing countries. In support of this narrative, scholars are quick to point to the wave of successes of the textile and apparel industries in Asia, starting with U.S. textile and apparel firms moving manufacturing capacity to Japan in the 1950s, then to Hong Kong, and then to South Korean and Taiwan (Bonacich and Waller 1994: 21–22). Since the 1990s, the wave has apparently moved from the Asian Tigers[21] to other Asian countries and most prominently to China. If all of this is true, then what is the problem with the narrative of industrial upgrading? The problem is multi-faceted and I will examine it using the example of the Chinese textile and apparel industries.

In a nutshell, the account of industrial upgrading creates an impression that the development of the textile and apparel industries (at both national and global levels) is as natural and unavoidable as biological growth. This is clearly not the case in reality. At the global level, it is true that the Asian Tigers and the developing countries in Asia (including China) have become industrialized through the development of the export-driven textile and apparel industries. However, the same type of industrialization and development did not occur in many other parts of the developing world, such as Latin America and Africa. Due to limited space, this chapter cannot fully explore why the textile and apparel industries in Latin American and African countries did not have the same trajectories of development as those in Asia, but suffice it to say that it had to do with the neoliberal policies that were put in place in the different contexts of these two regions. In the case of China, as we have seen previously in this chapter, the development of the textile and apparel industries did not occur naturally or occur in any form of natural progression of industrial upgrading. It was disrupted by war and political upheavals in the first and second stage of the development of the Chinese textile and apparel industries, and it wasn't until economic reforms were implemented in the late 1970s (the third stage) that the industries began to develop rapidly. Even in the reform period, the state still features prominently in the development of the textile and apparel industries. Simply put, the growth of the Chinese textile and apparel industries does not take place in a vacuum, but in the political and economic context of China, in which the state and the market both play significant roles. To understand the relative roles of the state and the market in the growth of China's textile and apparel industries, some elaboration is needed.

The state and the market are the two most important forces in bringing about the phenomenal growth in the Chinese textile and apparel industries. Frequently, the two are seen as fundamentally contradictory forces; in the eyes of the free market theorists (such as Milton Friedman), the state needs to get out of the way of the market so the (free market) economy can grow. In the context of China, there was a time when the opposite was true. During the second stage in the development of the Chinese textile and apparel industries, the socialist state nationalized the economy by taking over all the distribution channels of the economy and in effect forcing the non-state-owned sector to cooperate with the state. Consequently, the entire economy was turned into a state-controlled planned economy. Under the planned economic system, the state was the owner, the manager, and the driving force of economic growth. With the change in leadership from Mao to Deng, realization arrived that the state-controlled planned economy was flawed and market-oriented reform policies were adopted in late 1978. Subsequently, Chinese textile and apparel industries entered the third stage (the take-off stage), during which the industries shifted from a planned economy to a market-based economy. Today, the market has replaced the state as the driving force of economic growth in the Chinese textile and apparel industries, a statement is supported by recent statistics. In 2000, state capital only accounted for 18.7 percent of the aggregate capital of all statistical worthy enterprises in the textile and apparel industries, and the collective capital accounted for 9.94 percent of the total (Du 2004: v). Taking into account those non-state-owned firms with revenue below 5 million yuan, which employed half of the workforce in the entire industries, the percentage of state capital would account for only about 8 percent (ibid.).

However, the shift from a controlled, planned economy to a market economy should not be taken to mean that the role of the state is no longer relevant in China. On the contrary, market mechanisms were not part of the Chinese economy until they were introduced and cultivated by the state in the reform era. In each of the three phases of the market reforms in the textile and apparel industries, the state played a crucial role in allowing, inducing, and facilitating the growth of the market. Attesting to the powerful role of the Chinese state, the non-state-owned sectors emerged in leaps and bounds rather than developing gradually. In the state-owned sector, the state did not simply retreat and make way for the market, but actively reformed the SOEs and turned them into competitive participants in the market. This is most evident in the state-initiated Project Breaking Point between 1998 and 2000.

Without the strong hand of the state, it is hard to imagine that such drastic restructuring during Project Breaking Point could have taken place so quickly and relatively smoothly. To dramatize the painful adjustment the SOEs underwent, the media compared the dismantling of textile spindles in Shanghai to a warrior cutting off his wounded arm in order to prevent "infection."[21] The state-controlled media evidently intended to use the metaphor to invoke a heroic image of the SOEs and their workers, as they were bearing the brunt of the restructuring. At the conclusion of the restructuring project, hundreds of factories were closed, over one and a half million workers lost their jobs, and billions of yuan were spent on bad loans and compensation. The metaphor of a wounded warrior was an apt depiction of the SOEs, and in a way of the state. It was true that the SOEs went through some restructuring, but that was not the same as the neoliberal "structural adjustment" that emphasizes privatization. The SOEs preserved after restructuring become even stronger than before. It was also true that the state lost some power to the market through the economic reforms, but by cutting off the wounded arm, the state preserved the integrity of its power from being "infected." The state's insistence in calling its economy a "socialist market economy with Chinese characteristics" (and its ability to do so) is an indication that the dynamic between market forces and the state will likely be central to the development of the textile and apparel industries and the Chinese economy in general in the foreseeable future.

Based on the analysis above, the narrative of industrial upgrading is incongruent with the reality of the Chinese textile and apparel industries (as well as those in other parts of the world). Furthermore, this narrative explains the underdevelopment of the industries of a particular country by its own deficiency—the lower developmental stage of a country's textile and apparel industries is "caused" by its lack of the features of the more advanced stage. This explanation is problematic not just because it is tautological, but also because it puts the blame on the victim, so to speak; your industries do not advance because of your internal problems. By doing this, the narrative obscures the role of the state and other powerful players such as the multinational corporations (MNCs) that are involved in the textile and apparel industries. The outsourcing of manufacturing from a Western country to a developing country is clearly an external but important factor to the local industry. But the decision as to what to outsource and where to outsource it to remains firmly under the control of large MNCs based in the West, which will be further discussed in Chapter 7.

CONCLUSION

This chapter outlined the trajectory through which the Chinese textile and apparel industries developed into their current form. From the initial stage of infancy prior to the founding of the PRC, to a shortage economy in the first three decades of the PRC, during which cloth was rationed on a per capita basis, to becoming the world's largest manufacturer of clothing today, the development of the Chinese textile and apparel industries is nothing but a story of miraculous growth. The process of this development, however, was not in the form of a series of smooth and gradual industrial upgrades, but punctuated by structural shifts and adjustments.

The founding of the PRC by the Communists led to the nationalization of the Chinese economy, which resulted in a state-controlled planned economic system, which in turn expeditiously created an economy of scale in the textile industry. However, there were some intrinsic problems with the planned economic system, among which were the lack of incentives and a mechanism to cope with increasing surplus production capacity. These problems, combined with the general social environment that emphasized political struggle over economic development during much of the Maoist era, prevented further development of the textile and apparel industries. In the third stage, the industries started to take off after Deng returned to power and steered China toward market-oriented economic reforms in 1978. During the reform period, the textile and apparel industries as well as the Chinese economy as a whole gradually shifted from a centrally controlled planned economy to a market-based one. Today the market has replaced the state as the driving force of growth in the textile and apparel industries, but the state played an instrumental role in cultivating, facilitating, and encouraging the growth of the market, and continues to play an important role in the development of the industries. The example of Project Breaking Point illustrates the shifting dynamic between the state and the market in the reform period; it reflects the gravitation toward the market but at the same time underscores the power of the state in radical restructuring of the industries.

It is precisely because of the unique dynamic between the state and the market underpinning the structural changes that I argue that the growth of Chinese textile and apparel industries is not a simple modernization process that spread from the West to China. Rather, it emerged in the political-economic context in which China adopted reform policies that facilitated the growth and China's participation in the global economy. I also critiqued the narrative of industrial upgrading. It does not explain the rise of Chinese textile and apparel industries because it separates economic development from the political-economic context of China and obscures the role of power in the process of development.

The history of the development of the Chinese textile and apparel industries provides a backdrop to the emergence of the Chinese fashion industry, and it also highlights the shifting dynamic between the state and the market, two major forces that shape the broad changes in Chinese clothing and the fashion industry that I will discuss throughout this book. In the next chapter, I will examine the evolution of clothing styles in China. While the diverse styles today suggest the force of market segmentation can no longer be controlled by the Chinese state, the state was deeply involved in bringing about the changes of clothing styles as well as fashioning a narrative of modernity based on the stylistic changes in contemporary Chinese clothing.

–3–

What Do Changing Chinese Fashions Really Tell Us?

We are modern not only because we have achieved this status historically, but because we have developed consciousness of our historical depths and trajectories, as also our historical transcendence of the traditional.

—Nicholas B. Dirks (1990: 25).

[F]or much of the twentieth century. . .[Chinese] citizens might blithely disregard sumptuary and sartorial rules and regulations, but like their counterparts the world over, they generally heeded the call of the nation. In complex, sometimes unobvious or contradictory ways, they wore the nation on their backs.

—Antonia Finnane (2008: 16–7).

INTRODUCTION

During my year-long stay in Shanghai in 2004, I rented a small apartment at Xujiahui, a busy business district in Shanghai. In just a few minutes' walk from my apartment to the heart of Xujiahui, I would pass several types of stores. The first type comprised a few discount stores that sold branded shoes, bags, and clothes, which were right outside my apartment complex.[1] These were small store fronts, about 100–200 square meters, on the first floor and facing the street. Tempted by the huge signs of "closeout sale" on the window, I bought a pair of shoes from one of the shops shortly after my arrival in the neighborhood, but a few months later the shoe store was still in operation, and the closeout sale signs still on the window looked as fresh as ever (Figure 3.1).

I wondered how they could have closeout sales every day and why nobody asked the store to take off the misleading signs. While I was not one of their returning customers, from the large glass windows I could tell that the business seemed to be always quite brisk. Clearly, they didn't need my business or that of any other loyal customers to do well, because thousands of people would pass by these stores every day.

The second type of commercial establishment was a state-owned department store, which was inside a three-story building, located just off the main

Figure 3.1 A small discount store at Xujiahui. Courtesy of Jianhua Zhao.

thoroughfare. Even though the store was well-lit and looked updated, in some ways it reminded me of the state-owned department stores in the old days under the planned economy. The merchandise was not well displayed, signs were usually small (even with sales going on), the aisles were narrow, and above all, the salespeople never seemed to be excited about their jobs or eager to sell their products to the customers. On the other hand, the quality of the goods in the store seemed to be quite good, and the prices were generally pretty reasonable. In addition, the fact that it was a state-owned store might give the customers a sense of trust that it would not source their goods from unreliable suppliers. I understood why people would come and shop here, as I bought most of the essentials—bedding, pillows, quilts, and towels, etc.—to furnish my apartment. But, it is not a store where people would go for good service or luxury goods.

The third type of stores included several large, upscale department stores and shopping malls,[2] excluding stores that sold electronics exclusively, such as Bainaohui, BestBuy (a recent addition), and Taipingyang Diannaocheng. These stores were located right at the heart of Xujiahui. They were generally housed in huge multiple-story structures. They were clean, bright, and spacious, with modern fixtures and amenities. At the basement level was usually either a supermarket or a food court. Above the ground, the arrangement of the stores was not too different from that in other international shopping centers, with cosmetics and accessories prominently displayed on the first floor, then branded men's and women's wear on the upper floors. The goods in these stores were much more expensive (Dongfang shangsha being the most expensive of them all) than those in the other two types of stores, and the staff of the stores were typically more friendly as well. These stores were either state-owned, joint ventures, or solely owned by foreign capital. Although these stores were located on different sides of a major intersection, they were connected by an overpass and through the maze-like subway exits.[3] On weekends and major holidays, there always seemed to be sales events going on right outside the malls, which usually involved interactive performances, loud music, and huge crowds. The sale signs and advertisements (sometimes as high as two or three stories of the buildings) and promotional events were literally right in your face. It would not take more than a quick walk around Xujiahui to notice the highly diversified products and markets, and the diverse styles and colors the shoppers were wearing. Many of the younger shoppers, typically in jeans and t-shirts, with their hair dyed brown, would stroll around the shops with ease and appeared to be quite indifferent to all that was going on around them.

The shops at Xujiahui do not represent the full range of shops in Shanghai, as they do not deal with the rag trade (with hubs in the suburbs) or the top international designer labels, for which one would have to go to the Bund, Xintiandi, or upscale shopping malls on Huaihai Road and Nanjingxi Road. However, the range of shops at Xujiahui and the diverse styles and colors of the shoppers' dress clearly illustrate a lively and segmented clothing market in the twenty-first century Shanghai. The shopping scene at Xujiahui today contrasts sharply with that just a few decades ago when China was still under the planned economy, during which most people were in their drab Mao suits and everyone would have to use government-issued cloth coupons to buy cloth and clothes. The spectacular changes in the Chinese clothing industry are not only reflected by the phenomenal growth in its size and scale, but also evidenced by the dramatic changes in clothing styles in contemporary China. While Chapter 2 examined how the Chinese textile and apparel industries developed into their current state, this chapter focuses on the changes of clothing styles in contemporary China. Needless to say, given the space of this chapter, I can only focus on the major clothing styles in this period. The omission of some styles should not affect the broad point I will make about change. Specifically, I'll examine how Chinese clothing styles have evolved over time, and what such changes can tell us about notions of tradition and modernity in China. But first, I'll review briefly how anthropologists have studied style, particularly clothing style.

CLOTHING STYLES AND HISTORY

Contrary to the common assumption that style is trivial compared to the substance of a product, style can provide important insights about the product and its creator. The origin of the word "style," according to Alfred Kroeber, is "from stylus, the ancient writing tool, used metaphorically to express the individual manner peculiar to a writer" (Kroeber 1963: 66). The meaning of the term has clearly expanded from the style of one's handwriting (or calligraphy) to the style of expression. Consequently, an appreciation of the style of a handwritten essay does not only involve an examination of the aesthetics of form (as in an appreciation of the calligraphy), but also an intellectual engagement with the meanings of the writing. Similarly, clothing styles require both aesthetic and intellectual appreciation. A fashion designer is like an author (as opposed to a writer),[4] except that a fashion designer uses the medium of fabrics in place of words to express his or her individual style. The styles and strategies of individual Chinese fashion designers will be examined in Chapter 5. This chapter focuses on the social and historical aspects of clothing styles, the very aspects of style that Kroeber in general emphasizes. He writes,

> So far, we have the original meaning attaching to the word style; and this meaning with reference to individuals has never died out. In addition, however, with lapse of time the word style has come also to denote a social or historical phenomenon, the manner or set of related patterns common to the writers or musicians or painters of a period or country (Kroeber 1963: 66).

Elsewhere, Kroeber shows his specific interest in clothing styles. He examines stylistic changes in Western women's evening dress in long periods of time that exceed the lifespan of individual designers (Kroeber 1919; also Richardson and Kroeber 1940),[5] and he finds that the patterns in the stylistic changes in women's dress indicate that designers are "immersed in a cultural matrix that predetermined most of their conceptualization and behavior" (Lowe and Lowe 1982: 527). To be clear, the cultural matrix Kroeber refers to, which shapes the individuals in their creations of styles, is not equivalent to the external social and political conditions in which they live. Kroeber thinks that stylistic changes are largely dictated by and within "the structure of fashion" and that "the unsettling larger influences *impinge* on them [fashions]" (emphasis mine) (1957: 19). In other words, Kroeber believes that there is a relative autonomy within the fashion industry. For example, changes in Western women's full dress from 1844 to 1919 appeared to be "a slow pendulum-like swing between extremes" (Kroeber 1957: 9). Kroeber's study of Western women's full dress suggests that fashion cycles appear to be independent of the efforts of individual designers. At the same time, he acknowledges that external social and political forces can influence fashion cycles, even though he does not explain how the influence takes place in his study of Western women's dress. In a society like China that has undergone radical social and political transformation, would changes in fashion styles still be in the process of either approximation of or deviation from the ideal equilibrium that Kroeber suggests?

In what follows, I will outline the evolution of clothing styles in contemporary China. Following Finnane (2008), I will examine how clothing styles are related to the social and political milieu in contemporary China. Moreover, I will analyze Chinese official representations of the evolution of contemporary clothing styles, and examine the ways in which a moral tale of progress and modernization is constructed through these representations. I argue that it is through such representations and discourses that clothing becomes more than something that merely provides covering and livelihood for the Chinese citizens, and that time, modernity, and their associated morality are woven into clothing styles.

EVOLUTION OF CLOTHING STYLES IN CONTEMPORARY CHINA

Since the late nineteenth century, clothing styles have undergone dramatic changes in China,[6] not in terms of the cyclical change of fashion, but in historical changes that are entangled with politics of the time. Perhaps because of the largely linear nature of the stylistic changes of clothing in contemporary China, dress historians commonly illustrate the evolution of contemporary Chinese clothing as predicated on the four historical periods: the late Qing dynasty (1644–1911), the Republican period (1912–1949), the Maoist or radical socialist period (1949–1978), and the Reform era (post-1978). Here in this chapter, I follow this convention to describe the evolution of clothing styles in contemporary China, underscoring the connection between clothing styles and their respective social and political contexts in each period.

THE LATE QING

As the last imperial dynasty, the Qing, like many of its predecessors, maintained a rigid clothing code for its rulers and subjects alike. The elaborate sumptuary rules of the imperial family have been well documented (e.g., Garrett 1994: 29–61). Similarly, the Qing mandarins and subjects were supposed to dress according to their rank and status. This hierarchical way of dressing was not only legitimized by law, but also coded in morality and propriety: A person who dressed appropriately knew his or her place in society, which pertained to the Confucian concept of *li*, a complex concept that governed all social relations and behaviors; otherwise he or she would be no different from uncivilized barbarians (Steele and Major 1999: 18). Therefore, clothing was not just a reflection of one's taste, but also an integral part of the imperial social order that was governed by the system of *li*, just as described by a classic Chinese adage, "*chui yi chang er tian xia zhi*," meaning "[as long as] the clothing system is maintained, the social order is maintained."

However, to the above general characterization of clothing in the Qing dynasty, I have to add three caveats. First, the legal and moral constraints on clothing did not exclude possibilities of violation or transgression. For example, Wu (2005) did a study on consumption behaviors of wealthy families with lower ranks in the Jiangnan region in the Ming and Qing dynasties, and he found that their consumption behaviors often transgressed (*jian yue*) what their rank or status would allow. Similarly, Finnane (2008: 47) also mentioned the "new and strange" (*xinqi*) clothing, much of which was due to social climbing, of the commoners or merchant families in the sixteenth and seventeenth centuries. Second, sartorial distinctions in this period were mainly reflected through color, fabric, patterns, embroideries, and ornaments or accessories, but not through clothing styles *per se*. The major styles for men in the late Qing (Figure 3.2) included the *changpao* (or *cheongsam*), *magua* (the Qing-style jacket), a hat (skullcap), and a long queue (in a single plait); and the main clothing style for Manchu women was the *qipao*, while for Han women

Figure 3.2   A family portrait in late Qing. Courtesy of Ningbo Garment Museum.

the typical ensemble would include blouses and long skirts (frequently worn with pants underneath), and they typically had bound lotus feet.[7] In terms of the cut and silhouettes, clothing styles were rather limited during much of the Qing period as compared to other periods.[8] Third, new styles and demands for change began to emerge in the late Qing. Historians have argued that "the cutting of men's queues and changing of their clothing styles" (*jianbian yifu*) as well as the women's "natural feet movement" (*tianzu yundong*) were part of the revolution that led to the collapse of the Qing and the establishment of Republican China.[9] Following contact with Japan and Western imperial powers (including Britain, the United States, France, Germany, Austria, Italy, and Russia) in the late Qing, Western clothing styles started to gain popularity, so much so that a group of tailors called *hongbang caifeng* from the Zhejiang and Shanghai areas became well known for their fine skills in making Western styles of clothing.[10]

THE REPUBLICAN PERIOD

After the demise of the Qing and the establishment of the Republican government, Western styles of clothing, such as Western suits, became even more popular, since they were legalized by the new government as one of the formal attire, or *lifu*, in October 1912. The *changpao* was also officially included as a formal wear, as the new Republican government yielded to the pressure of the domestic silk industry (Wang 2003: 89–94; Gerth 2003: 68–121). In addition to the two different types of clothing, the Republican era is particularly known for the invention and popularity of the *zhongshanzhuang* (for men) and the *qipao* (for women). The popularity of these two styles made them the *lifu* of Republican period by default, a legacy that is still recognized today.[11] Elsewhere, I have discussed how the *qipao* was reformed and appropriated by Han Chinese women during the Republican era (Zhao 2004). According to professor Mingxin Bao, Han women's "reformed *qipao*" (*gailiang qipao*) in the Republican era is different from its Manchu predecessor in four major aspects, ranging from silhouettes, fabrics and patterns, ensemble, to status symbolism (1998: 11–14).

Here, I want to emphasize that the silhouettes and overall appearance differ between the two versions—the Han women's *qipao* in the Republican period was more fitted and revealing than the Manchu version, which was baggy and concealing—and that the differences are caused by the incorporation of Western design techniques, such as darts, set-in sleeves, and shoulder pads, in the making of Han women's *qipao*. Specifically, Han women's reformed *qipao* in the Republican period utilized techniques of three-dimensional cutting (*liti caijian*) while the Manchu *qipao* employed only two-dimensional cutting (*pingmian caijian*) techniques. The differences between the two types of cutting techniques will be further illustrated in Chapter 4, but the point I want to make here is that the adoption of Western design techniques did not make the *qipao* less Chinese; on the contrary, in the face of these changes the *qipao* became a Chinese cultural icon. Similarly, the making of the *zhongshanzhuang* also included some of the Western design techniques. Some dress historians even acknowledge that the style of the *zhongshanzhuang* was influenced by Japanese student uniforms and "*qiling wenzhuang*," a jacket worn by overseas Chinese in Southeast Asia (Wang 2003: 96–101; An and Jin 1999: 29–32). However, the personal promotion of the *zhongshanzhuang* by Sun Zhongshan (Sun Yat-sen), who is considered the founding father of Republican China, and the symbolisms of his revolutionary ideals as represented by different features of the jacket have no doubt contributed to its quick reception by the Chinese as truly their own.[12]

To summarize, the Republican period experienced a genuine plurality of clothing styles; three distinct genres coexisted: *changpao* and *magua* from the Qing dynasty, Western-style clothing such as Western suits (continued through the late Qing), and new inventions of the *qipao* and the *zhongshanzhuang* (as hybrids of the first two genres).

THE MAO ERA

In 1949, the Communist Revolution led by Mao Zedong defeated the *Guomindang* (the Nationalist Party or the KMT) Republican government[13] and the People's Republic of China was founded in mainland China. The PRC is divided into two periods: the radical socialist period or the Mao era (1949–78), and the reform period (post-1978). This historical division is also meaningful in terms of sartorial changes in the PRC. The Mao era is known in the West for one particular clothing style, the ubiquitous unisex Mao suit. Media reports and video clips of mass movements in the Maoist era always gave the impression of a sea of "blue ants" (or "green ants" during the Cultural Revolution).[14] Although there is some truth to those images, they do not capture the entire sartorial picture of the Maoist period.

In the 1950s, clothing styles from the Republican period such as the *qipao* and the *zhongshanzhuang* continued to be worn by many people. In fact, unlike the Qing and the Republican governments, the PRC government never issued any laws or regulations pertaining to clothing (Wilson 1999: 174). However, this is not to suggest that there was no connection between the dwindling popularity of the *qipao* and Western suits and the overall political environment in which the proletarian ideology dominated. According to A. C. Scott, the waning popularity of the *qipao* was because the people "tacitly understood" that "it was not patriotic to dress smartly" so that they put away their elegant *qipao* along with their silk stockings and high-heeled shoes and wore their shabbiest clothes (1958: 96). Garrett also shows historical evidence that the *qipao* was tolerated in the PRC until 1965 (1994: 106). It was not until the Cultural Revolution (1966–76) that the *qipao* and Western suits were labeled as belonging to the "four olds" (*sijiu*),[15] and subsequently were abandoned and in some cases destroyed (An and Jin 1999: 82; Steele and Major 1999: 59–60). High-profile cases included Wang Guangmei, wife of Chairman Liu Shaoqi, who was forced to dress in the *qipao* with a necklace of *pingpong* balls when she was interrogated and ridiculed by red guards during a class struggle session, which was recorded in photographs and video documentaries.

Political campaigns such as the Cultural Revolution without a doubt had impoverished Chinese clothing styles. However, the impoverishment, which created an illusion of uniformity to an untrained eye, was not primarily achieved by a heavy-handed government using forceful means as scenes and anecdotes of violence during this period would suggest (e.g., Kunz 1996). Instead, the state influenced people's attire indirectly through political ideology and discourse. The most important impact on what people wore during this period was probably the glorification of the peasants and workers, and by extension their clothing. In this political climate, clothing that could be interpreted as decadent or bourgeois, like the *qipao*, was considered by the people as inappropriate and even risky; wearing clothing that was just like everybody else's would address both practical (not to draw attention to oneself) and symbolic (to show solidarity with the working class) concerns. In addition, the state also actively promoted frugal lifestyles. Wilson argues that the discursive power of the state-initiated discourse of *pusu* (frugality) and the creation of role models of both cadres and ordinary people who lived frugal lifestyles, such as Lei Feng, helped to establish moral restraints against lavish dressing (Wilson 1999: 170–4). While the political and ideological influences on clothing in the Maoist era are recognized by scholars of Chinese dress, very little is written on the economic impact on clothing in this period. In fact, the seeming uniformity during this period was at least exacerbated by the shortage of textiles (discussed in Chapter 2). To address the shortage problem, the focus of the state was to increase production capacity and build large-scale textile plants, which consequently resulted in greater uniformity in fabrics, as those plants produced the same fabrics in large quantities and had no incentives or directives to diversify their products. Therefore, politics, economy, as well as the discursive power of the proletarian ideology and the discourse of *pusu* all contributed to the paucity of clothing styles during the Maoist period.

A major style in this period is the Mao suit (Figure 3.3). The Mao suit known to the West is called the *zhongshanzhuang* in China, or more precisely the

Figure 3.3 Mao's *Zhongshanzhuang*, reproduced in 1998. Courtesy of Ningbo Garment Museum.

Mao-style *zhongshanzhuang*. This style is a reformed version of Sun Yat-sen's. In the early 1950s, the central government transferred a group of *hongbang caifeng*, the group of tailors who made Sun's version of the suit, from Shanghai to Beijing and established a factory called *Hongdu* (Figure 3.4) specifically for the purpose of making garments for top government officials (Wang 2003: 169). The Mao suit was the work of these tailors. The differences between the Mao style jacket and the Sun Yat-sen jacket were mainly in the collar and fabric: the former had wider and looser collars and used all sorts of cheaper materials available at the time (mainly cotton and synthetic materials), whereas the latter had smaller and tighter collars and was mostly made of wool (primarily imported then). Simply put, the Mao jacket was but a proletarian version of Sun's *zhongshanzhuang*. Mao's status and charisma probably had a lot to do with the popularity of the style and the misnomer. That being said, it is not entirely accurate to say that all Chinese wore the Mao suit in the Maoist era or even during the Cultural Revolution decade.

Figure 3.4 Commemorating the thirty-year anniversary of Hongdou. Courtesy of Ningbo Garment Museum.

Despite the ubiquitous nature of the Mao suit among China's civilian population and its similarity to the military uniform,[16] it was not a uniform for civilians. According to Verity Wilson, no dress regulations were promulgated by the Chinese government during this period (1999: 174). In addition to the Mao style *zhongshanzhuang*, *qingnianzhuang* (the youth style) and *junbianzhuang* (the casual military style) were also very popular during the 1960s. Together the three styles were called the "three old styles" (*laosanzhuang*), and all of them bore great resemblance to Sun's original version of *zhongshanzhuang* (An and Jin 1999: 82). Common colors of clothing in this period included blue, grey, and black, which constituted the three old colors (*laosanse*). Green also became very popular when the red guards appropriated the military styles during the Cultural Revolution. Evidently, there was not a great variety of clothing styles and colors during the radical socialist period. Yet, ordinary people were still able to express their personal tastes and choices in muted and nuanced ways, a point made by Verity Wilson that deserves to be quoted at length:

> It was one of the ways people were able to engage in banter in a state system where gossip could be synonymous with informing. Dress concerns, of this sort at least, were seen as a relatively safe arena for exercising judgment, skill, and choice. The placement of pockets, the stitching of a seam, the depth of a collar and the suitability of the buttons were all details to engage the discerning dresser.

> A personal touch could be instilled by striped gloves knitted from leftover pieces of wool, and hand-knitted jumpers themselves could be uniquely fashioned . . . Even Mao badges, those most ideologically correct accessories, could be collected, swapped, pinned at various angles and in varying formations. (1999: 174)

Similarly, Juanjuan Wu also comments that the Cultural Revolution did not kill fashion in China; instead it "made people aware of the prevailing fashions down to the minutest details with a singular intensity" (Wu 2009: 2).

THE REFORM PERIOD

Although there was no regime change as in the previous three periods, the post-Mao Chinese state adopted economic reform policies domestically and open-door policies internationally. Subsequently, the state moved away from the political and ideological struggles of the Maoist era to a renewed focus on economic development,[17] which also entailed learning from the developed West. Chapter 2 examined the economic impact of the reform on the textile and apparel industries. Here, I focus on what the reforms mean to what people wear.

The CCP's attempt to settle ideological debates and move onto economic development did not immediately translate into a situation of anything goes in terms of people's clothing styles. In the early 1980s, people were still rather conservative with regard to what they wore, partly because of the lingering effects of previous ideological struggles and the overall morality of austerity and frugality (*jianku pusu*), and partly because new clothing styles were not yet readily available. One popular type of clothing that was unique to the 1980s was "double-use spring and fall wear" (*chun qiu liang yong zhuang*), which generally referred to jackets and shirts that could be worn in the two seasons of spring and fall. The uniqueness of this type of clothing lay in its name and functionality rather than its stylistic characteristics, which suggested that an overall abundance of garments was yet to come. As far as the early 1980s is concerned, the *zhongshanzhuang* and its various versions still ruled the scene. Compared to the conservative general public, top Communist Party leaders were at the vanguard in their attire. The return of Western suits was the result of personal promotion by the General Party Secretaries Hu Yaobang and Zhao Ziyang (the successor of Hu). On one occasion, Hu said,

> . . . Don't neglect the reform in lifestyles. Lifestyle has to change according to the changes in the means of production. Social revolution is historically linked to and even frequently starts with the reform in lifestyles. For example, Mr. Sun Zhongshan led the revolution and overthrew the Qing dynasty. He abandoned the

changpao and *magua*, and promoted the *zhongshanzhuang*, [and ordered] men to cut their queues . . . We have to adapt to the development of modernization, [we] should not be afraid to reform our lifestyles, and [we] should not be bound by backward stuff [*dongxi*, including ideas, habits, etc.]. Take eating for example, in our old tradition, eight or ten people eat from the same plate. Why can't we share and eat from our own plate? Take clothing for another instance, Western suits are convenient, why not promote them? (Editorial Board of Yearbook of Shanghai Clothing 1985: 1)

The fact that a top party official had to come out and make such comments points to the powerful effect previous ideologies, which he referred to as the backward stuff, had on people's attire. Paradoxically, to undo the constraints of previous ideologies on people, he had to use the same line of reasoning and emphasize that ideology was linked to what people wore, and hence he proposed that people's clothing styles and lifestyles in general should change with the times, as they were integral parts of the nation's reform agenda and modernization project. Therefore, while his message was couched in political and ideological terms, he in fact shifted the choice of clothing to primarily one of practical and personal rather than ideological matters (Figure 3.5).

Evidently Hu's efforts (as well as those of other party officials) worked; the *xifu* or the *xizhuang*, general terms for all types of Western suits, and especially for the tuxedo, have not only become the formal wear of government officials, but also a sought-after style for the general population.[18] In fact, the overall trend toward formal styles, as represented particularly by Western suits, was so prevalent toward the end of the 1980s and in the beginning of the 1990s that it was not uncommon to see migrant workers wearing Western suits or sport jackets as they worked on construction projects or performed other types of manual labor (Wu 2009: 51). Wu attributes the popularity of Western suits to a desire of the Chinese to modernize, she writes, "Just like adopting fast food (Kentucky Fried Chicken, McDonald's, and Coca-Cola were all present in China by the early 1990s), wearing the Western suit was viewed as a similarly fast and easy way to modernize" (Wu 2009: 50). Though it might be true that the Chinese wanted to project a modern image of themselves by donning Western suits, many contemporary or Western fashion styles (e.g., bell bottoms) did not come to China directly from the West, but through Hong Kong and Taiwan influences, especially the influence of popular Hong Kong and Taiwan TV dramas in the 1980s and 1990s. There has been increasing popular culture influence from Japan and Korea as well as from the West since the 1990s, but by then Western suits had been commonly accepted as work attire. Therefore, if there were a modernization of Chinese clothing in the reform era, it would be a mistake to interpret such efforts as the Chinese

Figure 3.5   A master tailor making a Western suit for a top Chinese government official. Courtesy of Ningbo Garment Museum.

trying to look like Westerners. Furthermore, there is never a straightforward connection between people's attire and what it symbolizes. A case in point is migrant workers' dress, which often becomes the laughingstock of the fashion-savvy urbanites (Guang 2003).

One frequently ridiculed outfit of the migrant workers, who are from the countryside, is an ensemble of a dark Western suit and white sneakers (the style is sometimes worn by U.S. comedian Ellen DeGeneres), which is considered by Chinese urbanites to be inappropriate at best, but more often *tu* or *tuqi*, or *ba* in Shanghai dialect. *Tu* means earth; in this context, it is used as an adjective, meaning earthy, backwards, unfashionable, and that which is associated with the countryside and the peasants. The opposite of *tu* is *yang* or *yangqi*, which means fashionable, modern, and that which pertains to the foreign and the West in particular. Therefore, the two terms of *tu* and *yang* are not only descriptive of fashion styles, but also indicative of one's taste, mindset, and even the level of one's inner quality or *suzhi*; they represent a series of opposite traits respectively: backward vs. modern, narrow-minded vs. open-minded, rural vs. urban, and finally low-*suzhi* vs. high-*suzhi*. Ironically, however, the Western suit as an imported style, which is supposed to be inherently modern and fashionable, when worn by migrant peasant workers turns into something unfashionable and backwards. Even more ironic, when the same outfit (a Western suit and white sneakers) was worn by Andy Lau (Liu Dehua), a Hong Kong pop star, no one seemed to have described him as *tu* or low-*suzhi*. Thus, what the Western suit means varies depending on whom the wearer is and the context in which it is worn. Nevertheless, there is no doubt that Western suits have staged a major comeback in China since the late 1980s.

Another major comeback in the reform period was the *qipao*. However, it is generally acknowledged that the craze for the *qipao* in the late 1980s was short-lived (Bao 1998; Finnane 1996: 125). Since then, the *qipao* has been commonly worn by hotel staff and other young women working in the service industry, yet only worn by middle-class women during formal occasions as a fashion item and/or a formal dress. While Finnane thinks that the inconvenience of the *qipao* is to blame for its diminishing popularity, as it is unsuited for the fast tempo of modern life (1996: 125), others believe that the *qipao* has been elevated to the status of the "national formal dress" (Bao 1998) and "a signifier of cultural identity" in mainland China (Clark 1999: 164).[19] As a matter of fact, many Chinese women today choose to wear the *qipao* for their weddings or their formal wedding pictures, which is usually a one-day affair that involves several outfits and scenes (both indoors and outdoors) scheduled before the wedding (Constable 2006). The *qipao* shops, some of which are rather upscale, are frequently seen at tourist spots in mainland China and Hong Kong. As a cultural icon of China, the *qipao* has also been adopted by high fashion both within and outside China. At the turn of the twenty-first century, China has witnessed a renewed interest in retro styles, culminating in the *tangzhuang* craze in 2001 and 2002, which will be discussed in greater detail in Chapter 4.

In addition to the revival of the Western suit and the *qipao*, new styles were slowly but surely catching on, initially through Hong Kong (and the influence of its popular movies and TV dramas) and the newly opened-up south and coastal areas. Bell bottoms were popular for a few years and quickly gave way to jeans and skirts. T-shirts also became popular, acquiring an interesting name of *wenhuashan* (cultural shirt), frequently carrying sometimes funny or politically subversive messages (Barme 1999: 145–178; Wu 2005: 53–4). More often than not, the messages were written in foreign languages, primarily English, but they frequently did not make any sense due to misspellings. In this context, the form or appearance of being *yang*, or foreign and modern, seems to matter more than the actual content and meaning of the message.

A similar pattern has been observed by Nicole Constable in her study of Chinese bridal pictures that often bear grammatically incorrect English captions (Constable 2006). In terms of clothing styles, jeans and T-shirts have marked a growing trend toward casual styles of clothing since the late 1980s, a trend that was also supported by an emerging interest in sports and outdoor activities (Brownell 1995). Besides professional sportswear (such as international brands Nike, Adidas, Puma, and the domestic brand Li-Ning), casual wear and sportswear also emerged in everyday life: tights and bikinis became acceptable and even popular;[20] jumpers, jackets, and blazers all became good outerwear; wool sweaters and down jackets turned into essential items for the winter.

Concurrent with the rapidly shifting fashion trends in the reform period, China is also experiencing a boom in the fashion media. The first domestic fashion magazines were established by state-owned entities; these included *Shizhuang* (*L'Officiel*) in 1980, *Xiandai fuzhuang* (*Modern Dress and Dress Making*) in 1981, *Liuxingse* (*Fashion Color*) in 1982, and several more later on. Many foreign magazines, such as *Elle* and *Cosmopolitan*, quickly established themselves (in collaboration with Chinese publishers) in the 1990s, taking over much of the market share in China. The Chinese version of *Vogue* was launched in September 2005. The most popular fashion magazine is called *Ruili fushi meirong*. Though the magazine seems to be owned by a Chinese publisher, the fashions and models in the magazine are strictly Japanese. Newspapers, on the other hand, are highly controlled by the Chinese government. Two state-owned newspapers, *Zhongguo fushi bao* (*China Fashion Weekly*) and *Fuzhuang shibao* (*Fashion Times*), are the dominant national trade papers, which were established in the mid-1990s. In addition to these two, there are regional newspapers, lifestyle newspapers, and shopping guide newspapers (*gouwu daobao*) that cover fashion on a regular basis. In the 2000s, major TV stations also started broadcasting fashion programs. The growth of fashion media has certainly contributed to the popularity of fashion styles and quickened the pace of fashion cycles in China.

Following the successes of Western name brands and designer labels—Pierre Cardin was the first foreign designer to enter the Chinese market (see Chapter 6)—domestic luxury brands and designer lines started to pick up steam in the second half of the 1990s. Yifei, for example, was one of the early leaders as a domestic designer label, but it fell apart after the untimely death of its owner, Mr. Chen Yifei, in 2005. Today there are many Chinese designers who are very successful commercially. For example, Wang Yiyang's (the first Chief Designer at Yifei) Zuczug (Figure 3.6) and Ma Ke's Exception are both quite mature brands that have survived the early phase of intense free market competition. There are also well-known designers who are very artistically driven (Figure 3.7), but not as successful commercially. Domestic

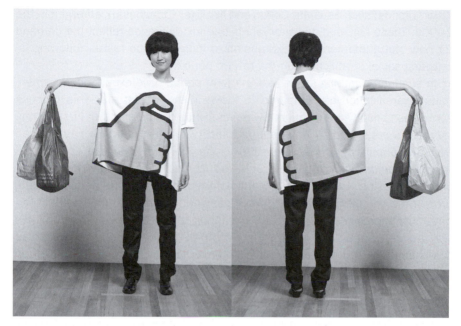

Figure 3.6   Sample design of Zuczug. Photo by Lu Canghai. Courtesy of Wang Yiyang.

Figure 3.7   Wu Haiyan's *Dongfang siguo* fashion show. Photo by Zhang Dapeng. Courtesy of Wu Haiyan.

luxury brands, such as White Collar, and Ne Tiger (Dongbeihu), emerged in the 2000s. These high-end designer labels and luxury brands reflect the demand for new status markers and expression of individualistic tastes following increasing social stratification in the reform period.

In summary, clothing styles in the reform period have experienced tremendous diversification as compared to those in the Maoist era. This process continues to evolve today, but a few major trends can be spotted. First, formal wear, as represented by *zhiyezhuang* (office wear), a trend that has evolved from the popularity of Western suits in the 1980s, remains a major category of everyday wear today. Second, casual wear and sportswear have become increasingly popular, even to the extent of becoming the dominant style among the younger population. Third, designer labels and imported brands have flourished since the late 1990s, catering to specific needs of individuals and groups. Last but not least, various cultural or sub-cultural styles such as the grunge look and punk style have become more common in China's urban centers. To sum up the changes in women's fashions in contemporary China, Finnane writes,

> The volatility of fashions in the twentieth century matched vicissitudes in national politics, to a point where a series of political regimes through the century was matched by a parallel series of vestimentary regimes. A comparison of photo montages with the headlines in Shanghai's popular press would immediately suggest a political chronology of Chinese women's fashions in the twentieth century. (2008: 15)

From the evolution of major clothing styles in contemporary China outlined above, we can see that both women's and men's clothing styles have changed dramatically throughout the four historical periods. Though the stylistic changes of clothing were and are connected to the social and political contexts of each period, the reform period is particularly different from the other three periods in its relatively loose association between political context and styles. In the three previous periods (with the exception of certain urban areas in the Republican era) clothing styles were relatively more stable and closely tied to political ideologies, but in the reform era they are much more changeable, diverse, and relatively independent of political and ideological control (yet more subject to market and popular culture influences). Given that changeability is essential to the functioning of fashion (Kawamura 2005), it is not surprising that it is in the reform period that Chinese fashion professionals such as fashion designers and models have emerged (which will be discussed in Chapters 5 and 6 respectively).

How does one make sense of the differences between the reform era (the present) and the three preceding periods (the past) in terms of the changeability of clothing styles? Does it mean that clothing styles in the past were non-fashion or traditional clothing whereas clothing styles in the present are fashion or modern clothing (c.f. Niessen 2003)? To put it differently, does China's adoption of Western-style clothing in the reform era symbolize modernity as suggested by Wu (2009: 2)? The Chinese official historiography of the evolution of clothing in the contemporary period gives insights into what a Chinese notion of modernity entails, to which I now turn.

A TALE OF MODERNITY?

From the *changpao* and *magua* in the Qing dynasty to the diverse styles today, clothing styles in China have changed significantly, not in the form of cyclical change observed by Kroeber, but more in the form of linear progression largely along with the transitions of the four historical periods in contemporary China (though some styles crosscut different periods). The linear rather than cyclical association between clothing styles and time lends itself to an objectification of time through clothing. In fact, the relationship between clothing and time is explicitly portrayed in the Chinese official representations of the sartorial evolution in contemporary China. Two examples will suffice to illustrate just that.

As a part of the China Cultural Year programs in Paris, which were sponsored by the Chinese Ministry of Culture and took place between October 2003 and July 2004, an exhibition of contemporary Chinese fashion was organized. In conjunction with the exhibition, a book was published both in French and Chinese, entitled *Costumes chinois: Modes depuis 100 ans* (*Chinese Costumes: Fashions of the Past 100 Years*). Yuan Yang, chief editor of the book, summarizes Chinese fashion in the past century in this way:

> In the 20th century, the spiritual look of the Chinese changed dramatically; clothing fashions were closely connected to the changes of political events, and every shift and innovation in clothing represented the mode of the time. This is a century in which Chinese clothing went through (*zouxiang*) being traditional (*chuantong*) toward modernity (*xiandai*), and from being feudal (*fengjian*) toward openness (*kaifang*). It is also the golden age for Chinese clothing fashions, numerous fashions rose and fell, much more diversely and swiftly than any other time in Chinese history. (2003: 10)

According to Yang, clothing is not just about one's appearance or look, but also reflects the spiritual outlook of the wearer. It is on the spiritual level that the changes in contemporary Chinese clothing tell a moral story: the Chinese (hence the nation) are changing from being traditional toward embracing modernity, from being feudal toward favoring openness. It is worth noting that

Yang did not use definitive past tense; instead, he uses the term *zouxiang*, which means moving toward, suggesting a progression through time, with the ultimate modernity and openness yet to come. Meanwhile, he also emphasizes that the current situation is very exciting and encouraging because "we" are in a "golden age," better than ever before. Therefore, Yang's account of contemporary Chinese clothing chronicles a dark and feudal past, a golden present, and a bright future, where modernity lies.

In a similar way but with a clear Marxist overtone, Zhao Wang writes in the preface to a college textbook on the history of contemporary Chinese clothing,[21]

> The development of contemporary clothing followed the reforms in lifestyles (*shenghuo fangshi*). Historical developments and reforms of clothing all closely tied to the changes in lifestyles. Modern clothing, in particular, develops and changes under the pre-condition of reforms in life [styles] and [means of] production. Especially in the post-1990s, people's lifestyles have changed greatly. Advanced means of production (*shengchan fangshi*), rich and colorful life, led to newer, more scientific, and more hygienic ideas in people's attire and appearance, and consequently, people in our great motherland are wearing in the new century [clothes that reflect] the spirit of our time, cultural taste, national fashion, and artistic aura. (Wang 1999: 2)

Different from Yang's account cited earlier, Wang explicitly attributes the progress in people's dress to the advancement in the "means of production," a Marxist concept, which is in sync with the Communist Party line as seen in Hu Yaobang's speech quoted earlier in this chapter. Given the fact that Wang's words appeared in a textbook, which is censored by the state, his Marxist overtone (and euphoria) is not surprising. However, like Yang, Wang clearly believes that clothing styles today are better than those in the past. Therefore, from these official narratives, evolution of clothing styles in contemporary China not only illustrates the broader historical changes, but also serves as "political acts" of ordering the past, the present, and the future (Fabian 1983: x). Indeed, these official narratives of the evolution of contemporary Chinese clothing represent a historiography that provides a moral commentary on time: the past, the present, and the future are in a continuum of progress and modernization in China.

The extent to which the official historiography of Chinese clothing reflects reality is not what I intend to explore. A far more important and interesting question is: To what extent does the historiography of contemporary Chinese clothing reflect the overall Chinese official historiography of this period? In other words, how are the narratives of contemporary Chinese clothing related to the way in which contemporary Chinese history in general is written in China?

Once again, as history textbooks are approved and censored by the Chinese government, they are a good source to examine for the Chinese official historiography. As indicated in Chinese high school textbooks, contemporary Chinese history began when the first Opium War broke out in 1840,[22] and this history is narrated as China's continuous quest for modernity.[23] This quest includes the Nationalist revolution led by Dr. Sun Yat-sen, which overthrew the Qing dynasty but quickly fell into warlordism. Since then the Chinese have awakened, which was marked by the May Fourth Movement (1919) and the birth of the Chinese Communist Party (1921). After the passing of Sun Yat-sen (1925), Chiang Kai-shek consolidated his power within the Nationalist party. Although Chiang was able to maintain some control of the Republic of China (1928–49) and fought alongside the Communists against the Japanese invasion (1937–45), it was the Communists who finally put an end to China's humiliating semi-colonial status and established a truly independent nation-state known as the People's Republic of China in 1949. According to this official Chinese historiography, contemporary Chinese history is a continuous story of progress, modernization, and liberation; the wars during the Republican period, the Great Leap Forward (1958), and the Cultural Revolution (1966–76) are all but trials and errors in the due process. The message in this historiography is clear: Thanks to generations of revolutionary forerunners, especially the Communists, China is making continuous progress toward liberation and modernization.

From the description above, it is clear that the historiography of contemporary Chinese clothing is consistent with the overall official Chinese historiography; both regard history as continuous and marching toward progress and modernization. One may say that the official Chinese historiography is the dominant historiography that permeates Yang's and Wang's accounts of contemporary Chinese sartorial history. In the dominant Chinese historiography, the rise of the Chinese nation-state is not just a historical event (such as the founding of the PRC in 1949), but a continuous process. Differently put, contemporary Chinese history as in the textbook version is written in a way that equates it with the rise of China. Benedict Anderson (1983) has taught us that nation-states are "imagined communities." Following Anderson, I think that the history of the rise of the Chinese nation-state is a historical construction that gives legitimacy to the nation-state. By historical construction, I do not mean that the historical events are fabricated; instead, I refer to the way in which these events are narrated assuming a logic that is not necessarily inherent or self-evident in the course of history. Aside from the apparent nationalistic sentiments, the logic in the dominant Chinese historiography has to do with a Chinese notion of modernity.

What, then, do the narratives of contemporary Chinese sartorial history and the dominant Chinese historiography in general tell us about Chinese modernity? These narratives do not give a straightforward answer; they only suggest that Chinese modernization is a continuous process, not any state or endpoint where modernity ends up. But if "modernity" is not here and now, then where and what is it? In a study of Chinese modernity, Lisa Rofel treats modernity as "a located cultural imaginary, arising from and perpetuating relations of difference across an East-West divide" (1999: xii). As such, she thinks Chinese modernity is "a story people [the Chinese] tell themselves about themselves in relation to others [the West]" (1999: 130). Can Rofel's interpretation of Chinese modernity, which was derived from a different context, be applied here? In other words, is the West of the present, real or imagined, what the Chinese believe to be their future modernity? The answer to the question requires some elaboration.

The Marxist teleology of societies, to which the PRC subscribes, places socialism and communism in a more advanced stage than the European capitalist societies. It is therefore tempting to claim that the Chinese locates modernity in socialism and communism. Scholars of China have also noted that radical socialist China fought for modernity by claiming an ideological high ground: "modern Marxism" (Rofel 1999: 25). It is true that the Chinese leaders had and still claim to have aspirations to reach the communist utopia one day, but the economic reality never convinced the Chinese, including the national leaders themselves, that they were actually more advanced than the capitalist West. If they ever had that illusion, the illusion was broken along with the failed Great Leap Forward campaign in 1958, which exacerbated, if not induced, severe famines that killed millions of people in the following three years.[24] It is perhaps surprising to some that it was Premier Zhou Enlai and Chairman Mao who first put forward the economically oriented goal of Four Modernizations in various versions in the 1950s and the 1960s. The final version, as we know it today, of "agricultural modernization, industrial modernization, modernization of science and technology, and modernization of national defense," first appeared in Zhou's "Government Working Report" in December 1964 (Cao 2006). The Third Plenum of the Eleventh Central Committee in 1978 simply restated the Four Modernizations as the national goal to be reached through economic reforms. The Goal of Four Modernizations suggests that even in the radical socialist period, the Chinese leaders recognized that China was still not modern and needed to be modernized, at least in economic and materialistic terms. A predicament arose immediately for the Chinese Communist Party leaders: How could China be ideologically more advanced while at the same time more backward economically than the capitalist West? Isn't it the Marxist doctrine that the ideological superstructure is determined by the economic base? Given the apparent paradox, how can China define its modernity in relation to the Western others?

The solution for the CCP and the state is not to define modernity as some sort of fixed condition or state, but to emphasize modernization as a process; to do so the CCP and the state constantly refer back to the progress that China has made, which gives legitimacy to the state and its modernization project. This pattern of legitimizing the present by comparing it to the past is a common practice in China, even when the specific plans for modernization are drafted. The paramount example is the state's "three-step" blueprints to realize modernization,[25] with each step referring back to the previous step, using such phrases as "doubling the GDP" of the previous period. The message behind this blueprint is that Chinese modernity locates in the future, but it is built on previous and current modernizing efforts, and that with "our" efforts, "we" the Chinese can ensure that the present will be better than the past and the future better than the present. The same logic is inherent in the narrative of China's modernization—a continuous process of progress. Therefore, the CCP's and the state's solution to China's predicament of modernity is to construct the past, present, and future as a continuous progress, and give temporality a certain logic and order, in the same fashion as the official narratives of China's sartorial evolution do. Seeing time in this manner, modernity becomes more than something desirable to be attained; it indeed becomes a trope, or to borrow Rofel's phrase (per Geertz 1973b), a story that Chinese people tell themselves about themselves. But different from Rofel's version, the reference point here is not the Western other; instead, it is China's own past. The moral of this story is two-fold: On the one hand, if we (the Chinese) desire the future, the better, and the modern, then we have to work hard toward it. On the other hand, what we are doing is clearly the right thing because we have seen progress as compared to the past. In short, a Chinese notion of modernity is encoded in the state's discourse of modernization, the official narratives of the evolution of contemporary Chinese clothing, and the dominant Chinese historiography.

CONCLUSION

This chapter reviewed the dramatic changes of clothing styles from the late Qing to the reform period. These changes did not take place in the form of fashion cycles as Kroeber predicted; instead, they appeared to be in a linear progression as various styles rose and fell along with the changes in the broad social and political environments. The linear correlation between clothing styles and politics through time paves the ground for official representations of the evolution of contemporary Chinese clothing styles as a story of progress and modernization. Consequently, the official narratives of the evolution of contemporary Chinese clothing create a structure of time that carries a moral message that the present (the PRC) is better than the past and it will become even better in the future. These narratives are consistent with the broad Chinese historiography that constructs the history of contemporary China as a continuous process of progress and modernization, culminating in the rise of the PRC. Furthermore, the way in which contemporary Chinese history is written in textbooks is also consistent with the CCP's and the state's discourse of and approach to modernization: modernization is not just a grand and fixed goal to be achieved (the specific goals of modernization have changed over time), but more importantly a continuous process to be carried out. In this discourse, as long as the state can demonstrate that progress (such as the doubling of GDP) is being made, both the discourse of modernization and the state are justified and legitimated.

Clearly, the official narratives of the Chinese sartorial evolution and the dominant Chinese historiography are constructed in such a way that they serve nationalistic interests. Besides their connection to nationalism, these narratives of Chinese clothing and historiography also reflect a deep-seated Chinese sense of time and modernity. According to this historiography, the past, the present, and the future are not experienced in breaks or ruptures (cf. Appadurai 1996), but are continuous and related to each other so as to construct a coherent order of progress. That is to say, in the official narratives, contemporary Chinese clothing is given meaning in structuring time. It is in this sense that I argue the evolution of clothing styles in contemporary China yields insights to a uniquely Chinese notion of modernity.

Countering previous studies of modernity, which either locate modernity in the West and portray the rest as "people without history" (Wolf 1982) or people stuck in time (Fabian 1983), or assert an insurmountable and perpetuating distance between the West and the rest (Rofel 1999), Chinese modernity, as encoded in the narratives of contemporary sartorial evolution and the dominant Chinese historiography, is a story the Chinese tell themselves about themselves in relation to their own past, rather than the Western other. However, this by no means suggests that the Chinese are oblivious to the influence of the West; in fact, Chinese designers and dress historians are very conscious of the West, as they openly acknowledge influences of Western design techniques and clothing styles. Today, Western influence on Chinese fashion comes from a host of sources, ranging from print media to popular culture. Yet, according to this Chinese notion of modernity, these Western influences reflect Chinese modernity only because they are incorporated into Chinese fashion history and suggest an advancement from China's past.

This chapter argues that one key meaning that the Chinese have mapped onto clothing styles in contemporary China is a Chinese notion of modernity. In the Chinese notion of modernity, history is "one of the most important signs" (Dirks 1990), and the state is the single most important agent in fashioning the dominant historiography and subsequently the notion of modernity.

In the next chapter, I will examine the *tangzhuang*, a style that is promoted by the state and carries important symbolic meanings about tradition and modernity, as a case study of the state's power in fashioning its own notion of modernity.

PART 2

Creating Fashion in China

–4–

Designing a National Style: The *Tangzhuang* Phenomenon

INTRODUCTION

On October 21, 2001, the last day of the Asia-Pacific Economic Coopera-tion (APEC) Summit, then-Chinese president Jiang Zemin along with other Asia-Pacific heads of state donned brightly colored Chinese silk jackets and matching white silk shirts and black pants or skirts, and posed in front of the world media (Figure 4.1).[1] The jacket soon became known as the *tang-zhuang*, a style that is intended by the Chinese state to symbolize a national dress that reflects "both traditional Chinese flavor and modern ideals" (*The China Daily* 10/21/2001). The style was indeed very popular in the winter of 2001 and the following year. However, its immediate popularity did not stop the critics from questioning the accuracy of the name and nature of the style.

The name of the *tangzhuang* suggests that the style dates back to the Tang dynasty (618–907), which was arguably the greatest period in China's long history. One of the original designers thought it was all right to call the jacket the *tangzhuang* because it symbolized something "Chinese," just as overseas Chinese are called *tangren*, and Chinatown *tangren jie* (personal in-terview in 2002). On the other hand, Chinese dress historians believed that the name was a misnomer because the style of the jacket bore greater re-semblance to the *magua*, a popular style in the Qing dynasty (1644–1911), than to clothing styles in the Tang dynasty.[2] Other designers on the origi-nal team took a middle-ground approach and later "corrected" the name to the *xin tangzhuang* (new *tangzhuang*) because the jacket was not a rep-lica of a clothing style of the Tang dynasty but a new style. In other words, they were toeing the official line, which emphasizes both the newness and Chinese-ness of the jacket.[3]

The enormous publicity of and the debates surrounding the jacket give rise to a series of questions: Why has a jacket that is intended to be used for no more than a day ignited such heated discussion? Is the style chosen from the existing Chinese repertoire of clothing styles? If not, how are the jackets designed and made? In what ways is the style both modern and tra-ditional? What do average Chinese think of the style? And finally, to what

Figure 4.1   2001 APEC Summit in Shanghai. Courtesy of Getty Images.

extent was the Chinese state successful at fashioning the *tangzhuang* as a national dress? This chapter addresses these questions. In the following, I will first analyze the unique significance of the occasion for which the jacket is intended. This will be followed by a description of the ways through which the jacket is designed and made, utilizing both media reports and data gathered through personal interviews, as well as a presentation and analysis of the debates surrounding the *tangzhuang*. Finally, I will assess the extent of China's success in inventing a national sartorial identity by juxtaposing the state's interpretation of the jacket and an account by a Chinese consumer-citizen. Let us now turn to the occasion on which the jacket is worn.

THE OCCASION

The APEC meeting is an economic forum among the Pacific Rim nations. Over the years, a convention has been established that the national leaders attending the summit (on the last day of the APEC meeting) will wear clothes presented by the host country that reflect its culture and tradition. The gifting of the clothes is not just a gesture of hospitality by the host country, but, more importantly, displays and symbolizes to the world an image of solidarity among the heads of state attending the APEC summit as they stand together, united in attire, in front of the world media (Roces and Edwards 2008: 1). The APEC meeting is therefore an occasion that lends global significance to the dress; it is literally pageantry on the world stage—only this time the models are the leaders of the Pacific Rim nations. At the same time, because the dress is made and presented by the host country, it also serves as a unique opportunity for the host country to represent itself to the world. For that reason, the host country is compelled to come up with a style that truly and uniquely reflects its own culture. What is generally recognized as the traditional garb of the host country thus becomes the standard attire that heads of state would wear at the APEC Summit.

China, as the first-time host of the APEC meeting in 2001, made sure that the Chinese public was informed of this convention; various state-controlled media widely reported on the traditional styles of clothing worn at previous APEC Summits such as the Malay batik shirts, the Philippines Barongs, and the Canadian leather bomber jackets (e.g., *Xinhuawang* 10/21/2001; *Zhonghuawang* 10/21/2001). Months before the meeting, the Chinese media began reporting on previous APEC attire, China's preparation and plans for its APEC dress, and speculations about what China's choice would be. Media coverage intensified as the APEC Summit drew close. Because the APEC dress was a closely guarded secret, the suspense steadily built and intensified until the jackets' inaugural appearance was finally revealed to the world media on October 21, 2001. The high level of public interest in China's choice of the APEC dress had to do with the fact that no one could really name the national dress of China,[4] which added to the mystery of what China's choice would be. Although no specific information about the design of the Chinese APEC dress was leaked to the media before the meeting, the wide media coverage and the suspense it created all added to the public perception that this was a highly important occasion and that the choice of the attire by the Chinese government would represent an officially recognized national dress of some sort. In other words, the APEC garb would provide China with a potent symbol to fashion a national identity to the world, and simultaneously to educate Chinese citizens about China's national status and achievements, hence legitimizing the rule of the Communist Party and the state.

To serve both purposes, China came up with a new style called the *tangzhuang* that looked ambiguously traditional. Why was none of the "official wear" (*lifu*) in contemporary China chosen by the Chinese government for the APEC Summit? To answer this question, we need to examine the potential alternatives to the *tangzhuang* for this occasion.

THE ALTERNATIVES

As discussed in Chapter 3, several clothing styles served as the "official wear" for men in contemporary China: the *changpao* (frequently worn with the *magua* jacket on top), the *zhongshanzhuang*, the Mao suit (or the Mao-style *zhongshanzhuang*), and Western suits (*xizhuang* or *xifu*). For women, the official wear included the *qipao*, the Mao suit, and Western suits. In the late Qing, the *changpao* was the official mode of attire. During the Republican era (1912–49), both the *changpao* and Western suits were officially considered as *lifu*. In addition, the *zhongshanzhuang* was invented and promoted by the founder of the Republic of China, Sun Zhongshan (Sun Yat-sen), and by default became the official wear in the Republican era. The popular *qipao* became the de facto official wear for women during the same period.[5] In the Maoist era (1949–78), the Mao suit was the only dominant style for both men and women. The Mao suit was in fact a modified and proletarian version of *zhongshanzhuang* and is widely known as such in China, rather than as the Mao suit, as it is often called outside China. In the post-1978 reform period, Chinese national leaders appropriated Western suits as the official wear.

Given their status of being official wear in contemporary China, all these styles could theoretically be chosen by the government as the APEC dress. In fact, designs of the *changpao* and the *zhongshanzhuang* were reportedly among the choices presented to government officials who were in charge of the APEC dress. However, as Chapter 3 made clear, the sequential succession of these styles over time suggests that they are closely tied to the politics of the time (see also Finnane 2008). The *zhongshanzhuang* and the Mao suit are both named after political figures, and subsequently they became associated with the political ideologies of Sun and Mao respectively. Sun Zhongshan clearly articulated how various features of his namesake jacket represented his revolutionary ideals. Even though Mao didn't explicitly explain the political rationale for his appropriation and modification of the *zhongshanzhuang*, his promotion of the socialist ideas of equality and frugality was directly responsible for the popularity of the Mao-style *zhongshanzhuang* as well as the disappearance of the *changpao* and the Western suit (Wilson 1999), which became associated with feudal or bourgeois ideologies and were hence considered politically incorrect during the Maoist era. In the reform period, Communist party leaders Hu Yaobang and Zhao Ziyang adopted Western suits and ties as the official wear to signal their determination on "reform and opening-up." Their actions seemed to have worked: the Chinese frequently judge the political climate or political leanings of their national leaders by what they wear on the national television news; while wearing the Western suit signals an open attitude toward reform, wearing the *zhongshanzhuang* or the Mao suit in the re-form era is considered hardline or conservative. Western observers are quick to point out the example of former Premier Li Peng, who wore a Mao-style *zhongshanzhuang* when he ordered the crackdown on the students' protests at Tian'anmen square in 1989 (e.g. Wu 2009: 124). Today, the *zhongshanzhuang* is very much rendered as the uniform for the national civilian leaders of the military, including the Chinese president Hu Jintao, who consistently wears the *zhongshanzhuang* instead of the Western suit at military functions.

Therefore, although the *changpao*, the *zhongshanzhuang*, and the Mao-style *zhongshanzhuang* had served as official wear, their political and ideo-logical associations made them inappropriate for the occasion. The Chinese state also did not want to project such a politically loaded and anachronis-tic image at the 2001 APEC. While the Western suit was the current formal wear in China and in that sense ideologically correct, it had no claim to being a distinctively Chinese style, which was an unspoken requirement for the of-ficial dress of the APEC Summit. All these factors contributed to the design of a new style for the 2001 APEC Summit. In response to my question about the intentions in designing the APEC jacket, one of the original designers said (personal interview 2002):

> . . . Many countries in the world have their own national dress. When you think of Japan, you think of *kimono*; when you think of Korea, you think of *hanbok*. What do we have? Nothing. The Western suit is not ours, and the *qipao* is only for women. When we were designing the APEC jacket, we were thinking we had to design a garb of our own culture that could be worn at formal occasions.

Similarly, the *New York Times* also made its own observations on China's op-tions for the APEC dress:

> Unlike most other places in Asia, China made a great show of rejecting its tra-ditional garb as politically incorrect in the early days of Communist rule, so put-ting the leaders in long, elegant cheongsams would have seemed hypocritical. Mao suits, on the other hand, would have been laughably anachronistic in a day when capitalists are being welcomed into the Communist Party. (*New York Times* 10/20/2001)

Evidently, in the eyes of both the Chinese fashion designer and the *New York Times* observer, the Chinese government's options for a dress that is both attentive to Chinese culture and appropriate for the occasion were rather limited. China would have to come up with something new that appeared to be old.

THE MAKING OF THE APEC DRESS

Recognizing the significance of the APEC garments, the municipal government of Shanghai, the host city, organized a team of seven designers to work on the design and production of the garments. The team worked secretly under the supervision of the Shanghai city government and the central government for nearly two years to come up with the designs and produce the finished garments. To ensure the secrecy of their work, a special mode of communication between the team and various levels of the government bureaucracy was put in place. In my interviews with three designers on the team and one official from the Shanghai municipal government in 2002, it was revealed that one person on the team was appointed by the Shanghai government as the sole point of contact between the team and the government. Every time the team came up with a new design or sample, the contact person would present it to one official in the Shanghai government, who was the team's only point of contact with the Chinese government. In the same fashion, the Shanghai government official would pass along the designs and samples to one person at the higher-level government bureaucracy. The feedback and instructions would flow back from the top down to the designers through this single chain (*danxian*) of command and communication. Other security measures were also put in place. For example, after the designs were determined, military guards were used to secure the design studio and the adjacent factory in which the garments were made, and no one was allowed to go in or out of the premises without authorization. The fact that the project took nearly two years to finish reflected not just the care and consideration that went into the processes of designing, selection of designs, modifications, producing the right fabric, making the samples, further modifications, and producing the final garments, but also the complex decision-making and communication mechanism between the team and various hierarchies within the Chinese government in order to safeguard secrecy.

On October 21, 2001, when the Asia-Pacific national leaders assembled for the official photo shoot, the secret of the "Chinese" garment was finally exposed: "[They] wore an updated version of a traditional Chinese jacket in royal blue, scarlet, burgundy, olive or brown embossed with gold or black embroidered patterns of peonies—a Chinese national symbol—around the acronym 'APEC' " (*New Straits Times-Management Times* 10/21/2001). The colorful silk jackets had "round collars and were fastened down the front with traditional Chinese knots instead of buttons" (*ibid*). According to the *New Straits Times*'s description, the jacket is a fairly traditional style; it points out several "traditional" Chinese elements: the peonies, the mandarin collar, the knotted cloth buttons, and the silk fabric in bright colors. In addition, the peonies were surrounded by the letters "APEC" spelled in the shape of the Chinese character *shou* (longevity) in a traditional form.

On the other hand, the Chinese media, perhaps led by the Chinese government or the team of designers, were especially keen on revealing the modern aspects of the jacket while acknowledging its traditional look. In particular, the fabric from which the jackets were made received a huge amount of publicity through TV, newspapers, magazines, and the internet. In the words of one designer, the fabric is "one of a kind" (*jue wu jin you*): made of not pure silk but a new blend of silk and synthetic yarns. A few new technologies were adopted so that the new fabric had more enhanced performance than pure silk: it was softer yet stronger, wrinkle-free, more water absorbing, allowed for better ventilation, and provided brighter and faster colors (Ding et al. 2002; *Jiefang ribao* 11/06/2001; *Xinmin zhoukan* 10/30/2001).

Aside from the new and high-tech fabric, the designers of the jacket also emphasized several "Western" design techniques, such as set-in sleeves (*zhuangxiu*), draping, and darts (*sheng*), used to improve the style and fitting of the APEC jackets (personal interviews 2002). Specifically, set-in sleeves and shoulder pads were used in the APEC jackets in order to give a more defined shape to the shoulders. Such techniques were not used to make traditional-style clothing before the late nineteenth and the early twentieth century in China. Techniques of draping and darts were used in the APEC jackets to improve fitting. More specifically, they used darts in the women's jackets in order to give more curves to the chest and the waist. For the men's jackets, draping was especially useful for those leaders who had pot bellies. For instance, I was told that former Chinese president Jiang Zemin's jacket was made using the technique of draping. In the absence of Jiang, the designers had to find someone with similar stature and bond padding onto his belly, then drape the fabric on him and cut it accordingly. Like set-in sleeves, draping was a totally foreign technique and concept to the Chinese tailors before the late nineteenth and early twentieth century.

Western design techniques such as set-in sleeves, draping, and darts belong to a genre of design called *liti caijian* by the Chinese fashion designers and dress historians, which literally means "three-dimensional cutting" and is loosely translated into English as draping. In contrast, the traditional Chinese "flat-cutting" or "two-dimensional cutting" technique is called *pingmian caijian*. Clothes made using the traditional Chinese method are flat or two-dimensional and not fitted to the body, whereas clothes designed and made using the Western method of draping are three-dimensional and tend to have a better fit. Differently put, the two methods of garment making are defined by the different effects the finished garments have on the wearer's body, each involving a different conceptualization of the body and a different set of design techniques. The Western method of draping, which was used by the designers for Jiang's jacket, conceptualizes the body as three-dimensional (as it is), and uses fabrics to sculpt the body and the technique of darts to accentuate certain parts of the body. In addition to draping, the Western three-dimensional cutting method includes set-in sleeves, which together with shoulder pads gives the shoulders a defined shape. By contrast, the traditional Chinese flat-cutting method conceptualizes the body as a flat surface and hence not requiring draping. It conceptualizes the measurements of the girths of the body as widths, with minor consideration given to the differences between the girths/widths of the chest, the waist, and the hip. Consequently, the finished garment has a flat and baggy look. Sleeves made using the traditional Chinese method are called *lianxiu* (literally meaning attached sleeves), as the sleeves were not cut separately from the bodice prior to construction, but cut as a part of the bodice in one piece. The traditional Chinese flat cutting method does not allow darts on the front and back panels of the garments, as they would create an uneven (i.e., three-dimensional) surface. Consequently, the *lianxiu* sleeves give the shoulders a naturally sloped and baggy look. In addition, the traditional Chinese method does not use shoulder pads.

The distinctions between the Western three-dimensional design method and the traditional Chinese two-dimensional method, as well as the different effects they create, are generally recognized in Chinese fashion design textbooks (e.g., Tang 2002; Zhang 2001: 110–111). Thus, it is not surprising that both the Chinese fashion designers and dress historians would agree that the adoption of draping, darts, and set-in sleeves in the construction of the APEC jackets make them more fitted than they would if only traditional Chinese flat-cutting design techniques had been utilized. That is to say, both parties would agree that the Chinese APEC jackets are quite modern. Why then were there still debates about the *tangzhuang* jacket between its designers and Chinese scholars of dress?

DEBATES SURROUNDING THE *TANGZHUANG*

The debates between the *tangzhuang* designers and Chinese scholars of dress centered on two aspects of the *tangzhuang*: the nature of the jacket and its name. The original designers were eclectic in choosing their techniques and integrated them with traditional Chinese elements to make the *tangzhuang* jackets appear to be traditional. To some of them, the traditional Chinese elements were sufficient to call the jackets "traditional"; to others, the jacket might not be completely traditional, but there was nothing wrong with it being both traditional and modern at the same time. Both positions contrasted with that of the Chinese scholars of dress, who believed that the two design methods of flat-cutting and three-dimensional cutting were fundamental to the divergence between traditional Chinese-style and Western-style clothing. They insisted that traditional Chinese style clothing had to be made with traditional Chinese flat-cutting techniques, so much so that they called the Chinese APEC jackets "fake antiques" (*jia gudong*).

The other aspect of the debate had to do with the name. Scholars of dress believed that the name of the *tangzhuang* was inaccurate, and some were particularly bothered by the contradiction that the name of the *tangzhuang* alluded to the Tang dynasty, while the style of the APEC jackets resembled more the *magua* style in the Qing dynasty than clothing styles in the Tang dynasty (*Jiefang ribao* 10/22/2001; *Beijing qingnianbao* 02/10/2002). The designers of the jacket, however, thought that the term *tangzhuang* did not mean clothing of the Tang dynasty, but "Chinese clothing," just as Chinatown was called *tangren jie* overseas. In other words, the designers intended to use *tangzhuan*" as a substitute for "traditional Chinese clothing." After the scholars' criticisms were reported by the media, several designers on the team and government officials later refined the name to *xin tangzhuang* or new *tangzhuang* (Ding et al. 2002), clearly still maintaining the broad connotation of *tang* as Chinese rather than Tang dynasty.

The debates surrounding the *tangzhuang* jackets raise the issue of authenticity in the creation of a dress that claims a traditional or national status. Chinese scholars of dress are right to point out that the Chinese APEC jacket is not a truly traditional Chinese style or a style that existed in the Tang dynasty given all the new and modern aspects discussed above. They are also right about the inaccuracy of the name of the jacket, which is indeed a new invention in mainland China, where *chuantong fuzhuang* (meaning traditional clothing) or *zhongshi fuzhuang* (literally Chinese-style clothing) were the general terms used to refer to traditional Chinese-style clothing prior to the APEC Summit in 2001. At the same time, however, the designers' view that the APEC jackets are traditional and Chinese, despite their modern features and the Western design methods adopted, is supported by a common pattern in which many traditional clothing or practices in the world are in fact "invented traditions" in specific historical contexts (Hobsbawm and Ranger 1983). The kilt, for example, the "traditional" dress of Scotland, was an invention no earlier than the eighteenth century (Trevor-Roper 1983). Even the quintessential Western design technique of darts in the eyes of the Chinese dress historians was not used in Europe until somewhere between the thirteenth and fifteenth century (e.g., Zhang 2001: 60–2). It is true that Western three-dimensional cutting techniques were used in the making of the *tangzhuang* jackets, but the borrowing of these techniques did not begin with the designers of the APEC jackets; it began with the Chinese *hongbang caifeng* in the late Qing, who made not just Western suits, but also the *zhongshanzhuang* and later the Mao suit. That is to say, the so-called Western design techniques had become part of the Chinese design repertoire by the late nineteenth and early twentieth century. It is futile to insist on the fundamental differences between

Western and traditional Chinese design techniques after a century of borrowing of Western design techniques by the Chinese tailors and designers. Furthermore, there is no reason why the *zhongshanzhuang*, which is made with Western design techniques, is perfectly Chinese, whereas the adoption of Western techniques in the making of the *tangzhuang* makes it problematic. Nevertheless, the debates surrounding the *tangzhuang* revealed the tensions that often accompany the process of the invention of tradition, and the fate of the invented tradition usually depends on how the tensions play out in the course of history. Thus, it is important to examine what has happened to the *tangzhuang* after the APEC meeting.

THE *TANGZHUANG* AFTER THE APEC MEETING

After the debates and discussions about the name of the APEC jackets quieted down, the term of *tangzhuang*, not the corrected *xin* (new) *tangzhuang*, was accepted by the public, not only to refer to the APEC jacket, but to traditional Chinese-style clothing broadly. In fact, the *tangzhuang* and the traditional style it came to represent became a craze (*tangzhuangre*) in China after the APEC Summit in 2001. A "*tangzhuang* street" reportedly emerged in Shanghai after the event (Zhongxinshe 01/31/2002),[6] and many *tangzhuang* businesses around the country claimed they had been overbooked (Xinhuawang 02/12/2002). The fact that the majority of the live audience were wearing the *tangzhuang* at the National Show of Spring Festival Celebration (*chunjie lianhuan wanhui*) broadcast by the Chinese Central Television Station (CCTV) in 2002, one of the most watched TV shows in China, gave the best illustration to the popularity of the style.[7]

As a consequence of the immediate fad of the *tangzhuang* after the APEC meeting, all seven designers on the team left their former jobs in the state-owned or private enterprises and started their own businesses of making the *tangzhuang* with the newly acquired title of "APEC Garment (Chief) Designer" (APEC *Fuzhuang <Shouxi> Shejishi*) on their business cards. However, the fad was short-lived. When I revisited two of the designers in 2004, I learned that most of them were not making the *tangzhuang* anymore. One of the designers I interviewed was actually still making the *tangzhuang*, but he had only received one order in the past several months, not from the Chinese but from Citigroup, the American financial conglomerate. At the time of our interview, he was in the process of switching his business to OEM manufacturing for international brands.[8] The brief popularity of the *tangzhuang* (Figure 4.2) makes one wonder to what extent the Chinese state has succeeded in its project of inventing a national dress through the opportunity of the APEC Summit. To address that question, we will have to revisit the objectives the state hoped to achieve through the APEC dress.

Figure 4.2   A customer gazing at a *tangzhuang* shop in Shanghai. Courtesy of Jianhua Zhao.

At the press conference following the APEC Summit in 2001, the spokesperson of the Ministry of Foreign Affairs, Zhang Qiyue, made a statement that the APEC attire reflected "both traditional Chinese flavor and modern ideals." It is clear that the Chinese state intended to create a "national dress" that would showcase an image of modern China with a rich cultural heritage. In fact, a synthesis of tradition and modernity was also the guideline given to the Shanghai government official and the designers, when they were working on the designs of the APEC garb. As discussed previously, the APEC Summit is an occasion that calls for a traditional garb of the host country. The fact that the Chinese government took pains to create something quite modern with a seemingly traditional look was in part due to the limited range of choices available, and in part due to the state's desire to fashion a national identity that is not just defined by tradition, but also modernity to its citizens and the world. Fashioning a "modern yet traditional" national identity may have reflected China's desire to be respected by the world (especially the West), but more importantly it embodies the state's attempt to showcase to Chinese citizens (hence legitimizes its existence) an image of modernity (as seen in the state's heavy emphasis on the high-tech material). In other words, to the Chinese state, the *tangzhuang* jacket was meant to be a powerful symbol that represented Chinese culture to the world on the one hand and a proud and modern national identity to its citizens on the other hand. Thus, the extent to which the state is successful with the project of the invention of the *tangzhuang* as a national dress is dependent on how the Chinese citizens receive and perceive the *tangzhuang*, which is exactly why I find Ms. Yu Kun's view illuminating.

Yu Kun is a white-collar professional in her late 20s from Beijing, whom I interviewed in the fall of 2002. She bought a ready-to-wear *tangzhuang* jacket in a department store in the winter of 2001. Responding to my question of why she bought the jacket, she said,

> I like *tangzhuang* because it is colorful and looks joyful (*xiqing*) and prosperous (*fugui*), which makes it suitable for traditional Chinese holidays like the Spring Festival. I also like the jacket because it is warm—it is made of silk and has padded linings—and you can match it with different pants or skirts. It is much more versatile and convenient than the *qipao*. When I saw the *tangzhuang* jackets in the store, I immediately bought one for myself and another one for my mom. It is good that the Chinese can now wear the colorful *tangzhuang* to celebrate happy occasions like the Spring Festival. For years I was looking for something like it but couldn't find any.

Yu Kun liked the *tangzhuang* jacket because of its traditional appeal: its bright color and its joyful and prosperous look. The two terms *xiqing* and *fugui* she used to describe the jacket are frequently associated with the joy and abundance of the Spring Festival, the biggest traditional Chinese holiday in the winter, which she mentioned as the perfect occasion for wearing the *tangzhuang* both in terms of the atmosphere and weather. Her excitement upon seeing the *tangzhuang* was evident as she bought two immediately, and the *tangzhuang* seemed to have met her needs that were unmet by other existing clothing alternatives. Throughout our interview, she did not refer to her jacket as new *tangzhuang*. Nor was she aware of the distinctions between the traditional Chinese two-dimensional cutting and Western three-dimensional cutting techniques. Her appreciation of the *tangzhuang* jacket was limited to its functions and aesthetics that were related to the festive traditional holidays such as the Spring Festival. The colorful, warm, and silky jacket seemed to remind her of what a traditional holiday was all about.

Though Yu Kun's view is obviously not meaningful in a statistical sense, her view of the *tangzhuang* is very telling with regard to the debates surrounding the APEC jacket and the extent of success of the state-initiated project of "invention of tradition." Like most Chinese consumers, Yu Kun does not seem to know or care about the fine distinctions between the *tangzhuang* and the new *tangzhuang*, or those between the truly traditional and the not so traditional. To her, the *tangzhuang* is traditional because it looks traditional and is suited for traditional occasions. The inaccuracy of the name and the lack of authenticity in the style do not seem to matter to her. Hence, Yu Kun's view contradicts those of the Chinese scholars of dress. At the same time, her view also departs from the state's (intended) interpretation of the *tangzhuang* as a synthesis of modernity and tradition, as modernity is simply not part of the connotation of the *tangzhuang* jacket to her. By assigning the *tangzhuang* completely to "tradition" and traditional occasions, Yu Kun and others like her have precluded the possibility of the *tangzhuang* becoming everyday wear like Western styles of clothing that have been adopted by the Chinese today, which probably explains why the *tangzhuang* craze was short-lived after the APEC Summit. Relatedly, there was also a revival of interest in *hanfu*, the classic Han Chinese clothing that claims to date back to the Yellow Emperor. The *hanfu* movement is espoused by a small group of Han activists, whose view seems to be quite ethnocentric to the general population and not supported by the Chinese government (Wu 2009: 125–6).

However, this does not mean that the Chinese state's project of "invention of tradition" is a complete failure. Yu Kun's immediate embracing of the *tangzhuang*, despite that her interpretation of it diverges from that of the state, is proof that Chinese citizens are accepting this newly invented tradition. When I discussed the implications of the short-lived fad of the *tangzhuang* with a well-known fashion journalist in Beijing in 2004, she said that although the heat of the fad was over, the *tangzhuang* had become part of the cultural lexicon of China, and that many people became more conscious of traditional Chinese culture during traditional holidays because they wore the *tangzhuang*. She added that she felt she had to wear the *tangzhuang* during the Spring Festival.

CONCLUSION

This chapter examined one particular type of clothing, the *tangzhuang* jacket, which was created under direct supervision of the Chinese state for a unique and important occasion, the APEC Summit in 2001. Conforming to the convention of the APEC Summit, during which the heads of state would wear a traditional garb of the host country, China hoped to invent a national dress that reflected "both traditional Chinese flavor and modern ideals." Mapping political ideology onto clothing is nothing new in China. Sun Yat-sen attempted to symbolize his "Three People's Principles" through the *zhongshanzhuang*, the proletarian Mao suit is usually seen to represent the socialist ideology of equality and frugality, and the *tangzhuang* worn by Jiang (and the other heads of state) encapsulates China's attempts to redefine a national identity to the world and to its citizens that is simultaneously traditional and modern.

China's project of inventing a national identity through the APEC dress came at a time when China was experiencing enormous growth and becoming increasingly confident in its encounter with the West (and the world). In this particular historical juncture, nationalistic sentiments are dominated by pro-tradition sentiments, which are clearly different from the 1980s when the nationalistic sentiments among Chinese intellectuals were hinged on modernization and anti-tradition (Liu 2001). The pro-tradition sentiments together with the occasion propelled China to come up with a traditional-looking design for the APEC dress. However, limited by the available choices in the contemporary period and driven by a desire to draw attention to the achievements China has made, hence legitimizing the rule of the Communist Party-State, China took every effort to ensure that the APEC dress also reflected "modern ideals," both through the designs and media promotion.

However, the Chinese state's design and promotion of the *tangzhuang* faced challenges. Chinese scholars of dress quickly criticized the *tangzhuang* as not really traditional and the name as inaccurate after its debut at the APEC Summit. Although Chinese citizens, like Yu Kun, immediately embraced the *tangzhuang*, they by and large relegated it to a traditional dress for traditional holidays and ignored the "modern ideals" it was supposed to embody as intended by the state. In his work on the practices of the "invention of tradition," Hobsbawm talks about the measurement of success of such practices: "[I]t also seems clear that the most successful examples of manipulation are those which exploit practices which clearly meet a felt—not necessarily a clearly understood—need among particular bodies of people" (Hobsbawm and Ranger 1983: 307). Following this criterion, the Chinese state's project of the invention of the *tangzhuang* as a national dress achieved partial success. The need for "a national dress" was clearly there, which explains the quick acceptance of the *tangzhuang* by the Chinese people as part of their sartorial lexicon, but at the same time they came up with their own interpretation of the *tangzhuang* that deviates from the state's. Differently put, when it comes to the acceptance of the *tangzhuang* by the Chinese consumer-citizens, it is another project of "invention of tradition" in its own right.

The case of the *tangzhuang* suggests that there are limits to the state's ability in fashioning a modernity and national identity through dress, as it can be "bought and consumed" by the consumer-citizens. The extent to which Chinese consumer-citizens buy into the official interpretation of the dress cannot be guaranteed at the point of design and production. In the next chapter, I will focus on the Chinese fashion designers and examine how the logic of fashion design works out in the market.

–5–

For the Sake of Art or for the Market? The Cultural Economy of Fashion Design

Being good in business is the most fascinating kind of art. Making money is art and working is art and good business is the best art.

—Andy Warhol

INTRODUCTION

On April 10, 2005, world-renowned artist Mr. Chen Yifei passed away at the age of 59 in Shanghai. Following his untimely death, heated debates surged between his critics and admirers with regard to his contribution to Chinese art. Comments about Chen, often charged with emotion, quickly flooded China's newspapers and websites. Admirers acknowledged Chen as one of China's greatest artists, whereas critics believed that he had sold out to commercial interests and was not at all a first-rate artist.

With thirty-three of his paintings reportedly selling internationally for a total price of over 40 million yuan (about $4.8 million) between 1991 and 1998,[1] Mr. Chen was one of the most sought-after modern Chinese artists. At the same time, Mr. Chen was the founder and owner of Yifei Group, through which he applied his aesthetic vision to businesses in fashion, modeling, publishing, environmental arts and design, and film making, which he called collectively the "pan-vision industry" (dashijue chanye).[2] The debate surrounding Mr. Chen suggests that for many Chinese the mixing of art and commercial interests is a contested terrain that should be avoided, whereas for others, like Mr. Chen, the logic of art and economy is intrinsic to a cultural industry.

Critics of Mr. Chen can find support in Pierre Bourdieu's field theory and argue that art and economy are two separate and autonomous fields that are structured by fundamentally opposite principles or laws. The field of art functions, according to Bourdieu (1993), as "the economic world reversed," in the sense that its internal logic is the "refusal" or "disavowal" of commercial interests. From this perspective, by pursuing an interest in business, Mr. Chen lost his "disinterestedness" and "violated" the principle of the field of art, compromising the purity of his art.

On the other hand, many Chinese fashion designers that I interviewed are in agreement with Mr. Chen and believe that the fashion industry is a cultural industry that involves both economic and cultural logics, especially the logic of art.

The intention of this chapter is not to examine the degree of Mr. Chen's "disinterestedness" toward his art; instead I focus on his particular interest in combining the logics of art and economy in the other field in which he was actively involved, namely, the fashion industry. By treating the Chinese fashion industry as a field, I argue that Chinese fashion designers' strategy of combining the logics of art and economy in their work has to be understood in relation to the distinctions between the *caifeng* (tailor) and the *shizhuang shejishi* (fashion designer) in China on one hand and the perceived field position of Chinese fashion in the global fashion industry on the other hand. In what follows, I will present the views and approaches of Chinese fashion designers toward their work, particularly through the cases of two prominent fashion designers and their businesses. Then I will compare and contrast their business models with international business models of haute couture and fast fashion. In so doing, I argue that the two Chinese fashion designers' views of and approaches to fashion illustrate the unique "field positions" and "position-takings" of Chinese fashion designers in the fields of the Chinese fashion industry and global fashion industry. Finally, I will provide an understanding of the nature of fashion design and what it means to be a fashion designer in China. Since this chapter is built on a field analysis of fashion, it is important to understand first what a "field" is and how fashion as a field is constituted.

WHAT IS A FIELD?

In an edited volume, *The Field of Cultural Production*, Bourdieu (1993) employs the concept of "field" mainly to study literature and art. According to Randal Johnson, the editor of Bourdieu's volume, a "field" is defined as "a structured space with its own laws of functioning and its own relations of force independent of those of politics and the economy, except, obviously, in the case of the economic and political fields" (Johnson 1993: 6). By "structure of the field," Bourdieu refers to the hierarchical distribution of positions that the agents or producers of the field occupy and the different sets of strategies employed by the agents to improve their standing in the field. That is to say, once the hierarchical or "structured" positions of the field (he calls them "field positions") and the strategies of the agents (which he calls "position-takings") are identified, we are on our way to understanding not only the contour of the "field" but also the dynamics of its internal functioning.

According to Bourdieu's field analysis, a (literary or artistic) work is such not only because of its position or the position of its producer in the field, but also because of the inherent position-taking by the producer in competition with other producers. A position-taking is objectively manifested through and delimited by its negative association with all other possible positions in the field, i.e., by not taking all other field positions (Bourdieu 1993: 30). In other words, a position-taking is a differentiating strategy of the producer from other producers. In this light, Bourdieu's notion of the field, as a structured space, is defined by and objectified through the struggles between the different positions and position-takings within the field. As Bourdieu (1993: 83) notes, such struggles are frequently exemplified by those between the orthodox and the heresy, or the established figure and the newcomer, or the elite and the popular.

Building on Bourdieu's field theory, this chapter conceptualizes fashion, in particular, the Chinese fashion industry, as a field. In order to understand the inner workings of the field of fashion, one has to first locate the different field positions in the fashion industry, which are connected to the objectives of the fashion designers in their work.

FASHION AS A FIELD

Artistic originality and commercial success are both desirable objectives of a fashion designer. Even though closely related, the two objectives are distinct from each other; success in one does not necessarily translate into success in the other. In fact, as Bourdieu puts it, the two objectives work in opposite directions—pursuing artistic originality entails exclusivity and "restricted production," while pursuing profit maximization involves "large-scale production" (1993: 53). According to Bourdieu, "restricted production" and "large-scale production" are two distinct modes of production that constitute two sub-fields of cultural production. Randal Johnson summarizes the distinctions between the two as follows:

> The field of restricted production concerns what we normally think of as 'high' art, for example 'classical' music, the plastic arts, so-called 'serious' literature. In this sub-field, the stakes of competition between agents are largely symbolic, involving prestige, consecration and artistic celebrity. . . The field of large-scale production involves what we sometimes refer to as 'mass' or 'popular' culture: private owned television, most cinematic productions, radio, mass-produced literature. Sustained by a large and complex culture industry, its dominant principle of hierarchization involves economic capital or 'the bottom line'. (1993: 15–16)

Simply put, "high" art involves restricted production that aims at prestige and consecration, whereas "mass" or "popular" culture involves large-scale production that aims at economic gains (also see du Gay 1997). Similarly, Igor Kopytoff (1986) describes the differences between art and commodity as they involve divergent processes of "singularization" and "commoditization." While the process of singularization works to preserve the uniqueness of artistic objects and resist market exchange, the commoditization process pushes these objects into the market for exchange (Kopytoff 1986). Therefore, although designing for the sake of art (*yishu*) and for the mass market (*shichang*) are both desirable objectives, a fashion designer would have to make a choice between them.

Between the two ends of art and the market, three different approaches have been theorized, which result in three business models, or as some scholars put it, three "fashion systems," including haute couture, prêt-à-porter, and fast fashion (e.g., Reinach 2005). Designers of haute couture or high fashion, which is called *gaoji shizhuang* in Chinese, emphasize originality, exclusivity, and luxury. They want the clothes they design to be treated as art and themselves as artists. On almost the opposite end, designers of fast fashion, or low-end mass-produced ready-to-wear clothing, do not care much about the artistic value of their designs; instead they are most concerned about the cost and speed of turnover that directly impacts their financial results. Designers in this group are frequently accused by others as being imitators or counterfeiters, who simply copy very quickly whatever sells well on the market (Reinach 2005). Between haute couture and fast fashion, there is prêt-à-porter, or in Chinese, *gaoji chengyi*, meaning high-quality ready-to-wear clothing, which claims to embrace both originality and marketability.

The three fashion types of haute couture, prêt-à-porter, and fast fashion are hierarchically ordered according to their level of originality (as well as price). While haute couture and prêt-à-porter are generally regarded as creative, original, upscale, and expensive, fast fashions are frequently looked down upon as unoriginal, low-quality, cheap, and unethical replications or knockoffs of the former two. Given their distinctions, the three types of fashion can serve as three different "field positions" and entail three different strategies or "position-takings" that constitute the field of fashion. Moreover, in the globalized world of fashion today, these three field positions are not only structured within the confines of nation-states, they are also perceived as structuring the global field of fashion. As stereotypes have it, Paris is the capital of haute couture in the world, and Italy is identified with its high-quality prêt-à-porter, and, in this order, "China, by definition, is fast fashion," even while there is no proper term for the concept of fast fashion in Chinese (Reinach 2005: 11).

The characterization of China as a fast fashion system essentially caricatures China as flooded by a sea of unoriginal, cheap knockoffs and counterfeits of Western fashions. By extension, Chinese fashion designers are assumed to be copycats of their Western colleagues. According to this view, the Chinese field of fashion is constituted by a single type of field position, and Chinese designers adopt a singular strategy or position-taking—they always favor marketability over artistic originality in their designs.

However, my research on Chinese fashion designers and fashion companies finds that such a characterization does not do justice to Chinese fashion designers and the Chinese fashion system. On the contrary, my field research indicates that the reality is much more complex for Chinese fashion designers, who are much more sophisticated in their approaches to fashion design than being mere copycats. As a group, they exhibit diverse views and adopt varied strategies ("position-takings") rather than a uniform approach to fashion, to which I now turn.

DIVERSE VIEWS AMONG CHINESE FASHION DESIGNERS

During my field research, I had the opportunity to interview about eighty Chinese fashion designers, over twenty of them more than once.[3] Among them, many are seasoned designers, some even having attained the status of "celebrity designers," but more than half of them are junior designers who have just started their careers or have only a few years of experience in the profession. In a general sense, the cohorts of designers I have interviewed parallel the three generations of Chinese fashion designers that Christine Tsui (2010) describes. Tsui thinks that the first-generation Chinese fashion designers (the 1980s) are more artistically driven and concerned about their Chinese identity, but less successful commercially; the second generation (the 1990s) is more "pragmatic and professional" and tends to enjoy business success; and the third generation (the twenty-first century) is more "contemporary, diversified, and creative," but tends to "copy" Western design techniques. I do not completely agree with Tsui's characterization of these three generations of Chinese designers. While I agree with Tsui that the first-generation professionally trained fashion designers in general are concerned about Chinese identity (and their identity of being fashion designers), many of them are in fact very successful; they enjoy great media exposure, have access to many resources, and some have even attained the status of celebrity designer or master designer. Consequently, what they do has a significant impact on younger generation designers (e.g., Mark Cheung's show at China Fashion Week discussed in the next chapter). Moreover, many of the first-generation fashion designers are just as pragmatic as the second generation, despite their tendency to produce highly artistic and original designs for the runway. It is even harder to make generalizations about the third generation, as they are young and malleable, and things can change for them very quickly. Due to the apparent contradictions between my observations and Tsui's views and the unrepresentative nature of my sample (as well as Tsui's), I refrain from making sweeping generalizations about the Chinese fashion designers I interviewed. Instead, I will highlight the diverse views and approaches among them, and then try to provide a cultural understanding of their diverse views and approaches in the Chinese context.

Prior to each scheduled interview, I would design an interview guide, which included some general questions I had for all designers and some specific questions that I came up with after doing some preliminary research about the designer to be interviewed through newspapers, the internet, other publications, and/or other designers or friends. One of the general questions I asked was how they dealt with the problem of designing for the sake of art or for the market. Surprisingly, they expressed conflicting views in their answers. It was particularly interesting to me that two of China's most prominent designers, Ms. Ye Li and Mr. Yuan Xing, held rather contradictory views.

To answer my question, Ye Li said, "art leads design, and design in turn leads life" (*yishu lingyin sheji, sheji lingyin shenghuo*). Ye Li further explained to me that fashion design should be the artistic expression of the designer's originality, taste, and unique style, and that without art there would be no identity, no life, and no future to a fashion design. Clearly, Ye Li thought that fashion design should be for the sake of art. Contrary to Ye Li's view, Yuan Xing thought that "a designer should only dream others' dreams rather than his or her own" (*shejishi yinggai fa bieren de meng, er bushi ziji de meng*). He considered designers' originality only secondary to serving the interest of their bosses and consumers. When pressed as to why the designers should not dream their own dreams, Yuan Xing said that if the designer cared only about his or her individuality and creativity, he or she would lose sight of the market and subsequently his or her design would not be accepted by the market. In short, Yuan Xing believed that fashion design should be for the sake of the market, a view directly opposed to Ye Li's.

Ye Li's and Yuan Xing's firm but opposing views were interesting to me because they were different from many younger designers I interviewed, who tended to claim that they value both originality and marketability (though some also support Ye Li's or Yuan Xing's respective views). More importantly, their divergent views suggest multiple positions and position-takings in the field of Chinese fashion, which contradict the perceived, stereotypical view of Chinese designers as unoriginal copycats and Chinese fashion as a fast fashion system. In this chapter, I will primarily focus on the cases of Ye Li and Yuan Xing. By highlighting these two, I do not suggest that their views and strategies are more or less representative of all Chinese fashion designers. Rather, their views and strategies provide clear illustrations of different positions and position-takings within the Chinese fashion industry. That being said, the prominence and influence of both designers do add extra weight to their views and approaches. To put their prominence in context, I have to briefly outline the history in which fashion designers emerged as prestigious professionals in China.

THE EMERGENCE OF FASHION DESIGN AS A PRESTIGIOUS PROFESSION IN CHINA

As described in Chapters 2 and 3, from the late Qing to the radical socialist period of the PRC (1949–1978), China's textile industry did not develop to the extent that it could provide the necessary input to support a fast-changing fashion industry. The political and moral environment during those periods (with the exception of the turbulent Republican era, 1912–1949) also prohibited people from dressing freely. It was not until the post-1978 reform period that China's fashion industry began to develop. During this period, a few factors (discussed in previous chapters) set the stage for the development of the fashion industry. First, the state-initiated economic reforms encouraged market fragmentation and competition, which called for the creativity of fashion designers. Second, the Communist Party leaders encouraged the diversification of styles and redefined the ideological dimension of clothing to serve the interest of the country's economic development. And finally, the economic reforms opened China up to influences of international fashions and fashion industries. In this section, I only outline a few milestones in the processes of institutionalization of the profession of fashion design in China.

In 1980, Central Institute of Arts and Crafts (CIAC merged with Qinghua University in 1999) started the very first college program in fashion design in China. In 1984 both CIAC in Beijing and Donghua University in Shanghai established departments of fashion design. Since then, the numbers of college and university programs in fashion have increased dramatically. According to Professor Jia Jingsheng, an incomplete estimate is that 720 colleges and universities, not including private professional schools, offer training in fashion design (*China Fashion Weekly* 09/19/2003). The development in education and training in fashion design produced a large number of professionally trained fashion designers by the 1990s. In 1993, the China Fashion Association (CFA) was founded in Beijing, as a branch organization of the China National Textile Industry Council, with an initial membership of only 64 people, among whom fewer than 10 were actual fashion designers, with the rest being officials and college professors (personal interviews with CFA officials in 2004). In 1997, CFA started to organize the first China Fashion Week, the most important annual fashion event in China, during which the "China Top Ten

Fashion Designers Award" (*shijia shejishi*) and the most prestigious "Golden award" (*jinding jiang*) are awarded to accomplished designers. In 2002, CFA had a selected membership of over 1,100 designers (CFA's official website). By then, the profession of fashion design had been firmly established and institutionalized.

The emergence and professionalization of fashion design could not happen, however, without the agency of individual fashion designers (i.e., their position-takings), especially major designers such as Ye Li and Yuan Xing. As college graduates of fashion design in the mid-1980s, Ye Li and Yuan Xing belong to China's first generation of professionally trained fashion designers.[4] As such, their accomplishments as successful designers also reflect and in some ways have given definition to the development of the profession of fashion design in China. One particular event in Ye Li's and Yuan Xing's career illustrates this point.

In 1996, one of China's largest fashion corporations advertised in national newspapers to hire fashion designers for an annual salary of one million yuan (about US$121,000 at the time). Ye Li and Yuan Xing were among the candidates considered for the positions. To put it in perspective, the one-million-yuan job ad came out at a time when most Chinese were making about ten thousand yuan or less a year. Not surprisingly, everything associated with the news caught a tremendous amount of public attention. I was then a student in a college in Wuhan,[5] and I first heard the news on a radio talk show, which solicited debates among the audience as to whether a fashion designer could be worth one million yuan. Although the exact arguments of both sides at the time have eluded me, I do remember that the "side against" used the familiar and somewhat demeaning term of *caifeng* (tailor) to label the candidates, whereas the "side in favor" used the new and fancy term of *shizhuang shejishi* (fashion designer). Both the *caifeng* and the *shizhuang shejishi* are dress-makers, but the *caifeng* or tailors have been gradually marginalized and replaced by factory garment workers and fashion designers since the 1980s. At the same time, however, *shizhuang shejishi* was still a new term when the one-million-yuan hire took place in 1996. For many people, myself included, it was the first time that *shizhuang shejishi* registered in their mind as a prestigious profession, and one that could demand big money. In the midst of all the media hype, Yuan Xing and another designer took the jobs, while Ye Li declined the offer.

The media sensation of "one million yuan fashion designers" brought the profession of fashion design to the public consciousness.[6] Media coverage of fashion events, such as fashion shows, fashion fairs, and design and/or modeling competitions has since increased dramatically and further elevated the status of the profession of fashion design. In fact, nationally famous designers today are not only regarded as artists, but also celebrities, thanks in large part to frequent media coverage. That said, only a handful of Chinese designers can be called celebrity designers, and most others have a much more difficult time working their way up. Ye Li and Yuan Xing are among the lucky few who have attained the status of "celebrated Chinese fashion designers" over the years.

To be fair, their successes are not just due to their involvement in the media sensation of the one-million-yuan hire in 1996, but also because of their education, long experience of working as designer or chief designer in several fashion companies, high-profile visits to Paris and other world fashion centers, influential fashion shows, and above all the numerous titles and prestigious awards they have won. (The importance of the awards will be discussed in the next chapter.) To top it off, Ye Li won the Golden Award in 2001, the highest honor awarded by the China Fashion Association, and both Ye Li and Yuan Xing won CFA's Top Ten Fashion Designers Award in 1995, the first time such awards appeared in China. Currently, Ye Li is a professor at a fashion design institute, the owner of a design studio located in Beijing, and also serves as Vice President of the CFA. Yuan Xing is Chairman and Artistic Director of a fashion company based in Shanghai, and a member of the Fashion Art Committee at the CFA. In addition, he is also a guest professor at several academic institutions.

The successes of Ye Li and Yuan Xing are not simply personal accomplishments, they are also models for younger designers and designers-to-be to emulate. To borrow Bourdieu's terms, their paths to success are the "trajectories" through which they establish their highly visible "positions" in the field. Given the emergent nature of the Chinese fashion industry, their strategies are particularly meaningful by providing prominent examples of "position-takings" in the field of the Chinese fashion industry. In this sense, their views are more than personal views, and their business models are more than individual cases, which will be the focus in the following sections in this chapter.

YE LI AND YUAN XING

I met Ye Li in a hotel lobby when she was on a business trip to Shanghai. I made the appointment for an interview with her days earlier; we decided the best time was in the afternoon when she would have some time between her other meetings, during which we could meet and talk in her hotel lobby over coffee. Given our two previous failed attempts to meet on other occasions and in other cities, I considered this arrangement a perfect success, so I arrived before the scheduled time of our interview at the Galaxy Hotel where she stayed. Although I had not met Ye Li before, I recognized her immediately when two middle-aged women walked toward the open coffee bar in the hotel lobby. Compared to her image on various websites, she dressed more on the conservative side. She was in black: black shoes, black pants, a basic black shirt, and on top of it a black light cashmere cardigan. Her assistant came along in case she was late for her next appointment.

Ye Li is a fast speaker with a trace of a southern accent. She spoke about the Chinese fashion industry and fashion designers with enthusiasm. She was proud of the boom China was witnessing, and that Chinese fashion designers were catching up so quickly with Western designers, and she was optimistic about the future of China's fashion industry. After seeing and indeed being a part of such tremendous growth of the industry in the past two decades, she had good reason to be proud and optimistic. Yet, her pride was also tinged with nationalist sentiments, and her optimism was mixed with a sense of responsibility as a prominent fashion designer. In her brief narration of the development of China's fashion industry, she conveyed a very clear message: China succeeded in garment manufacturing and Chinese fashion designers can also be competitive with Chinese fashion designs in the world of fashion.

Curious about what she meant by "Chinese fashion designs," I asked her how she interpreted the "Chinese-ness" in her own designs. She said that she heavily utilized Chinese materials (such as silk), motifs (ethnic patterns and prints), and artistic genres in her designs (Figure 5.1). She used three terms to describe the characteristics of Chinese artistic genre, of which she saw her own design as a part: *piaoyi* (flowing and graceful), *jianjie* (simple but perfect), and *hanxu* (modest or reticent). Those three terms generally pertain to the Chinese sense of beauty and are frequently used to describe traditional Chinese paintings or other art forms.

After an interview of over an hour—exceeding her initial commitment of half an hour, and ignoring her assistant's reminders of her next meeting—I came to understand why Ye Li said "art leads design, and design in turn leads life." Her design philosophy is intertwined with the broader context of the Chinese economy and the responsibilities of Chinese designers that she saw in the grand mission of the revival of the Chinese nation. Her argument boiled down to this: China has already become a powerhouse in garment manufacturing, which is an extraordinary achievement, and China will also become a world fashion leader, but in order to achieve this goal, Chinese fashion designers have to find their own identities, which is not possible without "art," i.e., their own unique and creative designs. Ye Li's view builds in part on an optimistic reading of the Chinese fashion industry and the overall Chinese economy, a sentiment shared by many Chinese citizens, including fashion designers, who have benefited from China's recent economic boom. However, there are also Chinese fashion designers whose views are much less optimistic. Among them is Yuan Xing.

Figure 5.1   A wedding gown designed by a student of Ye Li. Photo by Ding Xiaowen. Courtesy of Ms. Xuan Yanni.

My interview with Yuan Xing was easier to schedule than the one with Ye Li. It turned out that Yuan Xing's company was only half an hour away by taxi from the apartment I rented in Shanghai. I called him up one day and he agreed to my request for an interview in his office the next afternoon. Our interview was interrupted a few times because Yuan Xing had to meet with three groups of visitors. But while I was waiting, he showed me a book he wrote on fashion and his design portfolios, which included many creative designs and interesting ideas inspired by the Peking opera that he was working on for a show at China Fashion Week in the spring season for a different company. I also took this opportunity to see his showroom.

Yuan Xing's office was very spacious, more like an artist's studio than an executive's office; all walls were fully decorated with paintings and Chinese calligraphy, brushes of different sizes took up much of the space on his huge desk. In one corner of the room, there was a reception area surrounded by comfortable sofas and chairs, where our interview and the reception of other visitors took place. Yuan Xing's attire fitted very well with the friendly, laid-back atmosphere of his office. He wore a velvet blazer over a mock turtleneck wool sweater, khaki pants, and leather shoes, all of which were in different shades of muted brown, nicely layered and subtly complementing each other. His attire and color scheme reminded me of pleasant outings to Shanghai suburbs in the warm sunshine of the early fall. Our interview was very relaxed, less structured, but friendly, and lasted the whole afternoon.

Yuan Xing's response to my question about the strategy of art vs. the market was that fashion designers could only "dream others' dreams." He viewed fashion as a business in which a designer had to put consideration for the market ahead of his or her own aspirations for artistic expression. This emphasis on the market was often conveyed to me by many other Chinese designers during my field research. Not totally satisfied with Yuan Xing's answer, I asked him what he thought of the Chinese fashion market and why he believed that it would clash with the designers' own dreams.

The Chinese fashion market, according to Yuan Xing, has "Chinese characteristics," a twist on a popular Chinese political slogan, "socialism with Chinese characteristics." Much like a politician, Yuan Xing related to me that China was still a poor country with the bulk of its huge population living in the countryside, and that these "characteristics" meant that most Chinese could not keep up with the latest fashions. He compared Chinese fashion designers to "fish without water." By "water" he meant affluent consumers with good taste for fashion, without whom he believed that Chinese fashion designers would not be able to find the market for their unique and innovative designs. Yet, Yuan Xing's deterministic logic is not solely based on economic factors, such as consumer demands. He shared with me an anecdote: He was once asked at a press conference by a cynical Chinese fashion journalist why China could not yet produce the world's first-rate fashion designers. He simply retorted, "Once the world has first-rate Chinese fashion journalists, then the world will also have first-rate Chinese fashion designers." After finishing the story, he turned to me, as if continuing to respond to the journalist, "We [Chinese fashion designers and journalists] are in the same boat, and all of us are the products of our time and history." Similar to his remarks on the "Chinese characteristics," the history Yuan Xing talked about is not just economic history, but also political and cultural history. He commented on the conservative styles of his and many of his peers, and attributed the fact that he could not bring himself to wear very bright colors to having grown up during the Maoist era.

Yuan Xing's retort at first seemed to be merely a quick and angry response to the fashion journalist, but after listening to his elaborations, I realized that he truly believed that the growth of fashion designers was a complex process that was deeply entwined with many other factors, including the maturation of the fashion media, other supporting industries, and the consumers. His analogy between Chinese designers and "fish without water" suggested that even if Chinese designers came up with original and innovative designs, Chinese consumers would not be able to either appreciate or afford them. More broadly, Yuan Xing thought that the legacies of China's past, the lack of an adequate consumer base, underdeveloped supporting industries such as high-quality fabrics, dyeing and printing, and the immature fashion media are all parts of the "water" that hampers Chinese designers' (the fish) ability to produce a world-class fashion brand. In Yuan Xing's opinion, it is in the "water" of Chinese society that Chinese designers have to swim; they have to work with what they have and thus cater to the dreams of Chinese consumers rather than their own.

Ye Li and Yuan Xing clearly have rather different ideas about fashion design. Ye Li believes that art should be the driving force of fashion design; whereas Yuan Xing thinks that fashion design is restricted by the market and can only serve the interest of the market. Interestingly, their arguments are both grounded on the development of China's fashion industry in particular and the contemporary history of Chinese society in general. Although they appear to agree with each other on the basic facts about Chinese society and economy, they have different interpretations of these facts. Ye Li looks at the economic boom China is witnessing, and she is optimistic about the future of China's fashion industry, in which she believes there is an important role for Chinese fashion designers to play. On the contrary, Yuan Xing's view of China's recent past and present is quite pessimistic. Consequently he derives a market determinist view toward fashion design, even though he does not seem to separate his personal interest in art from his business, as evidenced by his creative work for other companies and by the dominant presence of paintings, calligraphy, and brushes in his office. Despite their differences, Ye Li and Yuan Xing share something important in common: Neither of them believes that copying Western fashion is the path to success.

Given Ye Li's and Yuan Xing's keen insights and their long experience of working in the fashion industry, it comes as no surprise that their views are highly consistent with their current business models and strategies.

THEIR BUSINESS MODELS

As previously mentioned, Ye Li owns a design studio in Beijing, and Yuan Xing owns a designer label company based in Shanghai. A design studio and a designer label company represent two different business models, in which the chief designer or artistic director has different degrees of control over their designs. As a designer-owner of a studio, Ye Li has more control over her designs than a designer-owner of a designer label company, like Yuan Xing, has over his. This is because Ye Li's studio does not involve mass production and does not sell directly to the consumers. Instead, her clients are fashion manufacturers who lack design capacities, and with whom she works in a horizontal and cooperative manner. Just as her clients can choose and reject her designs, she can pick her clients directly or indirectly by choosing the particular types of clothes or fabrics to design in a particular season. For example, if she is interested in designing silk, she would target silk manufacturers; if she is interested in making dresses, she would look for dress-makers as her clients. Of course, there are times when orders come in first and require her to design particular types of clothing. But even those companies for whom she designs entire seasonal collections have to respect and rely on her expert opinion rather than dictate to her what her designs should be like. Furthermore, if her samples are rejected by one client, she can always seek other clients who may be interested. The bottom line is that the relative low cost of producing only samples would not negatively impact her financially in any significant way should some of the designs be rejected by any or all of her clients. Consequently, Ye Li has control over the designing process, independent of her clients, and she can explore and produce very original and innovative designs.

Ye Li's studio was four years old when I interviewed her in 2004, and it had already expanded into six branch studios, with a staff of over twenty designers. Although her studio might not be well-known to consumers on the street, she was clearly able to capitalize on her innovative designs, services, and to some extent her fame and visibility in the media and build the brand of her namesake studio among the mass producers. I asked Ye Li whether she wanted to design her own line of clothing someday. She said that would be every designer's dream. However, she didn't think it would happen for her any time in the near future because she did not have the capital needed for a designer label, and she did not want the support of external investors, as that would compromise her control over the designs and also require a different set of management skills and marketing strategies from those of her current business. All in all, Ye Li said that she was happy with the way her studio was running.

In contrast to Ye Li's studio, Yuan Xing's company is a mass producer that sells directly to the consumers. Consequently, he has to closely follow the market's reactions to each of the styles his company designs and produces. If one style sells well, he will produce more of it; conversely, if one style does not sell, he will have to stop further production, offer discounts on those garments already on the market, or even pull them off of the shelves altogether. Facing the direct financial impacts and rewards of the market, it is understandable that Yuan Xing believes that a designer can only "dream others' dream." However, to prioritize the market does not entail a completely passive response to market demands. On the contrary, to maintain success in the market, one has to carefully study the market that one serves. In Yuan Xing's case, it is the Chinese marketplace that he attentively studies and from which he has strategically sought out a niche for his own line of clothing.

When I asked Yuan Xing about his target consumers, he described them in this way: They are "men in my generation [in their forties and fifties], who are rich enough to afford world class name-brand suits, such as Hugo Boss and Ermenegildo Zegna, but can't afford or don't want to buy their entire wardrobe from Hugo Boss or Zegna, and yet they are very picky about the quality of the clothes they buy." This description is markedly different from the general terms such as middle-class or white collar that many other Chinese fashion companies frequently use to describe their target consumers. Yuan Xing clearly identified a specific market segment in China: a group of affluent but not extremely wealthy, status- and image-conscious male consumers who are looking for a combination of status markers, quality, comfort (both physical and psychological), and value. As Chinese society becomes more and more stratified, status symbols such as clothing are gaining tremendous significance in people's social life, a trend of which Yuan Xing is well aware.[7] He not only identified a niche market, but also set up a unique market strategy that further refined his target market and strengthened the competitive position of his product line. He decided not to directly compete with, but to supplement, world leading brands available in Shanghai, such as Hugo Boss and Zegna. To do so, he only included basic items, casual wear, and accessories, but not formal wear in his collection. In this way, he avoided what a new label could not offer, namely, a prestigious status symbol (as Zegna or Boss suits would); at the same time he offered something his customers would look for—quality auxiliary products at competitive prices. By aligning his products with leading world name brands, Yuan Xing also avoids competition from most domestic brands that are deemed cheap by his target consumers.

As Yuan Xing was describing his target consumers and marketing strategy, I had in mind a collection of basic items such as shirts, pants, ties, and belts, and casual wear including blazers, jackets, sweaters, and some sports gear. I took a tour of his showroom while Yuan Xing was receiving his last group of visitors of the day, and my expectations were largely confirmed (Figure 5.2). The clothes were well made, and the fabrics felt good. In terms of styles they were quite similar to the ones commonly produced by Ralph Lauren, but the prices were much cheaper than Hugo Boss or even Ralph Lauren. I was most impressed by the logo of Yuan Xing's line, which was neatly designed in both French and Chinese in a traditional font, very elegant and grand-looking. After an afternoon-long interview and a tour of Yuan Xing's company, I was convinced that Yuan Xing carefully studied his target consumers and strategically supplied what the consumers demanded that was not readily available in the Chinese market. There was little surprise that the company was already profitable even though it was just one year old.[8]

Figure 5.2   A showroom of a man's line similar to Yuan Xing's. Courtesy of Xu Ye.

Ye Li's studio and Yuan Xing's designer label company represent two distinct business models, in which the designers (particularly the chief designer or artistic director) face different sets of choices and constraints, benefits and risks. On the one hand, Ye Li's studio does not involve mass production or serve the consumers directly, which allows her to maintain independent control over her designs. But the financial returns are much more limited than what mass production can potentially offer. On the other hand, Yuan Xing's company involves mass production, and consequently it faces the direct impact and rewards of the consumer market. Working with this model, Yuan Xing felt that he was only able to design what the market wanted. That being said, he did not just passively react to market demands; instead, he actively studied the Chinese market and sought out a market niche for his clothing line, which turned out to have a great payoff. From the vantage point of fashion design, it is clear that Ye Li's and Yuan Xing's business models correlate nicely with their divergent views: Ye Li values originality and she has the freedom to be creative and original in her studio; Yuan Xing weighs the market over originality and he designs for the sake of the market in his designer label company. Judging by the performance of their businesses, both of them are winners as they have both found their market niches and are able to capitalize on them. Aside from their personal abilities and achievements, their success in business clearly has to do with the process of market segmentation, which typically occurs naturally in a capitalist market economy but only started to occur in the reform era in China. By quickly finding their market niches during this period, Ye Li and Yuan Xing became trailblazers in their respective niches, which certainly increased their chances of success. It is in this sense that Ye Li's and Yuan Xing's business models and strategies constitute new "position-takings" in the field of the Chinese fashion industry.

From the description of Ye Li's and Yuan Xing's businesses, it is clear that neither of them is a copycat of Western fashion design. But are they copying Western business models? Differently put, are they simply transporting Western "position-takings" to the Chinese context? From the outset, the different views and approaches of Ye Li and Yuan Xing seemed to parallel the differences between the Western models of haute couture and fast fashion, which hinge on originality and marketability respectively. It is thus important to compare and contrast Ye Li's and Yuan Xing's business models with those of haute couture and fast fashion.

HAUTE COUTURE AND FAST FASHION

Haute couture,[9] the French term for high fashion, is a luxurious type of custom-made clothing utilizing premium fabrics and sophisticated handwork. In terms of design, haute couture offers the most freedom for designers to pursue their creativity and originality. The uniqueness of each garment is guaranteed by its limited quantity, or in Bourdieu's term, "restricted production" (Bourdieu 1993: 53), and it is supposed to be identified with the particular artistic expression of the designer. Well-known couture designers (*couturiers* or *couturieres*) are frequently treated as artists, and their designs are sometimes collected by museums.[10] In the fashion world today, haute couture is frequently represented by about two scores of fashion houses located in Paris,[11] all members of Fédération Française de la Couture, the guardian of the exclusivity of couture. Due to its luxurious and exclusive nature, the customer base for haute couture is small, and the sales from the couture business are often not enough to cover the cost of making the couture garments and their mandatory and expensive showing at the fashion week twice a year (Dickerson 2003: 375–6; Frings 2005: 150–2). However, the couture fashion shows attract a tremendous amount of media attention worldwide, which in effect becomes free advertising and earns recognition and prestige for the fashion houses. As a business model, the couture houses rely on licensing and/or selling their namesake ready-to-wear bridge lines (the prêt-à-porter lines) and accessories such as perfumes and bags to stay financially afloat.

From the description above, we can categorically say that Ye Li's design studio is by no means a couture house even though she favors art over the market in her design philosophy, as any couture designer would. First, she does not design her own line of clothing. In fact, even if she chose to design a couture line, she would not have the supporting industries and skilled staff to support it (specialty fabrics, advanced dyeing and printing technology, and abundant skillful sewing staff are essential to the success of the couture houses in Paris), nor would she have a customer base large enough to sustain it. Second, her designs are "prototypes," not for individual consumers, but for the mass producers who lack design capabilities. Last but not least, she does not seek inspiration (or guidance) from Western art; instead, her designs are rooted in the tradition of Chinese art.

Unlike haute couture, fast fashion emphasizes quick response, efficiency, mass production, and cost saving. It is a mass consumer-oriented business model, in which artistic originality and exclusivity are not a concern, given its goal to mass produce or reproduce popular styles in the shortest lead time possible. As a business model, fast fashion is not a Chinese invention. The term was first used in 1990 by the Apparel Research Committee of the American Apparel Manufacturers Association in a task report, in which it is referred to positively as a "quick response" system of product line development.[12] The then-forward-looking report sees fast fashion as most adaptable to the future of fashion production. According to Reinach, the "finest fruit" of European culture was masterfully snatched by the Chinese and now ripens in China (2005: 12). However, perhaps due to its geographical movement, the forward-looking and positive business model of fast fashion lost its positive connotation and become identified with imitation, low-quality, and cheapness (Reinach 2005). In the meantime, however, there is no proper Chinese terminology for the concept of fast fashion.

Yuan Xing's company indeed has a lot in common with the fast fashion model, as both focus on mass consumers, efficiency, cost, and profit. However, there are also significant differences between the two. Yuan Xing's line is not cheap, as fast fashion would imply. More importantly, although his line builds on leading world brands, he does not counterfeit or copy them. Instead, he consciously maintains an image of his own brand, which is reflected by, among other things, the meticulously designed logo in French and traditional Chinese fonts. In fact, he also strategically differentiates his collection from those of his Western competitors. For example, he intentionally avoids suits in his collection. Hence, his commercial success is not derived simply from competing against his Western competitors with relatively cheaper garments, but more importantly from his in-depth knowledge of the Chinese consumers. After all, it is the Chinese consumers whom his brand is serving. His extensive knowledge of and experience in China's fashion industry allow him to identify a niche market that is composed of a particular group of Chinese consumers who seek status symbols as well as quality, comfort, and value. The identification of this niche market coupled with Yuan Xing's ability to offer what the consumers are looking for at a competitive price has ensured the success of his line. Because of its unique market segment, product assortment, and strategic planning and marketing, Yuan Xing's company is not based on a fast fashion model; it is instead a uniquely Chinese high-end designer label.

From the analyses above, it is clear that neither Ye Li nor Yuan Xing have imitated the international fashion models of haute couture or fast fashion. Their cases illustrate that there are multiple "field positions" and strategies of "position-taking" in the field of the Chinese fashion industry, which contradicts the stereotypical views of Chinese fashion as a singular system of fast fashion and Chinese fashion designers as copycats of their Western counterparts. These stereotypes do not provide an accurate depiction of the Chinese fashion industry; neither do they offer an understanding of what it means to be a fashion designer in China.

What, then, *does* it mean to be a fashion designer in China? Does it mean the same thing in China as it does in the West? Or does it mean something very different because of Chinese fashion designers' unique field positions within the field of the Chinese fashion industry and the global fashion industry? In order to answer the above questions, we have to understand: a) what a fashion design is and b) what a (Chinese) fashion designer is.

WHAT IS A FASHION DESIGN?

Although a fashion design is a concrete object, the conceptualization of fashion design is not always straightforward or unambiguous. As mentioned at the beginning of this chapter, Chinese artist Mr. Chen Yifei's contribution to art was questioned because of his involvement in the fashion industry and other businesses. This suggests that in many people's minds, art and economy are completely separate and autonomous spaces (fields), which can be explained in Bourdieu's term of the field as illustrated in Figure 5.3.

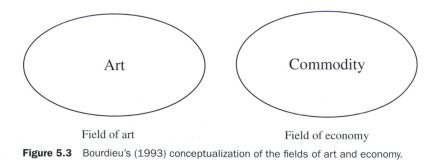

Figure 5.3   Bourdieu's (1993) conceptualization of the fields of art and economy.

Where should a fashion design be in this schema? It has to be either in the field of art or the field of economy (or neither). In other words, it is either a piece of art or a commodity (or neither). However, such a conceptualization of fashion design is not congruent with reality. A fashion design is evidently a commodity, aiming at pre-identified target consumers. At the same time, artistic originality is crucial to a fashion design, so much so that it categorically determines the quality of a fashion design, as seen in the hierarchical order of haute couture, prêt-à-porter, and fast fashion. Therefore, a different conceptualization of fashion design is needed.

In an edited volume, Phillips and Steiner propose an alternative conceptualization of art, artifact, and commodity. They write:

> [O]ne might say that the delicate membrane thought to encase and protect the category of 'art' from contamination with the vulgar 'commodity' has been eroded and dissolved from both sides. No longer treatable as distinct and separate categories, the art-artifact-commodity triad must now be merged into a single domain where the categories are seen to inform one another rather than to compete in their claims for social primacy and cultural value. (Phillips and Steiner 1999: 15–6)

Clearly, Phillips and Steiner believe that art, commodity, and artifact should all belong to the same conceptual domain (see Figure 5.4).

Since a fashion design does not fit well in the rigidly defined and separated conceptual spaces (or fields) of either art or commodity, does Phillips and Steiner's model explain what a fashion design is? Following their model, one may conclude that a fashion design is both an art and a commodity. Should that be the case, then there would be no meaningful distinctions between art and commodity. However, Bourdieu (1993) tells us that there are different operating logics in the two fields of art and economy where art and commodity reside respectively. In the field of art, there is a mode of restricted production, whereas in the field of economy large-scale production dominates. Similarly, Kopytoff (1986) describes the distinctions between art and commodity as

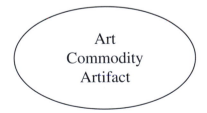

Figure 5.4 Phillips and Steiner's (1999) conceptualization of art, commodity, and artifact.

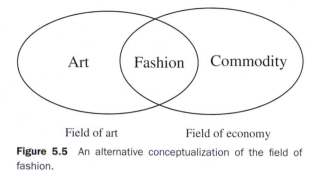

Figure 5.5   An alternative conceptualization of the field of fashion.

involving two opposing processes of "singularization" and "commoditization." To ignore the distinctions between art and commodity risks throwing the baby out with the bathwater.

As contradictory as it may seem, a compromise is possible between the two frameworks. If we do not insist that art and commodity belong to two separate and autonomous fields or one single field, then it is possible to conceptualize them as belonging to the two fields of art and economy that intersect, with fashion design lying at their intersection (see Figure 5.5).

With this conceptual framework, we not only are able to resolve the problems of the dissolving boundaries between art and commodity noted by Phillips and Steiner, but also to preserve their meaningful distinctions highlighted by Bourdieu and Kopytoff. Indeed, this conceptualization of fashion design as situated at the intersection of the fields of art and economy is most suited to analyzing the seemingly conflicting objectives of fashion designers—they want to be artistic and original, and at the same time they want to make money. It is worth noting that though this conceptualization of fashion design may seem to be novel at the intellectual level, fashion designers operate with diverse mixtures of the logics of art and economy all the time. World-renowned fashion designer Rei Kawakubo, for example, talks about her approach to fashion design in this way: "The decision [is] to first of all think of creating something that didn't exist before, and then after that to give the creation form and expression in a way that can be made into a business" (*The Wall Street Journal*, 08/25/2011). Now that we have somewhat demystified fashion design, let's turn to the conceptualization of a fashion designer.

WHAT IS A (CHINESE) FASHION DESIGNER?

The role of a fashion designer parallels that of an author or writer, both involving attaching the name of an individual to his or her work. Therefore, insights about an author or writer can help us understand what a fashion designer is. Building on the insights of Michel Foucault (1979) and Roland Barthes

(1982), Clifford Geertz underscores the distinction between "authors" and "writers" (Barthes's terms), or "founders of discursivity" and "producers of particular texts" (Foucault's terms). The former perform a function, and the latter an activity; the former produce a "work," and the latter a "text" (Geertz 1988: 18). By making this distinction, Geertz draws attention to the dimension of writing in ethnography and makes the point that great anthropologists (authors) are great in part because of the way in which they write. In the case of fashion designers, a similar point can be made: They are fashion designers because of the way in which they work. In fact, that is also a part of the argument of Bourdieu's field theory, which states that the "position-taking" of the player shapes his or her "position" in the field. But if we stopped at this point, though it is a very important point, we would miss a deeper commonality between an author and a fashion designer. That is: they both involve the issue of signature or authorship.

In an insightful study of the Western history of aesthetics, Martha Woodmansee notes that, "[i]n contemporary usage an 'author' is an individual who is solely responsible—and thus exclusively deserving of credit—for the production of a unique, original work" (1994: 35). She argues that the notion of "author" as the sole producer and owner of his or her intellectual work is a historical construct. It has to do with the emergence of the writers who sought to make a living off of their writings that were not protected by law in eighteenth-century Europe. The writers' efforts eventually gave birth to copyright laws. But prior to that, an author, according to Woodmansee,

> was first and foremost a craftsman; that is, he was [a] master of a body of rules, or techniques, preserved and handed down in rhetoric and poetics, for manipulating traditional materials in order to achieve the effects prescribed by the cultivated audience of the court to which he owed both his livelihood and social status. (1994: 36)

Therefore, the concept of the author has morphed from the "author as a craftsman" in the eighteenth century into the "author as a genius" today. In fact, a similar "craftsmen-to-artists" transformation has taken place for fashion designers. In France, this transformation began in the early nineteenth century; yet this process only began in China in recent decades. In other words, Chinese fashion designers are not just newcomers in the global fashion industry, but they are also relatively new in the Chinese fashion industry. In this context, in order to define themselves as geniuses or artists (i.e., authors), Chinese fashion designers have to confront not only the negative stereotype of them as copycats of Western fashion, but also a lowly regarded label of their trade that has been known for centuries in China—the *caifeng*.

Although both *caifeng* and *shizhuang shejishi* are Chinese terms that refer to specialists in garment making, there are significant distinctions between the two. The *caifeng* was the common term for dress-makers prior to the industrialization of China's garment industry, and it specifically refers to craftsmen (*gongjiang*) who learn their skills of making clothes through apprenticeship with a master, and who make clothes on an individual basis or in very small quantities. *Shizhuang shejishi* is a new term that emerged in the context of the industrialization of the Chinese fashion industry. A fashion designer is typically professionally trained in an institution of higher education or specialized training, and he or she generally works with the assistance of other specialists to produce designs or sample clothes that will be mass-produced by garment workers in factories. As craftsmen, the *caifeng* were officially ranked below the intellectuals (*shi*) and the farmers (*nong*) according to the traditional Chinese status hierarchy. On the other hand, the status of the *shizhuang shejishi* is aligned with the intellectuals by the mere merit of their education, even within the frame of traditional status hierarchy. Moreover, innovation is not required or expected of the *caifeng* (the quality was perhaps not even appreciated by previous social customs or ideologies that in general valued convention), whereas fashion designers are expected to be able to come up with innovative designs constantly. Thus, to a fashion designer, *caifeng* means small-scale production, "pre-modern" technology, and above all, no originality, so being called as such amounts to an insult.

In the context of the emerging Chinese fashion industry, in which fashion designers and the *caifeng*, albeit marginalized today, are both known as dress-makers, Chinese fashion designers like Ye Li and Yuan Xing would understandably resort to art and originality, directly or indirectly, in order to keep themselves distinguished from the *caifeng*. It is because of the specific historical context of the Chinese fashion industry that Ye Li's emphasis on art is more than just a personal inclination or a business approach. It is perhaps also why Yuan Xing seems quite ambivalent about the separation of art and his business, as he seems to enjoy the artistic aura of his office and creating original designs for fashion shows. The logic of art and originality is intrinsic to the very status of Chinese fashion designers, i.e., their positions in the field of fashion.

CONCLUSION

This chapter began with the controversy over Mr. Chen Yifei's contribution to Chinese art, which raised the question of why Mr. Chen and Chinese fashion designers cross the perceived "boundary" between the fields of art and economy. To answer the question, I applied Bourdieu's field analysis to fashion and identified three field positions: haute couture, prêt-à-porter, and fast fashion. The three field positions or types of fashions are hierarchically ordered, primarily based on the degree of originality of the designs, which correspond to three distinctive business models and strategies that can be called "position-takings" in Bourdieu's terms. In this hierarchy, Chinese fashions are stereotypically characterized as fast fashions that are unoriginal, cheap, and of low quality, and by extension, Chinese fashion designers are assumed to be imitators of their Western colleagues.

I challenged the validity of the stereotypes of Chinese fashion and fashion designers by presenting the different views and approaches of two prominent Chinese fashion designers, Ye Li and Yuan Xing. Ye Li values artistic originality over the market. She heavily utilizes Chinese materials and motifs, and tries to establish her identity by drawing inspiration from traditional Chinese art. Based on her view of fashion design, she chooses to set up a design studio where she can be innovative and original. Although she believes that art should be the driving force of fashion design, as with Western designers of haute couture, her design studio is not modeled after the Parisian couture houses. Her clients are primarily industrialized mass producers instead of super-wealthy individuals with vanguard tastes for fashion who are the patrons of haute couture. Different from Ye Li, Yuan Xing chooses to design for the market. With his in-depth knowledge of his target consumers and strategic planning and marketing, Yuan Xing carves out a niche market and successfully establishes his own brand. The success of his company is not a result of him blindly imitating Western fashion or following a Western business model, but dependent on the fact that his collection offers a unique set of values that Chinese consumers are looking for. In sum, neither Ye Li nor Yuan Xing are copycats of Western designers or business models. On the contrary, their diverse views and approaches contradict the stereotypes of Chinese fashion and fashion designers.

The disparity between the reality and the stereotypes of Chinese fashion and fashion designers is perhaps due to the instability in the field of the global fashion industry—on the one hand, Western fashion centers are trying to hold onto their glory and dominance; and on the other hand, Chinese fashion designers are attempting to find a name (or position) for themselves.[13] In other words, the rise of the Chinese newcomers poses a threat to the established powerhouses in the global fashion industry.[14] At the same time, the existing hierarchy in the global field of fashion poses significant constraints on Chinese fashion designers. For Chinese fashion designers like Ye Li and Yuan Xing to become credible in the global fashion world, they cannot simply copy Western fashion designers and their business strategies, which would relegate them firmly to the category of copycats and their work to fast fashion. It is in this sense that I argue that Ye Li's and Yuan Xing's views and strategies

illustrate different "position-takings" that are characteristic of their field positions in the global fashion industry as newcomers—they need to be original
so that they will not be so easily dismissed as copycats.

Furthermore, Ye Li's and Yuan Xing's divergent views and business models
also illustrate unique "position-takings" in the field of the Chinese fashion
industry, which came into being in the 1980s. As newcomers to the Chinese
field of fashion and clothing, which was dominated by the *caifeng*, Chinese
fashion designers like Ye Li and Yuan Xing have to directly or indirectly resort
to art and originality in order to distinguish themselves from the *caifeng*, who
are considered lowly esteemed dull craftsmen. It is particularly telling that
even though Yuan Xing prioritizes marketability over originality in his own business, his designs for fashion shows are highly original and artistic, a pattern
shared by many Chinese fashion designers that will be further examined in
the next chapter. Through the explicit emphasis on or indirect resort to artistic
originality, Chinese fashion designers are able to forge a new identity of their
profession in contrast to the *caifeng* in the reform era.

Therefore, although the work of fashion designers by nature requires both
the logics of art and economy in the Chinese and Western fashion industries
alike, for Chinese fashion designers to define themselves as "authors" or
"geniuses," they have to confront the negative stereotype of being copycats
internationally and the long association of their trade with the lowly regarded
caifeng at home. In other words, what it means to be a fashion designer in
China has to do with not only the way in which fashion designers work (that
is, to combine the economic imperatives with the logic of art in their work and
business), but also the context of the field in which they work. Because fashion crosscuts the fields of art and economy, a cultural-economic approach is
needed to understand the internal logic of the field of fashion. In this sense,
Andy Warhol's notion of the "art of business" perfectly captures the essence
of the fashion industry.

In the next chapter, I will continue to take a cultural-economic approach to
examine fashion shows during the China Fashion Week.

Creating Fashion on the Runway, Chinese Style

INTRODUCTION

If the Chinese fashion industry is a puzzle, then China Fashion Week (CFW) is an occasion when all the pieces of the puzzle come together. During China Fashion Week, all the major players of the fashion field, including designers, models, members of the media, potential buyers, fashionistas, and students and scholars of fashion, gather together to display and witness the latest fashion trends. It is also an important social occasion for reunions and celebrations among friends and colleagues. Toward the end of my field research in China, I had the opportunity to attend CFW in November 2004. The experience at CFW allowed me to observe first-hand how various pieces of the puzzle of the field of fashion are put together in China.

In a study of London Fashion Week (LFW), Joanne Entwistle and Agnes Rocamora (2006) make an argument that LFW is "a materialization of the field of fashion." They base their argument on a series of observations of LFW, including the site, the access, the spatial structure of seating arrangements, and the temporal order of arrivals. According to Entwistle and Rocamora, the spatial and temporal structures of LFW render the boundary of the field of fashion visible, reflect the relational positions within the field, and by so doing, also reproduce the field of fashion and its internal structure. China Fashion Week, as a newly established institution, has apparently learned from Western models, an assertion supported by the many parallels between CFW and LFW that will be discussed in detail in this chapter. At the same time, there are important characteristics of CFW that diverge from those of LFW. For example, the two tents at LFW, which house the trade show and the catwalk shows respectively, separate the business of fashion and the art of fashion. Thus they reflect the division of commerce and art in the broader field of fashion (Entwistle and Rocamora 2006: 739). However, the two sites in the Beijing Hotel and the China World Hotel, where CFW is held, do not separate different categories of fashion. In fact, there were plenty of creative couture shows as well as many prêt-à-porter (ready-to-wear) shows at both sites of CFW in 2004.[1] This observation is especially striking to me because there are no couture labels and practically no couture customer base in China.[2]

To a Western observer, seeing "unwearable" clothes on the runway is perhaps not surprising. After all, there is such a notion as haute couture, and despite the business model of haute couture is being challenged by the dominance of prêt-à-porter today, the runway at major fashion weeks remain the last outlets where haute couture can be seen and appreciated in the West. But in the context of China, the fashion industry developed in a dramatically different trajectory from that of Western fashion industries. Prior to CFW, there was no haute couture in China. As we have learned in Chapters 2 and 3, the Chinese fashion industry developed out of the shadow of the Mao era, during which the fashion scene was dominated by the ubiquitous Mao-style *zhongshanzhuang*. China Fashion Week is an even newer phenomenon; it was only eight years old in 2004. Therefore, although the Chinese couture designs on the runway of CFW appear to be consistent with what is happening at LFW, they do not "mirror the broader field of fashion" in China as LFW does in Great Britain. The couture shows at CFW are a distinctly Chinese phenomenon that has to be understood in the Chinese context.

This chapter will address these two key questions: Why do Chinese fashion designers create and showcase "unwearable" couture clothes at CFW when the domestic consumer base of haute couture is virtually nonexistent (not just in terms of purchasing power)? What is the logic with which fashion shows at CFW operate? Chapter 5 explained the cultural and economic imperatives that underline Chinese fashion designers' choice to resort to art and originality in the context of the emergence of the profession of fashion design and the rise of Chinese fashion designers in the global fashion industry. In this chapter, I will extend the cultural economic analysis to fashion shows at China Fashion Week. Following the example of Entwistle and Rocamora's study of London Fashion Week, I will demonstrate how China Fashion Week becomes a materialization of the field of fashion in China. At the same time, I will also examine how and why CFW diverges from LFW, and thus highlight the distinctive characteristics of CFW and the Chinese field of fashion.

This chapter is primarily based on my field research of the Eighth China Fashion Week, which was held in Beijing in November 2004. During CFW, I attended twenty-five out of the thirty fashion shows, the opening ceremony, the fashion forum, two design contests, and a number of press conferences. In addition to my observation of CFW, I interviewed fashion journalists, designers, and officials of the China Fashion Association. My observations of CFW are also informed by my experience at two Shanghai Fashion Weeks in 2004. Foreign designers also participated in CFW Fall 2004,[3] but I limit my discussion in this chapter to those shows by Chinese fashion designers. In particular, I will focus on my experience of the finale show by Mark Cheung, one of the most sought-after shows at CFW. However, one cannot fully appreciate Mark Cheung's show or any other shows at CFW without an understanding of the recent history of fashion shows and modeling in China.

FASHION SHOWS AND MODELING IN CHINA

The first Chinese fashion show, according to Kunrou Pan (2003), a retired fashion commentator in Beijing, was conducted in Shanghai in 1909, and modeled after U.S. fashion shows.[4] Western historians also recorded a variety of events that involved fashion shows organized by Chinese nationalists to promote national products (*guohuo*) during the 1920s and 1930s (Finnane 1996: 118; Gerth 2003: 203–4). At Ningbo Garment Museum, I also found photographic evidence of an early fashion show in Shanghai that dated back to the 1930s (Figure 6.1).

However, these early fashion shows in China were interrupted by the anti-Japanese war and the civil war in the 1940s. The very first fashion show the Chinese witnessed after the founding of the People's Republic of China was in 1979 when French *designer* Pierre Cardin brought French models to China to showcase his collections. Although Pierre Cardin's first fashion show was

Figure 6.1   An early fashion show in Shanghai. Courtesy of Ningbo Garment Museum.

restricted to a professional audience (*zhuanye renshi*) and cadres in the textile industry, it was so well received that he was authorized by the Chinese central government to do another show for a general audience at the Beijing Hotel in 1981. Pierre Cardin's fashion shows were an eye-opener for the Chinese because they not only displayed Western fashions that were completely new to the Chinese at the time,[5] they also re-introduced the format of fashion shows and modeling to China. As one industry expert who attended Cardin's show in 1979 suggested to me, her excitement at seeing Cardin's collection was tempered by an embarrassment that a country as large as China did not have any fashion models.

In 1980, China's very first team of fashion models was formed in Shanghai, named "Shanghai Fashion Performance Team" (*Shanghai shizhuang biaoyan dui*), and the models were called "fashion actresses" (*shizhuang yanyuan*). According to Professor Liu Xiaogang at Donghua University, the early "fashion actresses" worked only part-time, and when they were not participating in fashion shows they returned to work in state-owned garment factories (personal interview, 2004). One of the main missions of the team was to foster cultural exchange, which meant to work with foreign designers when needed. Due to the limited scope of their activities, these part-time "fashion actresses" were not at all in regular demand. Nevertheless, this team was an ice-breaker and certainly had its heyday. In 1983, they were "invited" to perform at *Zhongnanhai*, the headquarters of the Chinese central government (Pan 2003). In 1985, twelve of them were chosen by Pierre Cardin to work for his fashion shows in France, the first time for Chinese fashion models to work overseas.

The success of the Shanghai team soon inspired many other cities, including Guangzhou, Shenzhen, Beijing, and Dalian, to follow suit and set up their own "fashion performance teams." Like the Shanghai team, these teams were all part of the primarily socialist planned economy or command economy (see Chapter 2). The internal organizations of the teams were not in the form of a modeling agency, but a worker-cadre relationship (Bao 1999: 19). The work and leaders of the teams were assigned by the government. In addition, as indicated by their names, the early fashion models in the PRC were considered "actresses" and fashion shows seen as "performances," which suggested their closer kinship to other cultural performances (such as Peking Opera) than an activity that aims at commercial promotion. In addition, these names partly reflected the overall conservative attitude toward clothing and the body in Chinese society at the time. Calling the models "actresses" euphemistically suggested an attempt to elevate them from accusations of their "bad morality" in showing their body for money. Clearly, these names also indicated that commerce was not developed in China back then. As the textile and apparel industries shifted from a planned economy to a market-driven economy in the late 1980s, reforming the "fashion performance teams" became imminent.

In 1992, a "fashion performance team" that had been established a few years before in Beijing became China's first modeling agency, named Xinsilu. The new agency was based on a contractual model-agent relationship rather than the previous actress-cadre relationship (Pan 2003: 30). That is to say, the modeling industry in China started to shift from a command model to a market-based one in 1992. In 2000, the first national organization of fashion models, China Professional Fashion Models Committee, was formed within the China Fashion Association, which marked the professionalization and institutionalization of the fashion modeling industry.

Today, fashion modeling has become a distinct profession in China, and fashion shows have become a major and popular means to promote fashion products, brands, trends, and designers. There are fashion shows at fashion companies' wholesale buyers' fairs, in shopping malls, at trade fairs and exhibitions, and during city or national-level fashion weeks. Each year, there are about 200 fashion related trade fairs, exhibitions, festivals, and fashion weeks nationwide (Ding 2003: 13).[6] Along with the popularity of fashion shows, modeling contests and beauty pageants have also become very popular in China since the late 1990s (Brownell 2001).[7] In contrast to the early fashion shows in the PRC, fashion shows today are called *shizhuang xiu* rather than "fashion performances," and the models are called *mote* instead of "actresses." The new terms of *xiu* and *mote* are transliterations from the English terms of "show" and "model" respectively. These new terms indicate that the Chinese modeling industry is eager to learn from the West and to forge a new identity that diverges from previous perceptions of fashion shows as "performances" and models as "actresses," an outlook that carries vestiges of the planned economic system. Today, a full-fledged market-based modeling industry is thriving in China.

Although fashion shows are commonplace in China today, those at CFW are considered the most professional and widely reported. According to a press release by the China Fashion Association, the organizer of CFW, there were a total of 500 domestic and international fashion journalists registered for CFW in 2004. As a gala of fashion shows, CFW has become the biggest fashion event in China. Looking at CFW today, it is hard to believe that the very first CFW was held as recently as 1997.

CHINA FASHION WEEK AND ITS MISSION

One of the key arguments of this book is that the state has played a major role in the rapid growth of the Chinese fashion industry. It undertook dramatic measures to boost the growth of the Chinese textile industry (Chapter 2), and it also removed the political baggage of clothing from the radical socialist period and encouraged diversification in clothing styles in the reform era (Chapter 3). In fact, the Chinese state did more than just facilitate the growth of the fashion industry; it played a leading role in forming the China Fashion Association.

The CFA was formed in 1993, to assist and regulate the Chinese fashion industry, as a branch organization of the China National Textile Industry Council. Although the CFA was established as a voluntary organization, its parent organization CNTIC—also a "voluntary" organization—had close ties to the central government. As discussed in Chapter 2, the CNTIC descended from the Ministry of the Textile Industry, and its Chairman, Mr. Du Yuzhou, was the former Minister of the Ministry of the Textile Industry, who also served as the first and second President of the CFA until the end of 1998. Moreover, the CFA and CNTIC inherited a large number of personnel and an office building from the former Textile Ministry of the central government. The personnel inherited from the former Textile Ministry are still on the state's payroll.[8] The building is prominently located on Chang'an Street, only a few blocks away from Tian'anmen Square. In 1998, when Mr. Du Yuzhou resigned from his post as President of the CFA, his resignation had to be approved by the Chinese Communist Party and the State Council (CFA official website), which further revealed the CFA's close connection to the state. By partially funding the CFA, the state has a clear interest in CFW, a major event that the CFA organizes in order to jumpstart the Chinese fashion industry.

For the CFA, the immediate purpose of China Fashion Week is to provide a stage for both domestic and international brands and fashion designers to "showcase new products and display characteristics of new designs," and subsequently promote the growth of the Chinese fashion industry (CFA official website). In addition to fashion shows, CFW provides the stage for the CFA to give out awards to fashion companies, brands, designers, models, and journalists. These awards are direct measures for the CFA to carry out Mr. Du Yuzhou's "famed designers project" (*mingshi gongcheng*) and "name brands project" (*mingpai gongcheng*), which are designed to quickly build recognition of Chinese fashion designers and brands respectively (CFA internal documents).

In order to effectively execute Du's "famed designers project," the CFA established an elaborate structure of awards to be presented to fashion designers at CFW. The awards are hierarchically set up into a three-tier pyramid, each with varying degrees of prestige. At the very top is the most prestigious Golden Award (*jinding jiang*), which is awarded once a year to one highly accomplished Chinese fashion designer. In the middle are the "Top Ten Fashion Designers Awards" (*shijia shejishi,* or Top Ten for short), which are also awarded annually but are less prestigious than the Golden Award. At the bottom of the pyramid is the least prestigious but even more numerous

"New Designers Award" (*xinren jiang*). The first two awards are given to prac-
ticing designers, but the third-tier awards are given to the designers-to-be, i.e.,
college students majoring in fashion design. According to the CFA rules, to be
qualified for a higher-level award, one has to first win a less prestigious award
one tier below (CFA internal documents).[9] Because of this rule, the award system actually took quite some time to be fully established at CFW.

When the first CFW was held in 1997, the first Golden Award was granted
to Mark Cheung (also known as Zhang Zhaoda). According the CFA rules, he
had to be a former winner of the "Top Ten Designers Award." Indeed he was.
This only became possible because two classes of "Top Ten Designers Award"
and three classes of "New Designers Award" had already been awarded before the first CFW.[10] That is to say, the first two classes of "Top Ten Fashion
Designers" (and the first three classes of "New Designers Award") were selected based on criteria other than the designers' fashion show performances.
A university professor, who was an early winner of the "Top Ten Fashion Designers award," confirmed to me that those early awardees were selected based
on tests (including theoretical questions) and a few sample designs. Nowa-
days, however, the "Top Ten" are chosen mainly on the basis of their fashion
shows. The rules for selecting the Golden Award have changed as well. The
earlier Golden Awards were chosen internally by the CFA,[11] but since 2001
the Golden Award has been decided by more transparent procedures. First,
a committee of judges, composed of college professors, renowned fashion
designers, foreign experts, fashion journalists, and executives from the retail
sector (a recent addition), would nominate qualified candidates based on their
fashion shows, and then the CFA members attending the annual CFA meeting
during the CFW would vote to determine the final winner (CFA internal documents). Because of all the necessary preparations, including forming various committees, training fashion journalists,[12] and hosting design contests
in order to cultivate both the experience and "credentials" of the fashion designers, it took the CFA four years to launch the first CFW in December 1997,
with nine fashion shows being performed that year. In 1998, more fashion
designers participated in CFW and all three types of awards began to be synchronized and awarded together at CFW in the fall. Since then, the three-tier
pyramid of awards has become a mainstay at China Fashion Week.

In the early years of CFW, there was only one CFW a year. Since 2003, CFW
has been held twice a year: once in the spring (in March or April), introducing
Fall and Winter fashions of the same year, and once in the fall (in November or
December), showing the following year's Spring and Summer fashions. Historically, there have been fewer designers who participate in the spring event, and
CFW in the fall is typically larger in scale than the one in the spring. Also, all
the important fashion awards are given only at CFW in the fall. Consequently,
the CFW in November or December is much more sought-after by domestic

and international media as well as by the general audience than the CFW in the spring. The seasonal cycle and pattern of CFW today is similar to that of LFW and major fashion weeks in the West. However, based on my experience at CFW Fall 2004 below, the similarities between CFW and LFW extend far beyond the seasonal cycles.

CFW: A MANIFESTATION OF THE CHINESE FIELD OF FASHION

The Eighth China Fashion Week, formally known as "CFW 2005 Spring/Summer Collections," was held between November 19 and 25, 2004, at the China World Hotel and the Beijing Hotel,[13] which have been the conventional sites for CFW. The only exception was fashion designer Ma Ke, who chose a third site for her show, a move interpreted by observers as designed to capture more media attention. Ma clearly also played the double pun of showing her line of clothes, called "Exception" (*Liwai*), at the unusual site, which was clearly an exception to the rule. In addition, the site is called *Kaichang*, which was transformed from an old plant that used to make electrical switches, but the term can also mean the very first show. The very first show of CFW (as well as the very last show) is usually highly privileged and she probably would not have gotten it if she had chosen to stay at the CFW sites designated by the China Fashion Association. By moving outside the conventional sites, Ma Ke was able to determine the time of her show, which was ahead of everyone else's, but also maintain control of access to the show independent of the CFA. Indeed, Ma Ke's show turned out to be one of the most strictly access-controlled shows at the CFW. I managed to get into the show by getting a staff pass and was escorted by the producer through the back door, whereas many of my contacts in the media were denied access.[14] Evidently, Ma Ke's moves succeeded in capturing more media buzz, as so many members of the media were talking about how difficult it was to get a ticket to the show. Ma Ke's case suggests that the site of the show matters, but not in the sense of differentiating distinctive types of fashion as the two tents do at London Fashion Week.

Like Ma Ke's show, all the shows and events at CFW had access control of varying degrees. Depending on the level of exclusivity, a show could have one to three layers of access control. The least exclusive shows or other events would only require a ticket, which was issued by the China Fashion Association and checked by the security guards of the hotels. These events included the design contests and shows by lesser-known designers or brands, and a little more than half of the events at CFW used this type of access control. The more exclusive shows would require a ticket and invitation, with the ticket being issued by the CFA and the invitation by the host designer, and the gatekeepers would include both security guards of the hotels and the staff of the host designer, who would check the tickets and invitations respectively. Clearly, the invitations and additional gatekeepers were meant to be an added layer of access control by the host designer on top of what was provided by the CFA. This was perhaps not due to the designer's distrust of the CFA, which tended to issue more tickets than the room capacity, but an intention to ensure his or her (VIP) guests would have seats. About a dozen well-established designers chose this type of access control. The most exclusive shows and events would require not only a ticket (from CFA) and an invitation (from the designer), but also have police instead of security guards monitoring access. Only a few shows and events chose this highly restrictive access at CFW. The final show by Mark Cheung was one of them.

Common to all the shows and events at the two sites of CFW was that they required tickets issued by the CFA, which would be checked by gatekeepers at the entrance. The tickets were not for sale, but distributed by both the CFA and the host designer. The CFA would send the tickets ahead of time to its members, the registered media, and fashion institutions in Beijing (who would in turn distribute the tickets to their students). Similar to Entwistle and Rocamora's (2006: 740) observations of LFW, the tickets and gatekeepers at CFW literally marked the boundary of the Chinese field of fashion—those who have access to the shows are the "insiders" of the field, as opposed to the "outsiders" who have no access. As a foreign researcher, I was not a member of the Chinese field of fashion, so I could not get tickets directly from the CFA.[15] However, during the course of my field research in China, I was able to establish connections with many "insiders" of the field, including fashion designers, journalists, and fashion show producers. Through these connections, I was able to personally obtain tickets and invitations to most of the fashion shows and events at CFW. My ability to gain access to the shows without the official approval of the CFA illustrates perfectly my "insider-outsider" position relative to the Chinese field of fashion; a similar sense is also shared by Entwistle and Rocamora at LFW. While there are parallels between CFW and LFW with respect to access control, there are key differences as well, chief among which was the presence of the police as gatekeepers in some shows at the CFW. To the best of my knowledge, the police, which are an evident instrument of the power of the state, were not there at the request of the host designers, but to provide added security for government officials and dignitaries who graced the shows.

While tickets and invitations allowed "equal" entry to the shows, once inside the show theater space, the seating was hierarchically ordered. At the center of the rectangular show theater (at both sites) of the CFW was a "T-shaped" runway, which was surrounded by seats on three sides. Due to close proximity to the runway, the front-row seats commanded better views and thus were considered privileged seats. In fact, the seats in the front rows on the two opposing sides of the runway were marked as "VIP" seats (stated as such in red letters on the back of the chairs). There were also seats placed at the bottom of the "T" stage, right in front of the media stage, which was marked by a few dozen tripods and cameras. These seats were considered best of the best, as they enjoyed the most commanding view of the show and were marked as *guibinxi*, meaning seats reserved for distinguished guests. The remaining seats in the back rows were not marked by any distinction and were open to the general audience admitted into the show. The front-row *guibinxi* seats and VIP seats are privileged not only because they enjoy better views of the show, but also because they can be easily spotted by others in the audience. As Entwistle and Rocamora put it, the front row seats enjoy the advantage of both "seeing and being seen" (2006: 742–5).[16] They argue that by occupying the front-row seats, the occupants reaffirm their distinguished positions in the field of fashion, which consequently reproduces the field of fashion (and its internal hierarchical structure). In other words, the hierarchical structure of the seating in the show theater and the hierarchical structure of the field positions in the fashion industry reify each other during the fashion week. That much is common between CFW and LFW.

However, the occupants of the front-row seats at LFW vary from those at CFW. The front-row seats at LFW are typically taken by celebrities, fashion icons, renowned journalists and designers, and so on. Based on my own field research of CFW, the front-row seats include the *guibinxi* seats and VIP seats. For most shows, the *guibinxi* seats are reserved by the CFA for its own officials, officials of the National Textile Industry Council, judges, and other distinguished guests such as government officials, distinguished foreign guests, officials of major media, and corporate sponsors. Should these seats not be filled, they, along with the reserved VIP seats on the two sides of the runway, would be taken by the invited guests of the host designer, including his or her friends, fellow designers, and VIP customers. Compared to LFW, there is a clear lack of participation of celebrities and fashion icons at CFW. Therefore, although CFW and LFW are similar in that the seating arrangements in the theater map out and thus reproduce the hierarchy within the field of fashion, CFW is also very different from LFW because political power, represented by government and industry council officials, is literally front and center at CFW, and by extension, in the Chinese field of fashion.

In addition to the spatial display of distinctions inside the theater space, Entwistle and Rocamora point out that the temporal structure of fashion shows at LFW also suggests hierarchy, in the sense that those who enjoy the highest status in the fashion field tend to be fashionably late for the show (2006: 742). Once again, CFW differs from LFW. As my experience of Mark Cheung's show described below indicates, the ones who tend to be late at CFW are not necessarily those who are fashionable, but those who are in power (in fact, the show would not start without them).

In sum, by looking at the controlled access, the spatial arrangement inside the show theater, and the temporal structure of the fashion show, Entwistle and Rocamora (2006) argue that LFW is a materialization of the British field of fashion, which is an internally hierarchical, but externally autonomous space, hence independent of the field of politics. Similar to LFW, there are also controlled access and hierarchical spatial and temporal arrangements at CFW. It is in this sense that I make a parallel argument that CFW is a manifestation of the Chinese field of fashion. But unlike LFW, the profile of a fashion show at CFW is not raised by celebrities or fashion icons, but by high-level government officials, who consequently require even more strictly controlled access to the show. The importance and high visibility of government officials at CFW thus render CFW and, by extension, the Chinese field of fashion a structured but not completely autonomous space.

In what follows, I will present a portion of my field notes of the final show of CFW by Mark Cheung in Fall 2004, which is reproduced in past tense and then followed by an analysis of the show and my general observations of CFW.

THE FINALE OF CFW FALL 2004: MARK CHEUNG'S FASHION SHOW—*JIANGNAN*

Although CFW only has a short history of eight years, it has become a tradition that Mr. Mark Cheung, the first Golden Award winner, would be the host of the final show at CFW. According to journalists, Mr. Cheung wants to encourage younger designers to create new designs by example; the subtext is that even an accomplished designer like him works hard and churns out something new every year, so younger designers should not have any excuse not to do the same.

The finale show from the master (*dashi*) was perhaps the most anticipated show of CFW, conforming to the idea of saving the best for last (the concept in Chinese is called *yazhouxi*). Tickets to the show were in high demand. In fact, unlike many other shows, the tickets to Mr. Cheung's show were not distributed by the CFA, but by his team to ensure exclusivity of the audience. But for my acquaintance with a senior executive on Mr. Cheung's team, I would not have been able to get an invitation letter and a ticket to the show.

The show theater was in the Banquet Hall (*yanhuiting*) at the Beijing Hotel on the evening of November 24. I arrived at the Banquet Hall about thirty minutes in advance of the scheduled show time. Most of the seats, except the first three rows, were already taken. The theater was not as big as the other site of the CFW (the China World Hotel theater), housing probably about 500 to 600 seats, which surrounded the T-stage on three sides. Facing the T was the media stage camped with tripods and cameras. In front of the media stage, there were a few rows of empty seats prominently reserved by the

CFA for the distinguished guests. From previous experience, I knew that the distinguished guests would generally include CFA officials, Textile Industry Council officials, corporate sponsors, distinguished foreign guests, judges, and sometimes government officials. The first few rows of seats on the two sides of the runway were the VIP seats. Experience from previous shows told me that those VIP seats were reserved for people with invitation letters, including friends and VIP customers of the designer. Behind the VIP seats were seats for the general audience.

Feeling emboldened with an invitation in hand, I walked directly toward the front rows on one side of the runway. But before I got there, I was stopped by a policeman, not regular staff of the designer or security guards of the hotel (who would typically maintain order at the entrance) as in other shows. I showed him my invitation, but he did not even look at it, only told me in a cold voice, "Those are not for you." In puzzlement, I looked around for an empty seat further back and I located one in the fourth row on the opposite side. When I was about to make my way directly through the opening between the T-stage and the mostly empty seats for the distinguished guests, I was stopped once again by the policeman, who told me that I should take other "detours" but was too busy to explain to me where those "detours" were or why I could not use the pathway. In fact, I was familiar with the setting of the theater from watching previous shows and knew there were no real "detours." So, I had to elbow through the media stage, and on the way I found out from the journalists that the Mayor of Beijing was on his way to the show and that was why there was a heavy presence of police and so many front-row seats were reserved on very short notice—apparently the Mayor was not coming alone.

I finally sat down and took a good look at the setup of the stage. The backdrop of the T-stage was composed of three huge panels of watercolor painting, which stood out in the dimly-lit theater hall. The painting looked like a typical small rural town in South China (*jiangnan*, or south of the Yangtze River), characterized by three iconic *jiangnan* objects: a little bridge (*xiaoqiao*), a small river (*liushui*), and rows of houses (*renjia*). The bluish watercolor and dim light dramatized the romantic aura of a smoky *jiangnan* town fading into the distance. For a brief moment, my thoughts meandered: Were the people living in the houses cooking? Was it a drizzling day or was it getting dark? They all looked so familiar yet distant to me, as if coming out of a nearly faded memory. As someone who grew up in South China, I knew where this memory came from: not exactly from what I remembered of my hometown, but from a "collective memory" of the *yanyu* (smoky and drizzling) *jiangnan* passed down by generations of Chinese poets and artists. While the image of the rustic, romantic, and mystic *jiangnan* drew my thoughts away, the stage extended from the backdrop brought me back to the show theater. The runway carried the same motif as the painting; it looked like a little bridge, guarded by wood posts linked by ropes (Figure 6.2).

Figure 6.2 Backdrop of Mark Cheung 2005 Haute Couture Fashion Show. Courtesy of Jianhua Zhao.

Figure 6.3 Invitation to Mark Cheung's fashion show.

The setting reminded me that the name of the show, *Jiangnan*, was on the invitation. The invitation was placed in a beautiful envelope. On it was the title, *Jiangnan*, and the subtitle "Mark Cheung 2005 Haute Couture Fashion Show," written in beautiful Chinese brush calligraphy, with signatures (one in Chinese and one in English) and seals of Mr. Cheung arranged in a traditional manner. The invitation was a tri-fold (Figure 6.3). On the front was the image of the tiles on the roof of a typical *jiangnan* house, and the edge of the front fold was cut off in the shape of the end of the roof (the top left image of Figure 6.3). On the second fold was a traditional-style Chinese painting of a watery *jiangnan* scene (the bottom left of Figure 6.3). With the tri-fold fully open, from right to left (as in the traditional Chinese way) were the name of the show and then a poem by a famous poet Xu Zhimo, beautifully illustrating the scenery of *jiangnan*. To the end of the poem, Mr. Cheung added, " . . . My only choice is to let the silk thread take me back to [my] dream of the *jiangnan*." Below the poem was an image of a traditional scholar sailing on a small boat, and further below was a picture of Mr. Cheung and his impressive resume written in both Chinese and English. With a combination of calligraphy, painting, and poetry, Mr. Cheung's invitation presented the reader with a total aesthetic experience.

The room quickly filled up, even the seats for the prestigious guests. Right in the center of the front row, I saw Mr. Du Yuzhou, Chairman of the National Textile and Apparel Industry Council and former minister of the Ministry of the Textile

Figure 6.4   A sketch of day wear by Mark Cheung. Courtesy of Mark Cheung.

Figure 6.5 A sketch of evening wear by Mark Cheung. Courtesy of Mark Cheung.

Industry. In front of him was a large long-lens camera supported by a tripod. In the rear of all three sides, people were standing and squeezing into whatever room they could find. No standing tickets were issued at CFW (unlike LFW), so presumably, those people standing had their seats bumped by the late-arriving distinguished guests who did not need any tickets to get in. I turned to my two neighbors and quickly found out that both were college students majoring in fashion design. But before I could have a longer chat with them, the music was turned up, smoke came out of the runway, and the show began.

The show lasted about thirty-five minutes, and a total of sixty to seventy ensembles were displayed, which were divided into two sets—day wear and evening wear (as most shows did). Ruffles and layering were two dominant features of the entire collection (these are also clear in his sketches, see Figures 6.4 and 6.5), perhaps inspired by rows of roof tiles on those *jiangnan* houses or perhaps the waves of the river (as one journalist pointed out in

Figure 6.6   Mark Cheung 2005 Haute Couture fashion show. Photo by Jianhua Zhao. Courtesy of Mark Cheung.

her report). The overall darker tones of blue, black, and burgundy of the entire collection were clearly taken from typical *jiangnan* scenes. The colors of the clothes and the painting in the background were strikingly harmonious. For the most part, clothes in the first set were wearable, cheery, and youthful, represented by blue bell bottoms, embellished with ruffles (Figure 6.6). The second set of the collection shifted dramatically to evening gowns (Figures 6.7 and 6.8), accompanied by sudden shifts of music from solo flute to a dramatic and loud ensemble of traditional Chinese instruments. If it were not for the consistency in colors, ruffles, and layering (as well as the traditional Chinese music), the two sets of clothes would have appeared to be two completely separate shows. The styles of the gowns were mostly European style ball gowns, and many of them were truly elegant and sophisticated, but too busy in details and layering to be contemporary. Indeed, quite a few gowns resembled the eighteenth-century Rococo style. It was hard for me to picture an occasion for which those gowns could be worn in China other than on the runway.

Figure 6.7   Mark Cheung 2005 Haute Couture fashion show. Photo by Jianhua Zhao. Courtesy of Mark Cheung.

THE CULTURAL ECONOMY OF CHINA FASHION WEEK

I enjoyed Mark Cheung's show enormously.[17] Everything, including the invitation, the setup of the stage, the music, and the show, was meticulously put together, and all linked to the central theme of the *Jiangnan*. The entire show conveyed a rustic, romantic, and nostalgic aura. The theme of the show was so coherent that the clothes, which were supposed to be the centerpiece of the show, became subsumed by the whole artistic aura. If it were not for the heavy presence of the media and the frequent flashes of the cameras, it would have been easy to mistake the show for a theatrical performance. Indeed, the theatrical aspects of fashion shows have led scholars to ponder about the connections between fashion shows and theater performances (e.g., Kondo 1997; Troy 2003). But at the same time, fashion shows mean business: lots of money would have to be spent[18] and many people would have to work for a long time to make them happen; they are meant for spectacular commercial

Figure 6.8 Mark Cheung 2005 Haute Couture fashion show. Photo by Jianhua Zhao. Courtesy of Mark Cheung.

promotions. Mark Cheung, as a seasoned designer who oversees five prêt-à-porter lines,[19] of course knows the economic interests at stake. However, none of the styles from his five brands were displayed during his show. The names of his five prêt-à-porter lines were not even on the huge backdrop painting or the invitation. In fact, he calls his show an haute couture show (both on the backdrop and the invitation). The disparities between the collection he showed at the CFW and his prêt-à-porter lines that he sells on the market are striking. I couldn't help but wonder why he didn't show the clothes he was selling or sell the clothes he put on the show. From previous media reports and video recordings, I learned that haute couture shows have consistently been Mark Cheung's style at CFW. Evidently, he was not alone in doing couture shows at the CFW I attended either. In fact, as a "master" designer and the first Golden Award winner, his style of shows (or strategy of "position-taking") is emulated by many Chinese fashion designers. As a senior fashion designer of the same generation as Ye Li and Yuan Xing, Mark Cheung's emphasis on art supports my findings in Chapter 5 that Chinese fashion designers need to resort to art in order to set themselves apart from the negative stereotypes of being imitators of Western fashion and the traditional label of their trade as *caifeng*. However, it is hard to believe that the expensive couture shows at CFW are all about a "professional image." After all, both Ye Li and Yuan Xing, discussed in Chapter 5, have their own businesses. What is the economic logic of the couture shows when there are no couture labels in China? I discussed my observation about the disconnection between the couture shows at CFW and Chinese fashion businesses with fashion journalists and designers who attended CFW, among whom was Ms. Wang Mei.

Wang Mei is a veteran fashion journalist working for a major Chinese fashion newspaper, whom I befriended during Shanghai Fashion Week a month before CFW.[20] She accepted my interview in a café inside a bookstore after CFW. She responded to my question about inconsistencies between clothes on the runway and those on the market by explaining the differences between CFW and Paris Fashion Week:

> China Fashion Week does not make distinctions between different types of fashion shows and subsequently you see both haute couture and prêt-à-porter collections at CFW. By contrast, the two types of collections were shown separately at two different fashion weeks in Paris.

Wang Mei's point is clearly valid, but I was not concerned about whether Chinese fashion designers or CFA were confused about the distinctions between haute couture and prêt-à-porter; instead I was interested in finding out why Chinese fashion designers and others put so much emphasis on haute couture on the runway even while no couture brands or market existed in China. So I sharpened my question and raised it again to Wang Mei. "That's because the artistically oriented haute couture catches the attention of the media, and there was no cheaper but more effective way to spread your name than doing a successful fashion show during CFW," she replied.

Wang Mei's answer points to the role of the media. During CFW, nearly all the Chinese fashion related media, some entertainment-related media, and some international media would congregate in Beijing and cover the event. This means that fashion designers, brands, and sponsors would get a week of free advertising on TV, in newspapers and magazines, at both national and local levels (as well as some international exposure). In the case of the major Chinese trade papers, such as *China Fashion Weekly* and *Fashion Times*, the free advertising could last a couple of months. The hype would start way ahead of the event, covering the latest news of the designers, the models, and others who would participate at the upcoming CFW and speculating who would win the top awards. During the CFW, live coverage of the events by the media would be going on at the sites. It was in fact an odd experience for me during CFW that I would bump into friends and acquaintances who were speaking to a microphone or in front of a camera almost every few steps in the hallways at the two sites. I had to learn not to say hi but only nod and smile when I walked past them. Weeks after CFW, there would still be photographs of the shows, fashion commentaries and analyses written by experts and editors. Of all the media coverage, the ones that receive the most attention are the award winners at CFW, especially the Golden Award winner. In this context, it is understandable that fashion designers would gravitate toward couture shows that would more likely win them an award, because success at CFW, especially winning an award, would lead to immediate national fame and visibility for the designer (as well as others such as the models). The award and the fame ("symbolic capital") that comes with it in turn could be converted into economic gains ("economic capital") by the designer in numerous other ways, such as landing a better-paying job, winning financial backing to start a new line, and/or getting more customers. The successful careers of earlier award winners, such as Mark Cheung and Yuan Xing (in Chapter 5), powerfully validates this approach to fashion shows at CFW. Compared to the potential gains, the cost of producing a fashion show appears to be less a concern for the designer, especially when the cost may not be borne by the designer himself or herself alone.

Therefore, although the couture fashion shows at CFW appeared to be economically irrational at first, they become reasonable once we add the awards by the CFA and the media into consideration. The designers' quest for quick fame through couture shows is a logic of consecration that can only be sustained by their repeated conversions of symbolic capital gained through consecration into economic capital (Bourdieu 1986). The economic logic of couture shows is thus indirectly inherent. For designers, doing couture shows at CFW represents a viable strategy to jumpstart a career (or to stay at the top) in the Chinese fashion industry. Evidently, this strategy is also sanctioned by the state (via the CFA), as it is consistent with the state's effort to jumpstart China's fashion industry by instituting a complex competition and award system on the stage of CFW as outlined previously. This leads to another question: Why would other parties involved in the fashion shows, including the media and financial backers, be on board with the fashion designers and the CFA?

The media are fixated on the awards at CFW, not because they are ordered by the state, but because the media have an interest in doing so. Several Chinese fashion journalists confirmed to me that the issues of their newspapers or magazines that cover the Fall CFW reach the highest circulation in the entire year. Covering the awards at CFW is a win-win situation for the media, the designers, and the CFA. In fact, not just the media benefit financially from heavy coverage of CFW and the awards; the CFA also profits from it by attracting more participants (thus more registration fees) and more corporate sponsors. For example, two large Chinese fashion companies sponsored the "New Designers Awards" at CFW Fall 2004, and the CFA was able to attract a corporate sponsor of the closing ceremony just a few days before the event, according to two journalists who were familiar with the situation. Therefore, the cultural economy of the awards at CFW involves the fashion designers, the media, corporate sponsors, and the CFA; the collaboration among all the parties involved makes it possible for the CFA to fulfill its mission of creating more "famed designers" and "name brands" that Mr. Du envisioned. The cultural and economic logics of the awards are central to sustaining the couture shows at CFW.

However, fashion shows at CFW are not all couture shows; some shows at CFW Fall 2004 displayed ready-to-wear collections exclusively. In addition, while there were obvious corporate sponsors for some events, such as the design competition and the closing ceremony (with the names of the corporations attached to the events), it was not always apparent who the sponsor was for the fashion shows. I was curious what companies would sponsor a fashion show that merely promoted the designer, but not the company or its lines. My serendipitous encounter with Zheng Yifan helped me understand the dynamic between fashion companies and designers.

Zheng Yifan is Chief Designer of a women's wear company based in Dalian, and she was a winner of the "Top Ten Fashion Designers" award a few years before (I learned of her award through the CFA documents because she only mentioned that she had done fashion shows at CFW before). I met Yifan by accident during the 2004 CFW. We both went to a small restaurant in the lower level of the International Trade Center, which is adjacent to the China World Hotel, a major site of CFW. Since it was busy lunch hour and perhaps too many customers were there because of CFW, the waiter asked the customers to share tables, and I happened to share a table with Yifan. Through some courteous exchange of words, I found out that she was a fashion designer. I introduced myself as a researcher on China's fashion industry and asked if she would accept an interview with me. She agreed. I joined her two days later in her interview with a group of fashion models at the Starbucks inside the building of the China World Hotel. Yifan did not do a show that year, and she went to CFW mainly to interview and select models for photo shoots to be used in the coming season's advertisements and to reunite with her fellow designers.

She told me that when she showed her prêt-à-porter collection at CFW a few years earlier, there were not that many designers showing them, but it became increasingly a trend that the designers would show prêt-à-porter (which they sell on the market) rather than unmarketable haute couture collections. I asked her why the designers changed their approach. She said it was because the companies that financially supported the fashion designers realized that their actual lines on the market had not gotten any exposure in the previous years' fashion weeks; instead their support only helped the designers to achieve personal fame. Then, the designers might end up leaving the company for better jobs or might be tempted to start their own businesses on the side. I turned the subject to her personal experience and asked whether she felt the same constraint from her company when she showed her prêt-à-porter collection at the CFW. She said that she had a very good and stable working relationship with her boss, whom I later found out to be her elder sister and that she also owns a share of her company.[21]

During the interview, Zheng Yifan made it clear to me that the interest of the financial backers (fashion companies) is not always aligned with that of the fashion designers, and that the current state of fashion shows at CFW increasingly displaying ready-to-wear collections may be attributable to the clash of interests between fashion designers and their companies. Yifan's own example is also very interesting. Her interest is aligned with her financial backer (her sister), and she chose to showcase the ready-to-wear lines of her company. Evidently, she was not in the business of advancing her own career at the expense of her company by doing a couture show at CFW.

Therefore, the cultural economy of CFW that centers on the awards seems to be complicated by the fashion companies that are interested in promoting their marketable prêt-à-porter collections rather than the designers to whom they provide financial support. As a result, the current trend seems to be that there are increasingly more prêt-à-porter shows and fewer haute couture shows during CFW. This trend is also supported by fashion designers who own or partially own their prêt-à-porter lines as Zheng Yifan does. At the same time, as long as the awards remain as the center of attention of the media, fashion designers, and the CFA, couture shows like Mark Cheung's show described previously will continue to be highly conspicuous and prized at CFW. This pattern of CFW is different from London Fashion Week, which only shows prêt-à-porter collections, and its logic is also different from Paris Haute Couture Fashion Week because there are no haute couture lines in China. This pattern of CFW and its internal logic reflect the distinctive characteristics of the Chinese field of fashion, the logic of which has to be understood in the Chinese context.

CONCLUSION

In this chapter, I examined Chinese fashion shows and China Fashion Week, a major event that brings together various important players in the field of fashion in China. As an imported institution, China Fashion Week maintains many similarities to major fashion weeks in the West. Building on Entwistle and Rocamora's insights about London Fashion Week, I argue that China Fashion Week is a manifestation of the Chinese field of fashion, in the sense that various positions in the field are rendered visible through temporal and spatial arrangements at China Fashion Week. The structure of the field positions are also reified and reproduced by the same arrangements. However, China Fashion Week is also localized in significant ways; there are major differences between China Fashion Week and London Fashion Week.

One of the key differences between CFW and LFW is the position of political power in the field of fashion. As Entwistle and Rocamora observe, the boundaries set up at London Fashion Week indicate that the British field of fashion is an autonomous space that is independent of politics. By contrast, the Chinese fashion field as rendered visible by China Fashion Week reserves privileged positions for governmental and semi-governmental officials. The prominent presence of government officials at China Fashion Week not only indicates the connections between the state and the China Fashion Association, but also reflects the broader condition of the field of fashion and Chinese society in general, which are always permeated by the power of the state to a certain degree.

Another major difference lies in the elaborate award structure of CFW, which was set up by the CFA to jumpstart China's fashion industry. The awards at CFW lead Chinese fashion designers toward showing artistically oriented haute couture designs rather than showing their prêt-à-porter collections that are sold on the market. The divergence between the clothes on the runway and the clothes on the market is caused by the designers' belief that unique and artistic designs are better positioned to win awards at CFW, which could lead to instant national fame, and which in turn could lead to faster or greater economic gains. This approach to fashion shows at CFW has been proven to be a viable shortcut to success demonstrated by the career trajectories of many successful designers who were earlier award winners. In addition to the fashion designers, the CFA and the media also have an interest in seeing and reporting the eye-catching couture shows at CFW. This alignment of interests ensures the participation of all the major parties, which underscores the success of an award-centered CFW.

However, the recent increase in prêt-à-porter shows on the stages of CFW signals a potential clash of interest between fashion designers and their financial sponsors, i.e., the fashion companies. The interest of the fashion companies is evidently better served by showing their prêt-à-porter lines rather than the designers' couture designs at CFW. The trend toward more prêt-à-porter shows at CFW is supported by participation of designers like Zheng Yifan who own or partially own their company; subsequently their interest is aligned with that of their company. While this trend seems to be gaining momentum, couture shows will likely remain highly visible and coveted at CFW as long as there are powerful coordinated interests behind the awards.

The Chinese characteristics of fashion shows and fashion week suggest that fashion shows, particularly those during CFW, are not just commercial means to promote fashion, but also "localized" strategies for the designers and other players to obtain better positions in the field of fashion. Through examining the major parties involved at CFW, this chapter shows that a fashion designer's creative show is not just a shortcut for him or her to advance his or her career, but also a shortcut for China to jumpstart its fashion industry. Because of the "local characteristics" of China Fashion Week, an ethnographic approach is needed to unravel the cultural economy of China Fashion Week, and subsequently the Chinese field of fashion.

In the next chapter, I will explore the global connections of the Chinese apparel industry. I will examine how Chinese manufacturers and traders are connected to corporate buyers in the United States in an attempt to offer a clothing perspective on globalization.

Making Clothes for International Markets: A Clothing Perspective on Globalization

THE STORY OF A STEELERS JERSEY

The winter of 2005 was a joyful time for Pittsburgh Steelers' fans, because their team did the almost impossible. It went into the postseason as a wild card team and upset all the stronger teams on the road and was on its way to win the Super Bowl. The joy spread far beyond Pittsburgh and the United States. Mr. Zeng Gang, a contact and friend of mine who lives in Shanghai, China, and works in the business of international garment trade, was so excited for me that he sent me a Steelers jersey via FedEx. The Steelers jerseys, as I was told by Zeng Gang, were in high demand and mine was a sample for the follow-up orders from Reebok (merged with Adidas since 2006), the sportswear giant that makes jerseys for the National Football League (NFL) in the United States.

My Steelers jersey arrived just in time for the Super Bowl XL game, which was held in Detroit, Michigan, on February 5, 2006. As newly converted fans of the Steelers, my wife and I decided to go to a sports bar to watch the game in Pittsburgh. Right after lunch, we headed out for a bar, and I was wearing my brand-new Steelers jersey sent to me by Zeng Gang from Shanghai. After a few failed attempts for bars in nearby neighborhoods, which were fully booked, we luckily secured a table without a reservation in a sports restaurant/bar at Waterfront, a booming area for shopping and recreation in Pittsburgh. Our table was in a converted dining area where the restaurant had temporarily installed a big flat-screen TV to accommodate viewers of the game. The game was scheduled to begin in the evening. Like most people in the restaurant, we spent hours in the afternoon watching commercials and the warm-up shows, chatting, and drinking over snacks. By "people," I mean Steelers fanatics: They were all decked out in black and gold jerseys similar to mine; some were even holding the "Terrible Towels." For some of the fans, this was clearly a family affair. A neighboring table was taken by a family of four, and the mom had to find an extra chair for additional participants of the family event—stuffed animals dressed in Steelers jerseys and draped in a Terrible Towel. For others, this was a party event among friends. Judging by the black-and-gold regalia, the whole restaurant felt like a big gathering for Steelers fans, although many of them were first-time acquaintances. Whether they were friends or strangers prior to this gathering, it did not matter; what mattered was that everyone was a Steelers fan, marked and symbolized as such by the regalia they put on themselves. This became even more obvious once the game started. Each time the Steelers scored or made a big play, we all cheered, "go Steelers, go!" Similarly, when the Seahawks, the Steelers' opponent, were about to make a big play, we made a loud "boo. . ." By simultaneously cheering for the Steelers and booing the Seahawks, a sense of familiarity and oneness, or to use an anthropological term made popular by Victor Turner, "communitas," developed among the audience in the restaurant (1969: 97). Total strangers became very friendly, easily striking up a conversation with each other during commercial breaks or even in the men's room. My Steelers jersey evidently helped to mark me as "one of us": When the Steelers scored a touchdown, one man whom I had never met before came over and gave me a high five to celebrate. Yes, we had a good reason to celebrate: the Steelers won the Super Bowl!

Watching the 2006 Super Bowl game in a Pittsburgh sports restaurant is one of my most memorable Super Bowl experiences. Without a doubt, my experience was enhanced by the Steelers jersey made by Zeng Gang's suppliers in China. The jersey marked me as "one of us"—the Steelers fans, or as they call it, a member of the "Steelers nation." It helped to create a common frame of reference in which social distinctions outside this context or frame did not matter. The common frame—the Steelers team—was what brought everyone together. Consequently it facilitated a "bond"—the feeling of being an equal member of the Steelers nation—among the viewers in the restaurant, despite that many of whom were strangers. From my experience of watching the Super Bowl game in the sports restaurant, the most meaningful aspects of the jersey to me as a consumer were the black-and-gold pattern and the Steelers' logo; had I worn a Seahawks jersey, my experience in the restaurant would conceivably have been very different. Those most meaningful components of the Steelers jersey (to consumers like me) are controlled by the Steelers organization, marketed by the NFL, and licensed by the NFL to Reebok (both the NFL and Reebok also have their own logos on the jersey). All three organizations are based in the United States and are familiar to U.S. consumers. What the U.S. consumers may or may not know is that their NFL jerseys (as well as over one-third of their entire wardrobe) are made in China. The country of origin of their jerseys and other garments is usually marked on a small tag hidden from view. As the saying goes, out of sight, out of mind; it does not seem to matter to them where their jerseys come from. This is because unlike the logos of the Steelers, the NFL, and Reebok, the country of origin of their jerseys does not hold any symbolic meaning to them. In fact, this observation seems to be applicable to most U.S. consumers with regard to their views toward their clothes; nobody seems to care where their clothes are made.[1]

The hidden tag inside our clothes that indicates the country of origin, however, is not only the material evidence of the interconnections of the global apparel industry, but also reflects the way in which the global fashion apparel industry is structured. For example, my China-made Steelers jersey clearly demonstrates the connection between the Chinese clothing industry and the United States, but at the same time, the story of the Steelers jerseys also shows that the symbolic meanings of the garments are disconnected from the producers in China. In order to understand the apparent contradictions inherent in the export of Chinese made garments, this chapter examines the patterns in which the Chinese apparel industry is connected to the global fashion industry. I argue that the contradiction between the material connection between U.S. consumers and Chinese producers and the disconnection of meaning of the garments between the two are caused by the uneven power between Chinese suppliers and U.S. corporate buyers on the one hand, and the power imbalance between China and the United States on the other hand. Using a network analysis, this chapter offers a new perspective on globalization from the vantage point of clothing. In what follows, I will discuss the current pattern of garment trade between the United States and China. Then, I will examine the international trade regimes that regulate U.S. textile and clothing imports. This is to be followed by an analysis of the 2005 trade dispute between the United States and China concerning textile and apparel products and the implications of its resolution. Finally, I will explore what the transnational movement of Chinese made clothing can tell us about globalization. To start, let me explain why and how garments consumed in the United States (and most Western countries) are made elsewhere in the world.

"AN IMPERFECT INDUSTRY"

The apparel industry (as well as the textile industry) has been closely connected to industrialization and modernization since the Industrial Revolution started in Britain in the eighteenth century. Yet, no matter how advanced the technologies have become over the years, one of the key operations of the industry remains the same; it requires human operators sitting behind sewing machines to stitch the garments. Consequently, labor is one of the major components of the cost of the garments, and worse yet, a flexible cost. To reduce costs, the apparel industry in the United States (as well as in Britain and other developed countries) constantly seeks to exploit cheap labor both at home and abroad. The labor-intensive nature of and exploitation of labor in the apparel industry led Joanne Entwistle to call it "an imperfect industry" (2000: 212). The labor-intensive but not capital or technology-intensive nature of the apparel industry also means that the cost or barrier of entry is low, so much so that the apparel industry is frequently a major means for developing countries such as China to kick off their industrialization process and grow their economy. Consequently, the need for the U.S. apparel industry to outsource its labor-intensive manufacturing in order to reduce the cost of labor is met with the need for China (and other developing countries) to develop their economy.

U.S. apparel firms' strategy to outsource their manufacturing operations to developing countries where cheap labor is abundant is a part of the broad shift in the U.S. economy from Fordism or Taylorism, which emphasizes vertical integration and economy of scale, to a mode called post-Fordist flexible accumulation, which emphasizes horizontal integration and economy of scope (Harvey 1989: 45; Kilduff 2005; Piore and Sabel 1984). Though the outsourcing of textile manufacturing from the United States to an international destination has become significantly pronounced since the 1970s, the U.S. textile and apparel manufacturers' search for cheaper labor began within its borders as they relocated their operations from the north to the south (Collins 2003). As U.S. firms' (and Western firms in general) search for cheap labor turned to international destinations, a trend of intensified transnational flow of goods and capital grew, which became known as globalization.[2] As a beneficiary of this trend, China has become a major destination of sourcing for U.S. importers and retailers since the 1990s. However, this shift to China is but a continuation of a pattern of production that started in earlier decades in Japan, then Hong Kong, South Korea, and Taiwan (Bonacich and Waller 1994: 21–22). The dominant pattern in which China (and other East Asian NICs) manufactures and exports garments to the United States (and the West in general) is called a "full-package" production, in which the Chinese fashion professionals play a significant role. Once again, the example of the NFL jersey can serve as an illustration.

In 2004, Zeng Gang was an international trade agent in Shanghai, representing an international trade firm based in San Francisco, which would receive orders from Reebok, the licensee of the NFL apparel products. Generally speaking, Zeng Gang would receive designs from Reebok, which he would then take to his suppliers in neighboring provinces and ask them to produce some preliminary samples. After the samples were finished, Zeng Gang would send Reebok the finished samples along with their FOB prices[3] for confirmation. At that point, based on the qualities and quoted prices of the preliminary samples, Reebok would decide the number of styles and quantity for each style it would order from Zeng Gang's company. Once the decisions were made, Reebok would send Zeng Gang's company the orders along with the letter of credit and feedback on the chosen samples. Upon receipt, Zeng Gang would go back to his suppliers with the samples and feedback from Reebok and instruct them to make a second batch of revised samples. Then, he would send the revised sample to Reebok for further confirmation (several revisions may take place if necessary). Once the samples—at this stage they are called *dahuoyang*, meaning samples for mass production—were confirmed, Zeng Gang and his suppliers would buy the appropriate fabric and start mass producing the garments. Before and during mass production, Reebok might request to inspect the suppliers' factories to ensure compliance with quality, safety, and labor standards at the facilities, in which case Zeng Gang would accompany Reebok representatives to the factories. Should Reebok identify issues of noncompliance with their standards[4] in a factory, the factory would generally be given a reasonable amount of time to rectify those issues; in rare cases, Reebok could demand that Zeng Gang replace the supplier with a different one. In most cases, the mass production process would proceed as scheduled. Zeng Gang would then send a quality assurance agent, who was professionally trained in fashion design, to the factory for quality control and to ensure that the production schedule would be adhered to. After all the garments were finished and packaged in floor-ready condition, they would be inspected by a quality assurance company designated by Reebok to certify that the quality of the garments met Reebok's requirements. After that, the merchandise would be shipped to the port in Shanghai, and Zeng Gang would facilitate Chinese Customs clearance and a shipping company designated by Reebok would load the goods onto a boat en route to the United States. At that point, Zeng Gang's job would be done, and his company would be able to cash the letter of credit from Reebok (and his suppliers would in turn cash the letter of credit from his company). Yet, once the merchandise arrived in the United States, Reebok would conduct another round of quality inspection. Should the results be inconsistent with the terms set in their agreement, Reebok could request compensation from Zeng Gang's company, which they would generally honor because it would mean the end of business from Reebok if they didn't. In fact, in order to attract more business from Reebok (because of the large quantities of its orders), Zeng Gang and his suppliers did more than they were asked to do in recent years. They began to offer their own designs (thanks to the work of the anonymous designers working in the factories) and send them to Reebok along with the samples based on Reebok's designs. On two occasions, their designs in fact won orders from Reebok.

The pattern of international trade between foreign corporate buyers and Chinese garment manufacturers through trade agents like Mr. Zeng is perhaps the most common practice in the Chinese clothing export sector (Figure 7.1).

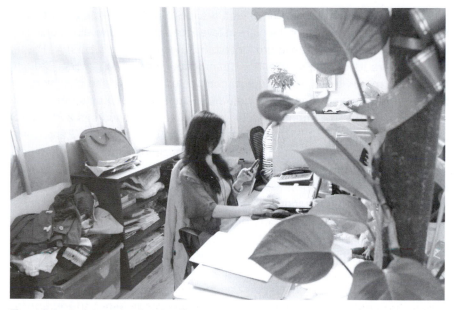

Figure 7.1   An international trade office in Shanghai. Courtesy of Mr. Wei Zengqiang.

However, there are also many trades that are conducted without trade agents. For example, some large U.S. buyers (large retailers or branded marketers) that have their own sourcing agents or offices in China usually buy from Chinese manufacturers directly. Similarly, many large Chinese garment manufacturers have their own international trade department, and would also like to cut out the middlemen as much as they can. However, neither party—large U.S. buyers with sourcing capacity in China and large Chinese manufacturers with in-house trading capacity—excludes trade through middlemen, and both have to rely on them as supplements to their existing businesses. For example, although Wal-Mart had its own sourcing center in Shanghai, they ordered from a trading company based in Beijing in 2004. An agent from the Beijing firm, whom I accompanied, went to Zhejiang province in order to locate the right manufacturer to fill the order. With or without trade agents, the services demanded by the U.S. buyers from the Chinese suppliers are largely the same—a full-package production service. A full-package production entails the suppliers being responsible for buying the fabrics and other inputs, making the samples, modifying the samples as needed, mass-producing the garments (which includes many processes), finishing and packaging, clearing Chinese Customs, and delivering floor-ready products to the shipping company. In other words, the Chinese suppliers are not just responsible for production, but also parts of product development, supply chain management, quality control, and logistics.

With respect to product development, there are various levels of participation by Chinese suppliers. At the highest level, foreign buyers would source finished products developed and produced by Chinese suppliers entirely. These foreign buyers tend to be smaller and the products tend to be generic. Though not yet a common trend, some foreign companies hire Chinese designers to develop products and then order them from Chinese manufacturers. At the medium level, Chinese suppliers would develop some products in addition to the product designs that they receive from foreign buyers, as Mr. Zeng Gang and his suppliers did for Reebok. This trend is becoming increasingly common in China today. At the lowest level, the Chinese suppliers would be involved in producing the samples for mass production based on designs or prototypes from the buyers. In the export of garments from China to the United States (and the West in general), the medium and lowest levels of participation by Chinese suppliers in product development are the most common types, especially when the garments are name-brand products. These different types of full-package production provided by Chinese suppliers are very different from the *maquiladora* or assembly production model in Mexico and Latin America, in which U.S. buyers merely outsource the assembly processes to Mexican or Latin American suppliers driven by specific tariff benefits offered by the U.S. government (Blair and Gereffi 2003: 152).

Although Chinese suppliers participate in product development as well as supply chain management, quality control, and logistics in addition to the production of the garments, they are considered original equipment manufacturers (OEMs), whereas their U.S. buyers are the original brand manufacturers (OBMs).[5] In the case of the Steelers jerseys, the Steelers organization, the NFL, and Reebok can all claim varying degrees of "ownership" of the meaningful symbols, i.e., the design patterns and logos/brands. By their ownership of the symbolic components or brands of the jerseys, they—as represented by Reebok—are the OBM. Zeng Gang's suppliers, the Chinese manufacturers of the jerseys, are the OEMs. This distinction between the U.S. buyers and Chinese manufacturers is critical, because it means that the OBM buyers control the most lucrative components and processes of the garments—the brand, the designs, the distribution, and marketing—whereas the OEM suppliers are in charge of the low-value-added processes of assembly and packaging. Despite the increasing participation by Chinese suppliers in the higher-value-added processes such as product design, supply chain management, and logistics, they cannot charge any premium for the additional services they provide; they are simply providing more services for minimum or no cost to the OBM buyers. For example, Zeng Gang and his suppliers could not demand that Reebok pay for the product development cost of the additional samples they made on their own for Reebok, not to mention demanding profit-sharing for those designs; they bore the cost themselves in the hope of getting more orders from Reebok. This indicates that no matter how much contribution the Chinese suppliers make to the development of the products, they have no claim to the most valuable components of the garments, i.e., the designs and brands (as reflected in my Steelers jersey). Moreover, because they have no access to the U.S. consumers and cannot participate in the marketing of the goods, they cannot map any meaning onto the garments at the site of consumption. The most meaningful components of the garments are firmly in the control of the OBM buyers and completely alienated from the Chinese manufacturers, to whom the garments are simply a means of livelihood. The alienation of the Chinese producers from the "meanings" of the garments they export is one of the key features of the "imperfect" global apparel industry. This imbalance of power between the Chinese suppliers and the U.S. corporate buyers is also reflected in the price of the garments—what the Chinese suppliers charge the U.S. corporate buyers, usually the FOB price, is only in the range of 20 to 25 percent of the U.S. buyers' retail price.[6] That is to say, the U.S. buyers' retail price would have a 400 to 500 percent markup.

The power imbalance between Western corporate buyers (the OBMs) and Chinese producers (the OEMs) is often explained by a global commodity chain perspective (Gereffi and Korzeniewicz 1994). A commodity chain refers to "a network of labor and production processes whose end result is a finished commodity" (Hopkins & Wallerstein 1986: 159). Gereffi and Korzeniewicz's notion of "global commodity chains" (GCCs) extends Hopkins and Wallerstein's idea to a context that is characterized by economic globalization. According to Gereffi and Korzeniewicz, the global apparel industry consists of "buyer-driven commodity chains," by which they mean it is an industry in which "large retailers, brand-named merchandisers, and trading companies play the pivotal roles in setting up decentralized production networks in a variety of exporting countries, typically located in the third world" (1994: 97). By contrast, in a "producer-driven commodity chain," large transnational corporations play the central roles in coordinating production networks (including backward and forward linkages), which is "most characteristic of capital- and technology-intensive commodities such as automobiles, aircraft, semiconductors, and electrical machinery" (1994: 7). By characterizing the global apparel industry as "buyer-driven commodity chains," Gereffi and Korzeniewicz not only point out the interconnections of the global apparel industry, but also highlight the imbalance of power between the OBM buyers and OEM manufacturers.

Though "buyer-driven" and "producer-driven" commodity chains illustrate the different degrees of control over production in the two types of commodity chains, frequently the lead firms in both types of commodity chains are large corporations based in the West. Even though in a buyer-driven commodity chain, such as those in the global apparel industry, the OEM manufacturers in developing countries have a high degree of control over the production processes, they are subordinate to large Western OBM buyers. If an OEM supplier does not yield to the demands of the OBM, the OBM can simply replace it with another OEM supplier. In a capital- or technology-intensive producer-driven chain, a Western lead firm would have even greater control over its suppliers, regardless of whether they are in a developing country or not. The general pattern of the imbalance of power between the lead firms in the West and the suppliers in developing countries in the global commodity chains mirrors the imbalance of power in the global political economy, in which Western countries have far greater influence than the developing countries do. In fact, the global political-economic order shapes the structure and flow in the global commodity chains of clothing, which is especially evident in the international trade treaties and regimes pertaining to textiles and apparel. Though the hidden tag in our clothes that indicates the country of origin is practically meaningless to the U.S. consumers and the OBM buyers, it is critical for the United States to identify and regulate its imports of clothing.

IMPERFECT INTERNATIONAL TRADE REGIMES

Although U.S. corporations (as well as consumers) benefit from outsourcing the production of garments, such acts also result in job losses in the United States, particularly in southern states such as North Carolina, South Carolina, and Georgia, where the textile and apparel industries are concentrated. To prevent job losses in the textile and apparel industries, the U.S. worker and labor unions, plus relevant interest groups, have aligned with local and federal politicians and made the textile and apparel industries one of the industries most protected against imports in the United States.

In the 1950s, the United States instituted protective measures such as the Voluntary Export Restraint (VER) against imports of Japanese cotton products. However, this measure failed because it actually led to a dramatic increase of imports from Hong Kong and Taiwan. In the 1960s, the Kennedy administration tried to remedy the shortcomings of the VER by instituting the Short Term Arrangement (STA) on Cotton Textiles and later the Long Term Arrangement (LTA) on Cotton Textiles, in order to expand the restrictions on imports of cotton products from Japan to other U.S. trading partners. But the STA and the LTA also failed because the textile and apparel industries quickly shifted from cotton products to wool and man-made fibers that were not restricted by those trade regimes. The continued loss of jobs in the U.S. textile and apparel industries led to further expansion of protection.

In 1974, the United States successfully negotiated an international treaty called the Multi-fiber Arrangement (MFA), which allowed the United States (as well as Western Europe and Canada) to restrict textile and apparel imports from developing countries to limited quantities adjustable only on an annual basis. The quota system of the MFA was the most comprehensive and long-lasting protective trade regime against U.S. imports of textile and apparel products.[7]

The MFA was an unfair trade agreement from the beginning, and it clearly violated the principles of the General Agreement on Tariffs and Trade (GATT), the dominant international trade regime since World War II, which included most countries in the world as members (socialist countries such as China were not members of the GATT). As acknowledged by the U.S. International Trade Commission, the MFA departed from the GATT specifically in two respects: "(1) they [the quotas] were applied on a country-specific basis, in contradiction of the nondiscrimination obligation (all GATT members be treated equally when any trade measures are applied), and (2) they contradict the general principle of reducing or avoiding absolute quantitative limits" (USITC 2004: 8). Developing countries, whose clothing exports were unfairly restricted by quotas assigned by importing Western countries such as the United States and Britain (Japan and Australia did not adopt the MFA), attempted repeatedly to eliminate the MFA through multilateral negotiations under the framework of the GATT, and such efforts became a major agenda of the "Uruguay Round" (1986–1994). In 1994, an agreement was reached between developing and developed countries under the framework of the GATT that the MFA quota system would be gradually phased out over a ten-year period and completely removed by January 1, 2005. As the GATT was superseded by the World Trade Organization in 1995, the agreement was replaced by the WTO Agreement on Textiles and Clothing (ATC) with the same goal of phasing out the MFA in ten years (Scott 1998). As a member of the WTO (since December 2001), China was supposed to enjoy the full benefit of quota-free export of textile and apparel products to the United States in 2005 when the new trade regime of the ATC went into effect. However, when China negotiated with the United States in 1999 for its accession to the WTO, the United States (the European Union later followed suit) added a safeguard clause specific to textile and apparel products called Paragraph 242 in the bilateral agreement, which allows the U.S. government to impose temporary quotas on U.S. imports of textile and clothing from China until December 2008 if such imports from China have caused "the existence or threat of market disruption" (Paragraph 242 of The Working Party Report on China's Accession to the WTO). Like the MFA, Paragraph 242, which specifically targets textile and apparel imports from China (but not from other countries), unfairly privileges the United States and violates the fair trade and nondiscrimination principles of the WTO, and contradicts the ATC agreement that aims to eliminate import quotas. Indeed, the contradiction between Paragraph 242 and the ATC became the source of a heated trade dispute between the two countries in 2005.

THE UNITED STATES–CHINA TEXTILE AND APPAREL TRADE DISPUTE IN 2005

By January 2005, under the ATC, all U.S. quotas on the imports of textile and clothing products were eliminated, which resulted in a dramatic surge of U.S. imports of textile and apparel products from China. Several product categories increased over 100 or even 1000 percent from a year earlier. The surge was caused in part by the rising U.S. demand for Chinese textile and apparel products and in part by the sudden elimination of all quotas, compounded by the fact that the U.S. government withheld quota restrictions on the majority of the product categories until the end of 2004 rather than lifting them gradually as they had agreed to in the 1994 GATT agreement (U.S. GAO 2005: 10). Obviously, China was unable to demand that the United States live up to its responsibility under the agreement either. Nevertheless, the surge of U.S. imports of Chinese textile and clothing was reported widely by the U.S. media as a "flood" and "threat" (e.g., Barboza and Becker 2005). On April 6, 2005, seven petitions were filed by American Manufacturing Trade Action Coalition (AMTAC), National Council of Textile Organizations (NCTO), National Textile Association (NTA), and the labor union UNITE HERE, requesting the U.S. government to take safeguard actions against the importation of seven categories of Chinese textile and clothing products.[8] On May 13, the Committee for the Implementation of Textile Agreements (CITA) of the U.S. Department of Commerce invoked Paragraph 242 and initiated threat-based safeguard quotas against the importation of three categories of textile and clothing products of Chinese origin. Five days later, CITA decided to impose safeguard quotas limiting the importation of four more categories of Chinese-made textile and clothing products, citing Paragraph 242 (http://otexa.ita.doc.gov).[9] Since then, a lengthy and heated textile and apparel trade dispute has broken out between the United States and China.

Soon after the U.S. decision on limiting Chinese textile and apparel imports, the two governments followed the procedure under the WTO agreement and began consultation and negotiation. While the U.S. government cited Paragraph 242 in the bilateral agreement to justify its decisions, the Chinese government invoked its rights as a member of the WTO and the quota-free trade agreement of the ATC that both sides signed as members of the WTO. The two sides were so adamant in their positions that it took eight rounds of consultation and negotiation for the two governments to finally reach a resolution, far exceeding the three-month period of consultation stipulated in Paragraph 242. The negotiation process took so long that some categories of Chinese products had already exceeded the limits of the quotas set by the safeguard measures and were subsequently withheld by U.S. Customs before the bilateral agreement was reached. At the same time, however, U.S. Customs did not reject entry of those over-quota goods outright, as the U.S. government did not declare the safeguard measures permanent and continued to negotiate with the Chinese government even after the three-month consultation period ended. On November 8, 2005, both sides reached a broad-based compromised agreement,[10] the terms of which included: China to accept quotas on 34 categories of textile and apparel products exporting to the United States from 2005 through 2008, much broader than the existing 19 product categories under temporary safeguard restrictions; and the United States to raise the percentage of annual increase of its importation of the Chinese textile and apparel products in those categories from 7.5 percent (as stipulated in Paragraph 242) to between 10 and 17 percent from 2005 through the end of 2008 (when all the quotas on Chinese textile and clothing imports would be finally lifted). The United States also agreed to allow entry of the Chinese-made products withheld by the U.S. Customs due to overage of the quota limits, with an understanding that the quantity exceeding the new annual quota limits would be half "subsidized" by the United States, with the other half counted toward the quotas of those product categories for the following year.[11]

Similar to previous protectionist trade regimes, the new agreement between the United States and China is far from a fair trade agreement. Above all, the privilege of the United States is protected by Paragraph 242, and the final bilateral agreement is by and large an enforcement of Paragraph 242, albeit with more generous quotas. Just as the U.S. OBM buyers have the upper hand over Chinese OEM suppliers, the United States clearly has the upper hand over China in the trade agreement, which may be attributable to the fact that the United States is buying more from China than the other way around.

However, the fact that the United States has the upper hand does not explain why it exercises that power. Evidently, it is not in everyone's interests to limit clothing imports from China because the U.S. quotas on Chinese-made garments become added costs to the garments.[12] The U.S. corporate buyers (importers, retailers, and branded marketers) would be better off without the extra costs of the quotas, and so would the U.S. consumers. Why, then, were the "voices" of the U.S. corporate buyers and consumers, let alone those of the Chinese suppliers, not "heard" by the U.S. government? Apparently, the global apparel chains do not just involve Chinese suppliers, the U.S. corporate buyers and consumers, but also other stakeholders, including domestically based manufacturers and workers in the United States (as well as manufacturers in other developing countries). It was their voices that were heard loud and clear by the U.S. government. To understand why the U.S. government adopted the protectionist policies it did, we have to examine the different positions and interests within the U.S. textile and apparel industries, and how these diverse interests are played out in U.S. politics.

STRONG OPPOSITION FROM DOMESTICALLY BASED U.S. MANUFACTURERS AND WORKERS

As previously mentioned, the rise in importation of Chinese-made clothing was reported by the U.S. media as a "flood" and "threat," something needing to be contained. No one else had taken this threat more seriously than the domestically based U.S. textile and garment manufacturers and workers' unions. From their position, the imports from China represented competition and a threat to their own market shares or jobs. To protect their own interests, they tended to overstate the threat of imports from China and eagerly demanded that the U.S. government provide more protection.[13] Representing their interests, various groups and organizations such as AMTAC, NCTO, NTA, UNITE HERE, and DMC (Domestic Manufacturers Committee of the Hosiery Association) vehemently lobbied policymakers in Washington, D.C., for safeguard protection against imports from China in 2005, efforts that turned out to be rather successful.

SUPPORT FROM U.S. CORPORATE BUYERS AND CONSUMERS

To the U.S. corporate buyers, including importers, retailers, marketers, and manufacturers that outsource their production to China, however, clothing imported from China is not a threat, but a good deal. In a survey of a large number of U.S. corporate buyers, conducted by the U.S. International Trade Commission to assess the competitiveness of certain foreign suppliers to the U.S. market, the Commission states, "China is expected to become the 'supplier of choice' for most U.S. importers because of its ability to make almost any type of textile and apparel product at any quality level at a competitive price" (p. xi). Clearly, the views of the China-made garments shared by the U.S. corporate buyers differ from those of the domestically based manufacturers, workers, and the interest groups that represent them. Moreover, consumers would be better off without the quotas, so consumers should have an interest in supporting Chinese imports as well, although consumers cannot be seen as a unified group because consumers may take many other factors such as quality, environmental concerns, and fair labor practices in addition to price, into consideration when they make their purchases.

The diverse views and interests raise the question of why only the voices of domestically based U.S. workers and manufacturers, and not those of its corporate buyers and consumers, appeared to have been heard by U.S. policy makers when it came to the United States–China textile and garment trade. Economist Pietra Rivoli's (2005) study of the global textile and apparel industries provides valuable insights into the U.S. trade policy making process.

Rivoli attributes the frequent wins of protectionism in the U.S. textile and clothing trade to two major factors. One factor is what she regards as the "snarling together" phenomenon among the interest groups, such as AMTAC, NCTO, NTA, and UNITE HERE (she calls them an "alphabet army"), who represent the interests of the domestically based U.S. manufacturers and workers (Rivoli 2005: 123). These interest groups are able to speak with a single voice because the U.S. textile and apparel industries are geographically and historically concentrated in southern states, such as the Carolinas and Georgia, and this concentration is further strengthened by a shared cultural and historical bond among the textile manufacturers. By contrast, the U.S. corporate buyers are not as unified; organizations such as the National Retail Federation (NRF) represent diverse interests ranging from the interests of a small tourist shop to those of Saks Fifth Avenue, and thus they have a much harder time speaking in unison. I would also add to Rivoli's point here that the geographical diversity of the importers (including the retailers) separates them into different voting districts, which makes them less effective than their geographically concentrated rivals in their concerted efforts to influence policymakers. Nevertheless, Rivoli notes the role of American voters by pointing out that the voice of protectionism in unison is generally met with sympathy from American voters, who would rather tolerate this type of protectionism than hear news that another American factory is being closed and another American community being destroyed due to job losses resulting from outsourcing.

The second factor that contributes to protectionism in the U.S. textile and apparel trade has a lot to do with the politics of deal-making in Washington, D.C. As Rivoli puts it, the access to the U.S. market is treated by the politicians as a "currency," to be traded for votes, foreign policy favors (such as Pakistan's help in the war against terrorism), and sometimes ironically for acceptance of broader trade liberalizing initiatives by the same interest groups who advocate protectionism against textile and apparel imports (2005: 124). In a word, protectionism in the U.S. textile and apparel trade is very useful, if not essential, for political purposes in the eyes of American politicians.

Although Rivoli did not study the 2005 United States–China textile and apparel trade dispute specifically, her analysis of the processes of U.S. trade policymaking helps explain how the different positions on the U.S. imports of Chinese-made clothing were translated into a largely protectionist policy favoring domestically based manufacturers and workers. In the politics of deal making and negotiation, the concerted voice of domestically based U.S. manufacturers and workers was much more powerful than the less organized ones of U.S. corporate buyers. Similarly, this also explains why the voices of average American consumers, who clearly had an interest in this issue, were largely absent in the U.S. government's decision-making process on the textile and apparel trade policies—they are too diverse to be meaningful to the politicians, especially when it comes to votes during elections. In fact, one would be hard pressed to find an average American consumer, who was not in the above-mentioned categories of interest groups, going to public hearings held by CITA in Washington, D.C. to voice his or her support for more imports of Chinese-made clothing because he or she would potentially be able to save a few dollars on a jersey. As a matter of fact, the imports from China could be easily replaced by equally cheap if not cheaper imports from elsewhere. So, it was unlikely that even cost-conscious consumers would voice their support for imports from any single foreign country, let alone those consumers who were more concerned about environmental or social factors than costs. As a result, the political economy in the United States, as usual, favored a protectionist trade policy in dealing with the textile and apparel trade dispute with China in 2005.

IMPLICATIONS FOR CHINESE SUPPLIERS

The power imbalance between the United States and China, as reflected in the trade regime, and in particular the bilateral trade agreement in 2005, had profound implications for Chinese garment manufacturers and trade agents. As a whole, they are highly diverse and unorganized, and other than calling on the Chinese government for help, there was little they could do to influence U.S. trade policies. The nearly six-month trade dispute between China and the United States in 2005 was especially long for them. Representing their interests as well as the interests of the roughly 19 million workers employed in the Chinese textile and apparel industries,[14] the Chinese government negotiated hard with its U.S. counterpart in the bilateral trade dispute in 2005. In the end, the Chinese government gave in to U.S. pressure and signed the new agreement that was largely favorable to the United States in exchange for a stable trade environment. In many ways, however, the resolution did not come as a surprise. First of all, the existence of the discriminatory clause of Paragraph 242 against China essentially framed the resolution. Second, in terms of trade with the United States, China was and is a net exporter to the United States. There were simply not enough bargaining chips at the disposal of the

Chinese government. Third, aside from the interests in the textile and apparel industries, China also received pressure from the United States on other issues such as intellectual property rights and currency appreciation.[15] The Chinese government had to balance the interests of the textile and apparel industries with the other interests. Moreover, the way in which the 2005 Sino-U.S. trade dispute was resolved should not be taken as an isolated incident; on the contrary, it reflects a broad pattern in the bilateral relationship in which the United States generally sets the terms. In the final analysis, the Sino-U.S. trade dispute in 2005 serves as a reminder that the United States remains the dominant power in the global political economy, which circumscribes the international trade in clothing.

Having no hope of getting help from the Chinese government, Chinese manufacturers and exporters had to deal with the fallout from the trade dispute on their own. Many of them were afraid to take new orders from the United States for fear of heavy losses during the prolonged negotiation period between the U.S. and Chinese governments. For those who did, they tried to beat others to the "finish line," i.e., U.S. Customs, to ensure that their goods would be there before the quota limits were reached. To do so, many of them did the otherwise unimaginable—they shipped their "cheap" products in the safeguarded categories by air instead of by sea, bearing the hefty shipping costs in order to avoid potentially even bigger losses (*Nanfang Daily*, 07/04/05). Mr. Zeng Gang, the trader of my Steelers jersey, shipped the order of the NFL jerseys when the quota of that category was over 90 percent filled in the fall of 2005. He was worried sick and prayed for ten days that his shipment would not be rejected by U.S. Customs.

Evidently, what the Steelers jerseys mean for Zeng Gang and his suppliers—a means of livelihood and a source of worry—has no bearing on the ways in which U.S. consumers use the garments. They are unable to map any symbolic meaning onto the garments at the site of consumption in the United States (or other Western countries) because of the uneven power between them and the OBM buyers. At the same time, the export of the garments, on which the Chinese suppliers' livelihood is dependent, is structured and regulated by international trade regimes that are shaped by the power imbalance between China and the United States. These characteristics of the export of garments from China to the United States support my argument that clothing offers a unique perspective on globalization.

GLOBALIZATION: A CLOTHING PERSPECTIVE

Globalization is popularly understood as the seemingly unfettered flow of goods, capital, people, images, and ideas across the world. In that sense, the global textile and apparel industries are the poster child of globalization. Take the Chinese textile and apparel industries, for example. They grew from minimum participation in the global economy before the 1980s to becoming the dominant exporter of textile and apparel products today; they have evidently become highly integrated with the global textile and apparel industries. As a "tracking" strategy of globalization, George Marcus (1995) suggests anthropologists "follow the thing[s]." Such an approach is in fact an extension of Appadurai's (1986) "social life" or Kopytoff's (1986) "cultural biography" approach to the global context. Following the movement of the Chinese-made garments from their sites of production by Chinese manufacturers to their consumption by U.S. consumers, the global flow of clothing is indeed very telling about the processes of globalization.

First of all, the meaning of the garments at the site of consumption, as illustrated by my Steelers jersey, is completely alienated from their producers at the site of production in China, where they figure largely as a means of livelihood. This suggests that the "de-territorialization" (i.e., the global movement) of goods must be "re-territorialized" in their local ways of consumption (Inda and Rosaldo 2002). In a study of the consumption of McDonald's in East Asia, James Watson and his colleagues provide excellent examples of appropriation and integration of McDonald's into the local ways of life in East Asian societies (Watson 1997). In this respect, there exists a parallel between the consumption of Western goods such as McDonald's in East Asian societies and the consumption of Chinese-made garments in the United States. In both instances, the meanings of the goods at the site of production (or origination) do not automatically transfer to their site of consumption. In other words, contrary to the belief that globalization would lead to a global homogenization or Westernization (see, for example, Ritzer 2000), the transnational movement of Chinese-made garments illustrates that meanings of the goods are always locally constructed.

Second, the transnational movement of Chinese-made garments is not at all a free flow. It is generally initiated and structured by large corporations (the OBM buyers) based in the United States (and other Western importing countries). At the same time, it is regulated by international trade regimes that privilege Western countries such as the United States. Even though Chinese suppliers are playing a big part in the global commodity chains of apparel, the power between Western OBM buyers and Chinese OEM suppliers is uneven, and so are the powers between Western countries (such as the United States) and China (and the developing countries in general) in the global political economy. Therefore, contrary to Friedman's (2005) idea, the world is *not* flat, despite the increasing participation of China in the global economy.

Finally, the global commodity chains of clothing provide a global network that links together diverse and locally constructed meanings of clothing.

In this global network, Chinese suppliers, U.S. corporate buyers (including big retailers, marketers, and importers), domestically based U.S. textile and garment manufacturers, their workers, and U.S. consumers are all connected together, despite their different views of Chinese-made garments. This global network, or more precisely the "network of networks" (cf. Hannerz 1992) is crucial to furthering our understanding of globalization that tends to be studied separately from either a social life or a political-economic perspective.

In a study of Coca-Cola, Robert Foster (2002) argues that the soft drink connects the company's executives in the United States and consumers like Elizabeth Solomon in Papua New Guinea (PNG). As a result of the connection, the two parties become each other's context to construct their own meanings of the commodity. In this network linked by the soft drink, consumers such as Elizabeth were imagined by the company executives as vessels to be filled with more and more cola. For average PNG consumers the commodity is another thing to be appropriated into "a set of cultural dispositions and practices that preexist and even shape the spread of capitalism" (Foster 2002: 162). Foster's network analysis not only heeds the different "local" meanings of the commodity constructed at different sites, but also underscores how the diverse meanings are linked to each other through the global network of the commodity. A similar network analysis that combines both a social life perspective and a global commodity chains approach can be applied to the Chinese-made garments. I will use the United States–China textile and apparel trade dispute in 2005 to illustrate this approach.

The domestically based U.S. textile and apparel manufacturers' and workers' interests clashed with those of the U.S. corporate buyers on the issue of more or fewer garment imports from China. Subsequently, they each constructed their meanings of the Chinese-made garments based on their own interests and life experiences. Whereas the U.S.-based manufacturers and workers perceived these commodities as a "flood" and "threat" (to their market shares or job security), the U.S. corporate buyers saw them as "quality products with cheap prices." Each side lobbied hard and tried to convince the U.S. policymakers of their views of the Chinese-made garments. In response to the trade dispute and the drawn-out negotiations, the Chinese producers, though with limited options, also tried to do whatever they could to preserve what the products mean to them—a means of livelihood.

Evidently, based on their own experiences and interests, the three parties constructed different meanings or interpretations of the Chinese-made garments at different sites. At the same time, the three parties were also connected into a common network linked by the commodities, and subsequently each became the others' context in which one's actions based on their own view of the commodities would prompt certain reactions from the other parties who had different views of and vested interests in the commodities.

Therefore, although various interested parties (stakeholders) constructed different meanings of the Chinese-made garments from their own positions, these diverse meanings *were connected* in the sense that they became each other's context in which an action prompted by one meaning was simultaneously a reaction to those prompted by other meanings. It is in this sense that I argue a network analysis of the export of Chinese made garments combines the merit of the social life approach, which brings to light the diverse meanings constructed at different sites, and the strength of the "global commodity chains" perspective, which underscores the uneven power of various parties who are connected to the commodities. The network analysis of the garments provides a synthesis of "meaning" and "power" by revealing that the various local meanings of the commodities are connected into a global network, in which power is unevenly distributed, which in turn shapes and perpetuates the heterogeneity of meanings of the commodities in various local settings within the network. In this way, the network analysis of the Chinese-made garments offers an understanding of globalization that challenges both the homogenization thesis by revealing the diverse meanings of the garments constructed at various local sites or contexts, and simultaneously the view that "the world is flat" due to globalization by highlighting the uneven power that is vested in global apparel chains and the power imbalance in the global political economy in general.

CONCLUSION

In this chapter, I focused on the global connections of the Chinese clothing industry by looking at the exportation of Chinese-made garments to the United States. The export of Chinese-made garments illustrates the global connections of the Chinese apparel industry. At the same time, the meanings of the garments as constructed by U.S. consumers, like that of my Steelers shirt, were disconnected from the Chinese producers. I argue that the apparent contradiction inherent in the global flow of Chinese-made garments is caused by Western OBM buyers' control over Chinese OEM suppliers on the one hand and the imbalance of power between the United States and China on the other hand. The two types of power are layered over the Chinese-made garments. While the power of the OBMs renders the "made in China" tag invisible, the power of the state makes its existence essential to regulate the global movement of the garments. Although this chapter only focused on the export of Chinese-made garments to the United States, this pattern of trade resulting from the workings of these two types of power can be identified in the exports of Chinese garments to other Western countries as well.

Built on both the social life approach and the global commodity chain perspective, this chapter utilizes a network analysis of clothing that takes into account both the diverse meanings of the garments that are constructed in different local contexts and the uneven power that is vested with various parties connected to the network of clothing. The network analysis is applied to the United States–China textile and apparel trade dispute in 2005, during which the various parties connected to Chinese made garments, such as the U.S.-based manufacturers and workers, the U.S. corporate buyers, and the Chinese producers, all attempted to map their own meanings and interpretations— a threat, a good deal, and a means of livelihood and source of worry respectively—onto the garments from their particular vantage point. Simultaneously, these different interested parties as well as their views of the garments were all connected to a common network through the garments, so much so that they became each other's context or "approximate mappings" of meanings (Hannerz 1992: 42–3) in which one's action was at the same time a reaction to the others'. Such a network analysis not only helps us understand how the different meanings and interpretations are constructed at different sites globally, but also how the differences are connected and perpetuated. Therefore, the network analysis of Chinese-made garments offers a two-pronged critique of globalization. On the one hand, the diverse meanings of the garments constructed at local sites challenges the view of global homogenization or McDonaldization (Ritzer 2000; Schlosser 2001). On the other hand, the uneven power vested in the diverse stakeholders in the United States and China contradicts the argument that the world is now flat as a result of globalization (Friedman 2005).

On that note, I will conclude this chapter with the current development in the apparel industry in Shanghai. As the temporary quotas on apparel imports from China ended in the United States and the EU in 2008, Chinese-made garments are now traded in a quota-free environment. However, this does not mean that the Chinese OEM suppliers will no longer face any restrictions on their exports to the United States or the EU. The United States could use product-specific safeguard measures against Chinese imports until 2013 according to its WTO agreement with China (the same privilege applies to other WTO members including the EU). In addition, the United States could use other instruments such as anti-dumping duties against the surge of Chinese imports.[16] Should the United States declare China as a currency manipulator, then the United States could target imports from China with more tariffs. All these pose external risks to Chinese manufacturers and exporters. In addition, there are also internal factors that would dampen the prospects for Chinese manufacturers and exporters, chief among which are the rapid appreciation of Chinese currency against the dollar and the euro and rising labor and land costs. In the past few years, Mr. Zeng Gang moved his

Figure 7.2 A garment factory in suburban Shanghai. Courtesy of Mr. Wei Zengqiang.

office three times due to the rising cost of rent, from downtown to a suburban district, and then to a suburban county in Shanghai. As the export business has become increasingly sandwiched by falling demand and rising costs, Mr. Zeng opened a factory and became a true OEM supplier not just for international corporate buyers, but also for the domestic name-brand companies (Figure 7.2).

Though formal businesses like Mr. Zeng's remain the mainstream in the Chinese apparel industry, a new and disturbing trend has emerged in Shanghai. Experienced workers would quit their jobs and start their own underground, informal, and "homework" style businesses as subcontractors, repeating what happened in the United States and Great Britain in earlier decades (e.g., Bao 2001; Phizacklea 1990). The "imperfect" apparel industry is poised to become even more sinister in China.

–8–

Conclusion: Clothing, Modernization, and Globalization

"SOCIALIST MARKET ECONOMY WITH CHINESE CHARACTERISTICS"

When the Chinese Communist Party decided to reform the Chinese economy in 1978, it started a fundamental shift in China's economic structure from a state-owned and state-run planned economy to one that is composed of increasing shares of privately owned and foreign-owned sectors. China's apparel industry is particularly illustrative of this trend. Since the early 1990s, China's apparel industry has been dominated by non-state-owned sectors. Such a shift in China's economic structure has created a paradox for the CCP: on the one hand, the CCP still insists on a Marxist ideology that asserts that the economic base determines the superstructure, a concept that every Chinese high school student can recite, and on the other hand, the Chinese economy today is no longer state-owned and the "socialist" share has shrunk to a dismal minority. How then can the CCP and the state justify within the Marxist framework that China is still a socialist economy and should maintain a socialist ideology and superstructure?

Heartened by Deng's comments during his famous tour to South China in the spring of 1992 (see Chapter 2), former president Jiang Zemin came up with a solution in his speech at the 14th Party Congress in October 1992, which stated that the goal for China's economic reform was "to construct a socialist market economy with Chinese characteristics." Evidently, Jiang intended to create a compromise between the Chinese economic reality and the ruling ideology with the notion of a socialist market economy. However, not everyone agrees with Jiang's characterization of the Chinese economy. For example, British political scientist Shaun Breslin (2004) calls the Chinese economy "capitalism with Chinese characteristics." Be it capitalism or socialism, the introduction of market forces into the Chinese economy has simultaneously changed the structure of the Chinese economy and the socialist ideology, and consequently both have been endowed with "Chinese characteristics." Alternatively, one may say that it was because of the specific context of China to which the market economy and the socialist ideology, both of foreign origin, had to adapt, that they acquired the "Chinese characteristics." This raises the question: What are the basic characteristics of China?

Once again, Deng Xiaoping was the first Chinese leader who used the phrase "socialism with Chinese characteristics" in his opening address at the 12th Party Congress in 1982, but the idea of the "Chinese characteristics" was not fully developed until the then-Communist Party Secretary Zhao Ziyang's speech at the 13th Party Congress in 1987, in which Zhao proclaimed that China was in the "elementary stage" (*chuji jieduan*) of a socialist society because of the "basic characteristics" of China (*jiben guoqing*), which included "a huge population, an economy with little accumulated wealth, uneven regional development, and underdeveloped means of production." According to Zhao, those characteristics of China determined that for a long time China would be in the elementary stage of socialism, and consequently it had to adapt socialism to the Chinese reality and build a socialist society with Chinese characteristics. In other words, Zhao (and the CCP) thought that because Chinese socialism was not developed out of an advanced capitalist economy, it had some catch-up to do with regard to the economic base. This position of the CCP was translated into a policy that gradually allowed the market, instead of the state, to play the fundamental role in allocating resources.

Therefore, in a broad sense, the Chinese political economy represents a syncretism between Marxism and the Chinese reality, and between Chinese socialism and market mechanisms. In this light, the phenomenal changes that have taken place in contemporary China are also the process in which both Marxism and market mechanisms become localized in China and vested with "Chinese characteristics." In this broad context, the dramatic rise of the Chinese fashion industry this book describes is shaped by and attains "Chinese characteristics." In what follows, I will highlight some of the "Chinese characteristics" that have been discussed throughout this book in order to address the three questions asked in the very beginning of the book: How did the phenomenal changes in Chinese clothing and the fashion industry come into being? What are the implications of these changes for the professionals, such as fashion designers, who work in the industry? And what can these changes tell us about the macro processes of modernization and globalization in China?

RISE OF THE CHINESE FASHION INDUSTRY: IS IT JUST A STATE PROJECT?

In the course of the rise of the Chinese fashion industry, the state played an important and unique role. It reformed the economic system from a planned economy to a market-oriented economy, which facilitated the rapid growth of the textile and apparel industries (Chapter 2). In fact, the state did not just adopt measures in order to facilitate the growth of the fashion industry; it also took the charge in boosting the growth of the industry. National leaders such as Hu Yaobang and Zhao Ziyang personally led and encouraged diversification of clothing styles, and they were responsible for removing ideological baggage from clothing in the early days of the economic reforms (Chapter 3). The state also reorganized the government bureaucracy and set up the service-oriented and voluntarily based China National Textile Industry Council and China Fashion Association to better assist the market-based textile and apparel industries. At the same time, the state, via CNTIC and CFA, intensified efforts to create "famed designers" and "name brands," which was evident through the award system at China Fashion Week (Chapter 6). All these indicate that the state was deeply involved in the Chinese fashion industry and its growth. On top of the measures designed by the state to boost the growth of the fashion industry, the state also attempted to map an "official" version of modernity onto Chinese clothing by constructing an official narrative of the evolution of contemporary Chinese clothing (Chapter 3). At the same time, however, there is another side to the all-powerful state in the rise of the Chinese fashion industry. Once the state allowed market forces into the economic system, the non-state sectors quickly flourished and captured market shares at the expense of the state-owned sector, and in a sense forced the state-owned sector to undergo dramatic reforms in order to become economically viable. Similarly, once the state removed the ideological constraints from clothing, style diversification took its own course and the state was left with few tools to regulate dress (not to say that it was in the state's interest to do so). Although it is true that the state brought CNTIC and CFA into being and still partially finances their operation, and that the power of the state can easily penetrate CFW (as representatives of the state can easily obtain privileged positions at fashion shows during CFW), the success or failure of Chinese fashion designers is largely dependent on their performance at CFW or in the marketplace. In other words, the Chinese field of fashion functions relatively independently of the state. Even in the state-sponsored project of creating a modern national dress for the APEC Summit in 2001, the state's ability to control the meaning of the *tangzhuang* was under challenge by Chinese scholars and consumer-citizens in various ways (Chapter 4). It is in this sense that I argue that clothing and the fashion industry are not just a means to achieve modernization by the state in China, but also a medium through which a Chinese notion of modernity is articulated and contested. The dynamics between the state and the market are unique Chinese characteristics that have shaped the rise of the Chinese fashion industry in the reform era.

WHAT ARE THE IMPLICATIONS FOR CHINESE FASHION PROFESSIONALS?

The dramatic rise of the Chinese fashion industry has profound implications for those who work in the industry. This book has mainly touched upon three groups of professionals: fashion designers, models, and trade agents. Many of them thrived in the booming fashion industry. In the case of Chinese fashion designers and models, their professions came into being along with the rise of the domestic fashion industry. As white-collar professionals, Chinese fashion designers and models now enjoy generally high income and high status in society. In the early days of the reform period, by contrast, fashion models were awkwardly known as "fashion actresses" and fashion designers had to justify what they did as different from the commonly known and lowly regarded *caifeng*. Therefore, along with the rise of the Chinese fashion industry, the professionals who work in the industry, such as the designers, models, and trade agents, have become upwardly mobile groups in society.

Though there are unmistakable positive implications for the professionals working in the Chinese fashion industry, the social and structural constraints over them should not be overlooked. As Chapter 5 made clear, Chinese fashion designers have to confront not just the association of their trade with the lowly regarded *caifeng* (domestic perception), but also the stereotype of them being copycats of Western designers (international perception). In their struggle against both stereotypes, Chinese fashion designers often directly or indirectly resort to art in order to claim higher social distinctions. In this environment, couture-style fashion shows at China Fashion Week (also favored by the award system of the China Fashion Association) become one of the few viable strategies for Chinese fashion designers to achieve social distinctions and greater financial rewards. For most Chinese fashion designers, to do a show at CFW or design their own line will remain a dream that may or may not come true. Many of them end up working "anonymously" in the export-oriented garment factories. But the dream is alive and the temptation is real, which often results in frequent job changes from a quality control person to a pattern maker, to a merchandiser, to an assistant designer, to a chief designer, to a freelancer, and to a studio owner or a designer of their own lines. As long as they feel that they are getting closer to that dream, they would jump at the next opportunity. It is through their dealings with the social and structural constraints as well as opportunities unique to the Chinese context that Chinese fashion designers (and other professionals) come to define the "Chinese-ness" of their profession.

FASHION, LOCALIZATION, GLOBALIZATION

The processes of globalization and localization are constant themes that emerge throughout this book. The global connections of the Chinese fashion industry primarily exhibit in two-directional flows: the inflow of Western ideas, styles, design techniques, business models, and fashion shows to China and the outflow of Chinese-made garments to the West. In both types of flows, which suggest intensifying global integration of the fashion industry, trends of globalization are met with various forms of localization.

In learning Western development models and ideas, the Chinese state adopted market-oriented economic reforms in order to modernize the textile and apparel industries. Yet, the Chinese model of modernization is not based on free market economy; instead, the state along with the market played and is playing a key role. The unique dynamic between the state and the market in the reform period indicates that "modernization" in China is a localized phenomenon. Similarly, by promoting Western suits and other Western fashions, the national leaders did not promote the idea of Westernization; instead the state endorses a Chinese notion of modernity in relation to their own past (rather than the West). Chinese fashion designers intently study Western fashions, design techniques, and business models, but they are not simple copycats of their Western colleagues. In order to succeed in the Chinese marketplace, they have to understand not just the needs and wants of the Chinese consumers, but also what it means to be a fashion designer and the unique social and structural constraints on them. It is in the Chinese context that Chinese designers' leaning toward artistic designs and couture shows takes on new local meanings, as discussed previously. Consequently, the huge inflow of Western goods, practices, ideas and models did not automatically translate into a Westernization of China or a global homogenization. On the contrary, they are "re-territorialized" in China and endowed with Chinese meanings. In this sense, this study of the Chinese clothing and fashion industry thus joins previous anthropological studies (e.g., Watson 1997; Miller 1998) that challenge the global homogenization or Westernization thesis that permeates the popular imagination of the so-called "global pop culture."

Moreover, this book has also explored the integration of China's clothing industry with the global clothing industry by examining the outflow of Chinese-made garments to the United States (Chapter 7). China is the largest exporter of garments to the United States as well as in the world. However, the dominant mode in which these exported garments are produced in China is called a full-package OEM production for Western OBM importers that control the symbolic and valuable components (the design and brand) of the garments as well as the high-value-added processes of design, distribution, and marketing. Because of the uneven distribution of power between Chinese OEM suppliers and Western OBM buyers, Chinese suppliers are alienated from the meanings of the garments they produced at the site of their consumption in the West. The work of the Chinese producers is potently reduced to a tag marked "made in China" that is hidden from view, only to serve as an instrument by which the state regulates the transnational flow of the garments. Therefore, the way in which Chinese-made garments are exported to the United States (and the EU) is conditioned, shaped, and regulated by the imbalance of power between Chinese OEM producers and the U.S. (and the EU) OBM buyers, and simultaneously the uneven power between China and the United States (and the EU). While the rapid expansion of the export of Chinese-made clothing suggests an increasing participation of China in the global economy, it also reminds us that the world is indeed *not flat* (cf. Friedman 2005).

Therefore, in very broad strokes, this book uses the Chinese fashion industry as a site, and has studied how the rise of the Chinese fashion industry is constituted by and constitutive of the dynamics between the state and the market, the life and work of Chinese fashion designers (and other professionals), and various processes of localization and globalization that have been taking place in post-Mao China.

CAVEATS AND SUGGESTIONS FOR FUTURE RESEARCH

As mentioned in the beginning of this book, the goal of this book is not only to understand the dramatic changes in the Chinese fashion industry, but also to understand what the changes in the fashion industry can tell us about the broader changes in Chinese society. It is my hope that this book has demonstrated that change is at the heart of the Chinese fashion industry, and that China has undergone phenomenal changes in the past few decades and is still changing rapidly. But the ultimate fear for anyone writing a book that studies change in China today and particularly one that studies the fashion industry, which is the quintessential embodiment of change, is that you are going to miss the moving target. At the same time, however, the rapid change in the Chinese fashion industry (as well as in Chinese society more broadly) provides a perfect illustration that "there is nothing immutable or primordial about cultural systems . . . What is 'in' today is 'out' tomorrow" (Watson 1997: 10).

To study the Chinese fashion industry as a cultural system, this book takes a cultural economy approach that is informed by the social life or cultural biography (Kopytoff 1986) approach and the global commodity chain perspective (Gereffi & Korzeniewicz 1994; Bestor 2001). This approach is supported by the fact that Chinese clothing and the fashion industry are situated at the intersection of culture and economy, and of the local and the global. It has, therefore, the strength to illustrate cultural and economic logic inherent in the Chinese fashion industry and at the same time engage with a wide range of broader issues and theoretical debates such as modernization and globalization. This approach also has the advantage of highlighting the interconnections of the fashion industry as a whole. Yet, a study that focuses on one sector of the industry, one segment of the commodity chain, or one particular group that is involved in the industry will probably be better suited to uncover the "cultural biography" of that one sector, segment, or group. Aside from the fashion professionals, especially fashion designers that are studied in this book, more ethnographic studies are needed to understand how the structural changes in the Chinese textile and apparel industries impacted the lives of the workers. Chapter 2 noted that over one million Chinese textile and garment workers lost their jobs during the restructuring of the state-owned enterprises in the late 1990s. In fact, that was only a part of the story. Because of China's dual "household registration system" (*hukou*), workers with urban residence registration were better protected by the state than workers with rural residence registration. Thus, future research on Chinese garment workers should examine not just the relationship between labor and management, between workers and the state, but also the distinctions among the workers themselves and the uneven impact on them due to the changes in the Chinese textile and apparel industries.[1] Another focus for future research could be on the Chinese consumers, examining the ways through which clothing is related to issues of class and social stratification (Davis 2000; Goodman 1999), which have become increasingly prominent in the reform era. According to some scholars, increasing consumer choices have become the "new social," in which private individuals exercise self-governing and self-responsibility in post-socialist China (Ong and Zhang 2008).

In addition to locally focused research, future research can also further expand the network analysis explored in Chapter 7 and examine the global connections or disconnections of the network resulting from the transnational movements of clothing. The global commodity chains are useful tools to study how the meanings of commodities are locally constructed and at the same time how the global political economy shapes and conditions the commodity chains.

Finally, Chinese clothing and the fashion industry involve many aspects that are frequently studied separately by various disciplines. As is demonstrated in this book, both the business and cultural aspects of dress are vital to Chinese fashion designers and the industry as whole. It is my hope that this book will be a step toward more interdisciplinary research on the emerging trends, conditions, and challenges in the Chinese fashion industry in the twenty-first century.

Notes

CHAPTER 1   INTRODUCTION

1. Some older Chinese believe that a person should wear a piece of red garment, either a red cloth belt or a red *dudou,* to ward off evil spirits when the year has the same Chinese zodiac sign as the one of his or her year of birth. In Chinese, this is called one's *benmingnian*, a time during which bad luck tends to befall. According to the Chinese lunar calendar, the zodiac signs are repeated in a twelve-year cycle, so every twelfth year, one is in his or her *benmingnian*.
2. To protect their anonymity, I use pseudonyms for all the people I interviewed in this book, except Mr. Chen Yifei, who passed away in 2005. I do use real names for public officials and those whose name appeared in print or online media.
3. For a review of Eicher and her colleagues' works, see El Guindi 1999: 49–61.
4. I use Chinese names except authors in this book as they are used in China, i.e., surname first followed by first name. In cases where individuals are called by their English names, I follow the English convention and put their first names before their surnames, such as Mark Cheung.
5. Similarly, Christopher Breward (1998) also observes divisions in British academia, especially in the different approaches to clothing or dress in art history and cultural studies.
6. Here, I adopt Bourdieu's notion of a "field" (1993), which is fully explained in Chapter 6.
7. For an overview of the political economic approach, see Roseberry 1988, 1997.
8. For a summary of the criticism of modernization theories, see Tipps 1973.
9. Some scholars, such as Lisa Rofel (1999), have mistakenly believed that the Four Modernizations were first proposed by Deng in 1978.
10. Marx and Engels's idea of social evolution was in part inspired by early anthropologist and evolution theorist Lewis Henry Morgan.

CHAPTER 2   THE GROWTH OF CHINESE TEXTILE AND APPAREL INDUSTRIES

1. The number is reportedly over one hundred million if those employed in supporting industries, such as the cotton growers, are included. These numbers are estimates by the China National Textile and Apparel Council.

2. The contribution of textile and apparel export to China's trade surplus has decreased since 2005, but still accounted for 78.8 percent of China's trade surplus in 2009.

3. Trade surplus has long been seen as positive in China because it earns the hard currency China needs to invest in its infrastructure and many mega projects such as the Three Gorges Dam. Recently, however, China's huge trade surplus has become a major cause of international trade disputes as well as disputes over the Chinese currency exchange rate.

4. As a part of the state-controlled distribution system, the state instituted cloth rationing in the form of "cloth coupons" on a per capita basis in 1954. This measure was deemed necessary in a shortage economy at the time, and was kept in place for the following three decades.

5. *CTIDR* is an annual publication issued by the China National Textile and Apparel Industry Council. Since 2000 it has replaced the *Almanac of Chinese Textile Industry*, which was published by the Chinese Ministry of the Textile Industry.

6. To protect their identities, the officials I interviewed are not named here.

7. Since 2004, the Council's English name changed to China National Textile and Apparel Council, but there was no change in its Chinese name.

8. Bast fiber refers to any of several strong, ligneous fibers, such as flax, hemp, ramie, or jute, obtained from phloem tissue and used in the manufacture of woven goods and cordage.

9. Vera Fennel's (2001) dissertation studies the struggle faced by some small tailor shops in Beijing.

10. In addition to production, government command comes in still another way. Because they are state-owned enterprises, the managers of the mills and factories (work units) are indeed cadres assigned by the state, holding additional offices in the Communist Party Committee (*Dangwei*), the Workers' Union (*Gonghui*), and the Women's Federation (*Fulian*), which mirror a lower-level government bureaucracy and carry out administrative functions such as the family planning policy within the work unit (*Danwei*). For more details about work units in China, see Bian 1994 and Lu and Perry 1997.

11. In Chinese, "*cong zhaozhong zhua sudu, zhua chanliang, zhua kuoda shengchan nengli, zhuanyi dao zhaozhong zhua pingzhong zhiliang, zhua jishu gaizhao, zhua jingji xiaoyi shanglai; yao cong danchun shengchan xing zhuanbing wei shengchan jingying xing.*"

12. *Zhiqing* (educated youth) refers to the young urban intellectuals, primarily high-school students, who were willingly or unwillingly sent by the Chinese government to rural areas for "re-education" from the 1950s through the 1970s. After Mao's death in 1976, most of the *zhiqing* returned urban areas, but many remained in rural areas with the families that they established through marrying rural residents.

13. There are more SOEs in the textile sector than in the garment sector, and they are typically very large in scale because the textile sector is much more capital intensive than the garment sector.
14. The SEZs include Shenzhen and Zhuhai in Guangdong Province, which are adjacent to Hong Kong and Macau, and Shantou and Xiamen in Fujian Province, which are close to Taiwan. Hainan Province was added to the list of SEZs later.
15. "Stories of the Spring," written by Jiang Karu and Ye Xuquan; performed by Dong Wenhua, January 1, 1998.
16. The democratic movements in the late 1980s were led by college students, who protested in large scale on Tian'anmen Square against government corruption. On June 4, 1989, the Chinese government used the army and forcefully suppressed the student movements. For details of this incident, see Brook 1992.
17. Collective enterprises (*jiti qiye*) in theory should include rural township collectives. However, the Chinese government regarded the TVEs (*xiangzhen qiye*) as outside the system (*xitongwei*) (e.g., *ACTI* 1994: 3, 5). The TVEs are different from the SOEs and urban collectives in that they do not receive funds from the state budgets and their workers typically do not enjoy pensions after retirement, which are typical of the socialist system. Nevertheless, the socialist sector or *xitongnei* firms are predominantly the SOEs.
18. Another place stated the aggregate loss as 780 million yuan (*ACTI* 1995: 78).
19. Generally speaking, these laid-off workers from the SOEs would receive some unemployment benefits from the government, which typically would not be sufficient to sustain a living, and those laid-off workers would thus have to temporarily rely on their savings and/or support from family members. Most of those workers ended up in a different job either through the help of the government or their own personal networks.
20. Liz Claiborne, Inc., sold its namesake brands to JC Penney in October 2011, and the company changed its name to Fifth and Pacific Companies in January 2012. The new company focuses on three lifestyle brands: Juicy Couture, Kate Spade, and Lucky Brand.
21. The Asian Tiger economies include Hong Kong, South Korea, Taiwan, and Singapore.
22. See *Zhongguo fangzhi bao* (*Chinese Textile News*), January 26, 1998.

CHAPTER 3   WHAT DO CHANGING CHINESE FASHIONS REALLY TELL US?

1. There was a major renovation and cleaning up of Xujiahui as well as other major streets as part of the beautification of Shanghai in preparation for

the World Expo in 2010. Some of the discount stores I mentioned were closed as a result of that.

2. I have re-visited Shanghai in three summers in 2009, 2010, and 2011. Compared to the first two types of stores, the big malls had the least changes in the past few years.

3. There were many temporary and semi-permanent stalls inside the subway terminal of Xujiahui in 2004 as well. Most of the stalls had semi-permanent structures, but some "shop" owners were peddling their goods on the floors. They appeared to sell their goods, which were typically cheap, to random customers and students. These "shops" were replaced by established chains in anticipation of the World Expo in 2010. However, peddlers still showed up in the evenings and on weekends during my most recent trip in 2011.

4. Geertz's (1988) distinction between writers and authors is relevant here, but will be discussed further in Chapter 5.

5. To analyze the stylistic changes, Richardson and Kroeber took six measurements of a dress: skirt length, waist length, décolletage length, skirt width, waist width, and décolletage width (Richardson and Kroeber 1940: 112).

6. The discussion of Chinese clothing here is limited to clothing of the Han, and does not include clothing of the ethnic minorities, save the Manchu.

7. Dorothy Ko sees foot-binding as a form of attire; see Ko 1997.

8. Using evidence from memoirs and novels, Antonia Finnane (2008) notes that despite the limited range of clothing styles in the Qing dynasty, people from the affluent Yangzhou area showed great interest in clothing and material objects such as watches.

9. This is a view presented in Chinese textbooks (e.g., An & Jin 1999: 7–8) that is shared by many dress historians. Gerth (2003) also details how the removal of the queue was central to the collapse of the Qing dynasty. Also see Wang 2003: 64–70.

10. They were also called *fengbang caifeng*, as they were originally from Fengtian, Zhejiang, and then migrated to the Shanghai area.

11. Japanese dress scholar Yamanouchi Chiemi surveyed 61 individuals in Xi'an and Shanghai on the issue of national dress in 1997, and most of them thought the *qipao* and the *zhongshanzhuang* were or should be the Chinese national dress (2001: 6).

12. For details of the symbolisms, see Wang 2003: 98–99.

13. The KMT leader Chiang Kai-shek fled to Taiwan and found a foothold for his government there, which continues to be called the Republic of China (ROC).

14. These images lend conveniently to Western interpretation of China as a totalitarian and brain-washed communist other.

15. They include "old thinking, old culture, old customs, and old behaviors."

16. The military uniform is also *zhongshanzhuang* in style, but includes the military paraphernalia, including the buttons, badges, hat, and belt.

17. Ideological debates and discourses did not go away entirely, and sometimes they even made strong comebacks. The repression of the 1989 Tian'anmen incident is a key example.

18. The military uniforms remain more or less the same; they still bear great resemblance to the *zhongshanzhuang* style.

19. The *qipao* is considered as a "symbol of cultural identity" beyond mainland China, such as in Hong Kong, Singapore, and other overseas Chinese communities; see Chua 2000, and *Hong Kong Fashion History* 1992.

20. Susan Brownell has an interesting discussion of the bikinis debates in the mid-1980s, which shows how the style emerged and became accepted. See Brownell 1995: 270–4.

21. Textbooks of all levels are closely regulated by the government in China. Unlike college textbooks in the United States, Chinese textbooks are generally much more standardized and are used nationally.

22. The war ended with the loss of the Qing to Britain, which marked the beginning of a series of cession of sovereign rights of the Qing to foreign powers, which turned the Qing into a semi-colonial status.

23. This periodization follows the position of Chinese high school history textbooks. But if modernity is to be equated with capitalism, then it could be dated back to the first emergence of capitalist sprouts in the Ming dynasty as Spence (1990) suggests.

24. For a recent account of the Great Leap Forward, see Thaxton 2008.

25. The "three steps" plan has been modified repeatedly by each Party Congress; however, overall consistency with respect to progress has been maintained in those various versions.

CHAPTER 4   DESIGNING A NATIONAL STYLE

1. A Chinese source reported that 3,000 journalists from around the world congregated in Shanghai to cover this event (*Beijing qingnianbao* 10/15/2001).

2. There were several news reports on Chinese scholars' disagreements on the use of the term of the *tangzhuang*. See *Jiefang ribao* 10/22/2001; *Beijing qingnianbao* 02/10/2002.

3. One of the original designers I interviewed holds this view, which is also reflected in the title of a book the team published. See Ding et al. 2002.

4. Japanese scholar Yamanouchi Chiemi (2001) thinks that there are traditional Chinese styles, but no one traditional style serves as the national dress.

5. The Republican governments actually decreed several sets of formal wear for women, but none of them were popular enough to be even remembered today.
6. In the summer of 2002, I observed that there were about a dozen stores along Changle Road making and selling traditional Chinese clothing. However, many of them were not recent establishments.
7. The Spring Festival is the most important traditional Chinese holiday. It is on the first day of the year by the Chinese lunar calendar, but the celebration starts on the last day of the lunar year (around the end of January according to the Gregorian calendar) and typically lasts half a month to the second important traditional holiday, *Yuanxiaojie* (the Lantern Festival), which is on the first full moon day of the lunar new year. In 1983, the China Central Television Station (CCTV) broadcast a large-scale live performance on the Eve of the Spring Festival. Since then, watching this show has become a tradition for most Chinese families.
8. OEM stands for original equipment manufacturer, a contract business for the original brand manufacturers (OBMs), who are typically large international fashion companies or retailers.

CHAPTER 5   FOR THE SAKE OF ART OR FOR THE MARKET?

1. Since Chen passed away, the prices of his paintings skyrocketed. One painting of his, "Thinking of history in my space," was sold at a price of over 40 million yuan (about U.S. $5.8 million based on the exchange at the time) in Beijing in May 2009.
2. I interviewed Mr. Chen Yifei on his involvement in the fashion industry in May 2004.
3. I met and talked to a greater number of designers in different venues (including fashion shows and trade fairs), but I consider an interview here in a more formal sense that it is scheduled ahead of time either by me or through a friend, and that I have designed an interview guide prior to the interview.
4. For some general comments on the first-generation Chinese fashion designers, see Tsui 2010: 131–136.
5. Wuhan is the capital city of Hubei province in South-Central China, a city that has a population of about 8 million people.
6. After the success of this corporation, several Chinese fashion companies followed suit and launched their own publically advertised hire of "million-yuan designers."
7. Class is a touchy issue in China. During the Maoist era (1949–78), "class" was only interpreted as related to the means of production in a Marxist

framework, such as "the haves" and "the have-nots." The Communist revolution was supposed to have done away with the class of "the haves," but the descendants of "the haves" were still labeled as "the exploiters" in the context of the ideological "class struggles" that were popular during the Maoist period. In the post-Mao reform period, the economic reforms brought about class distinctions in economic terms in China. Subsequently, there is an increasing interest in sociology and anthropology to study "social stratification" in China based on the income and prestige of various occupations (e.g., Bian 1996; Gao 2005; Li 2002; Zhang 2002), and social distinctions in people's consumption patterns (e.g., Davis 2000; Goodman 1999).

8. Yuan Xing told me about the profitability of his company during the interview, which was also confirmed to me by other designers who were close friends of Yuan Xing.

9. The term haute couture is protected by law in France to refer to the high-end made-to-measure fashion created by the fashion houses that meet the criteria defined by the *Chambre de commerce et d'industrie de Paris*. However, in the global fashion industry, the term is loosely used to refer to high fashion. Following Reinach and others, I use the term here in a loose and general sense.

10. For a brief history of haute couture, see Breward 2003; Dickerson 2003: 369–79.

11. There are also about one dozen haute couture houses in Italy, but they are smaller and less influential than the Parisian haute couture houses.

12. The 1990 Task Report of the Apparel Research Committee of the American Apparel Manufacturers Association is entitled, "'Fast Fashion'— Quick Response Product Line Development."

13. In fact, the goal of Shanghai Fashion Week in 2004 was clearly stated as "to construct the sixth fashion capital in the world."

14. Reinach's (2005) article clearly points to the threat of Chinese fast fashions to the Italian prêt-à-porter.

CHAPTER 6   CREATING FASHION ON THE RUNWAY, CHINESE STYLE

1. The specific numbers of each were hard to calculate, because many shows tended to combine both types of fashions. My general sense was that there were more couture shows than ready-to-wear shows at CFW in 2004.

2. Chinese celebrities today do buy couture dresses, but they buy from international designers and usually for social occasions overseas.

3. At CFW Fall 2004 I attended, there were three shows by Japanese designers, one color show by Kodak, one by a Korean designer, one by a group of eight young French designers, and one Italian men's wear show.

4. I interviewed Ms. Kunrou Pan twice in Beijing in 2004, during which she generously provided me with the reference of her article (2003) and other useful information to my research.

5. Several Chinese designers recalled their experience of Pierre Cardin's early fashion shows as exciting and surprising, which was reflected by a common phrase they used, "[I never thought that] clothes could be made that way!"

6. This estimate is supported by the calculation of a fashion journalist, whom I interviewed in 2004.

7. Modeling contests and beauty pageants are very similar in format, and sometimes the same candidates compete for both. In the Chinese popular imagination, the two are frequently grouped together as part of the "beauty economy." However, there are differences between them. Miss China Universe (in 2004), Wang Meng, pointed out to me during our interview that beauty pageants emphasize both inner and outer beauty and that beauty queens often have missions in charitable works. Models, by contrast, generally work through an agency that does not have a stated mission for charity.

8. According to a high-ranking official of the Council whom I interviewed in 2004, the Council and CFA then hired more personnel from job markets on a contract basis than those inherited from the former Textile Ministry. Funds from the central government only cover the salaries and benefits, including retirement benefits, of the former Ministry personnel, but not the contract-based employees.

9. For the third-tier awards, now there are awards that are considered equivalent to the "New Designers Award," all of which are sponsored by and named after particular companies in the fashion industry.

10. The first class of "Top Ten Fashion Designers" and "New Designers Awards" was awarded in 1995 after the CFA was formed, one class of "Top Ten" was awarded in 1997, and two classes of "New Designers Awards" were handed out in 1997. Two classes of "Top Ten" were awarded in 1998, but since then the three types of awards are synchronized with the CFW.

11. It almost became a scandal at the first CFW when the media ranked Ms. Wu Haiyan as number one, but in the end the Golden Award was given to Mr. Zhang Zhaoda (Mark Cheung) by the CFA.

12. Similar to the CFA, most fashion media were created in the 1990s. For instance, two major national fashion newspapers, *China Fashion Weekly* and *Fashion Times* were founded in 1994.

13. Journalists jokingly called the two sites *Zhongguo da* [fandian] (meaning "China big") and *Beijing da* [fandian] ("Beijing big").
14. According to members of the media, each major media only got two tickets to the show.
15. I formally requested tickets from the CFA. The staff person said she would need approval from the president (Mr. Wang Qing) of the CFA, who declined my request.
16. In a study of fashion shows, Kondo also notes that the audiences of the fashion show gaze at each other and thus perform for each other (1997: 103).
17. Mark Cheung accepted my request for an interview with him, but the interview never materialized before I had to leave China.
18. The cost of a fashion show at CFW ranges from several hundred thousand to well over one million yuan, which includes costs for the design and production of the clothes, the models, "tips" for the media, the invitations and gift bags (optional), press conference (optional), the post-show party (optional), and the registration fee paid to the CFA (about two hundred thousand yuan). The registration fee covers the rent of the space and the production of the show.
19. As of 2004, Mark Cheung had five lines of clothing: two lines in men's wear, one prêt-à-porter line for older women and one for younger women, and one line of women's jeans.
20. There are two Shanghai Fashion Weeks, organized by different organizations. One is called *shishang zhou*, and the other *shizhuang zhou*, but both are translated in English as "fashion week." I attended both fashion weeks in Shanghai in 2004.
21. After my interview with Zheng Yifan, I visited her company's stores in Beijing and Shanghai, and did more research on her company. I called her later and followed up with an interview.

CHAPTER 7   MAKING CLOTHES FOR INTERNATIONAL MARKETS

1. I have surveyed about 100 college students in the United States on their views of what factors are most important to them when they choose to buy their garments. The country of origin is consistently ranked the least important factor. In unusual circumstances, the country of origin of garments does have symbolic meanings. For example, after the media revealed that the opening ceremony uniforms for the 2012 U.S. Olympic team were made in China, the company that designed the uniforms, Ralph Lauren, was harshly criticized. In this case, the label "Made in China" was seen as unpatriotic.

2. Globalization means many different things to different scholars. For a brief review of globalization, see Lewellen 2002.
3. The prices quoted by Zeng Gang are freight on board (FOB) prices.
4. The standards are designated by Reebok, but most MNCs have similar standards, such as SA8000 or equivalent standards.
5. Sometimes, the OBMs are also called "original design manufacturers" (ODMs).
6. The percentage is even lower for high-end products, and the OBM sells the products in retail at a much higher multiplier.
7. For the brief history of the U.S. trade protection against textile and apparel imports, see Rivoli 2005: 127–130.
8. To keep the pressure up on the U.S. government, more petitions continued to be filed by the same groups later in June, July, and up until November, when a new broad agreement was reached between the United States and Chinese governments.
9. These seven categories include cotton knit shirts and blouses (category 338/339); cotton trousers (category 347/348); cotton and man-made fiber underwear (category 352/652); men's and boy's cotton and man-made fiber shirts, not knit (category 340/640); man-made fiber trousers (category 647/648), man-made fiber knit shirts and blouses (category 638/639), and combed cotton yarn (category 301). More categories were imposed with safeguard quotas later during the negotiation and consultation process.
10. This agreement is entitled "Memorandum of understanding between the governments of the United States of America and the People's Republic of China concerning trade in textile and apparel products," available at http://www.ustr.gov.
11. After the resolution between the United States and China, the EU resolved its trade dispute with China, modeled on the framework adopted by the United States and China.
12. The quotas were free from the U.S. government, but the Chinese government sold them to Chinese manufacturers. Quotas were also available in the "black market," sold by profiteers.
13. For example, the American Textile Manufacturers Institute, in a study entitled "The China Threat to World Textile and Apparel Trade," estimated that China would take over 2/3 of the U.S. market in 24 months after the quotas were lifted in 2005. Many scholars believe that such a scenario is unlikely, given that a host of factors besides cost are involved in the U.S. corporations' sourcing decisions (e.g., Abernathy 2004).
14. The Chinese Minister of Commerce Bo Xilai made the comment on the social significance of the Chinese textile and apparel industries during the press conference after he signed the new trade agreement with

the U.S. Trade Representative, Rob Portman, on November 8, 2005. The transcript of the press conference is available at http://www.ustr.gov/Document_Library/Transcripts/

15. During the sixteenth annual U.S.-China Joint Commission on Commerce and Trade (JCCT) meeting, which was held in July 2005, the Chinese media reported the debated issues including the intellectual property rights and the valuation of Chinese currency between the United States and China, e.g., http://finance.sina.com.cn, accessed on July 11, 2005; and http://www.xinghuanet.com, accessed on July 11, 2005.

16. Anti-dumping cases are established if the imported products are found to be selling below cost. Because China is not considered a market economy, anti-dumping cases against Chinese imports are determined by a proxy from a different country chosen by the U.S. competitors who are charging Chinese manufacturers "dumping." Consequently, anti-dumping cases against Chinese imports are fairly easy to establish.

CHAPTER 8   CONCLUSION

1. Workers with rural residence registration can work in urban areas, but they are considered migrant workers. In addition, there are factors other than household registration that differentiate workers. For example, gender is an important dimension in the lives of the workers.

Bibliography

Abernathy, Fred. 2004. *The Apparel and Textile Industries after 2005: Prospects and Choices*. Harvard Center of Textile and Apparel Research, Harvard University.

An, Yuying, and Genrong, Jin. 1999. *Zhongguo xiandai fuzhuangshi*. Beijing: China Light Industry Press.

Anderson, Benedict. 1983. *Imagined Communities: Reflections on the Origin and Spread of Nationalism*. New York: Verso.

Appadurai, Arjun. 1986. *The Social Life of Things: Commodities in Cultural Perspective*. Cambridge: Cambridge University Press.

Appadurai, Arjun. 1996. *Modernity at Large: Cultural Dimensions of Globalization*. Minneapolis: University of Minnesota Press.

Apparel Research Committee of the American Apparel Manufacturers Association. 1990. "Fast Fashion." Quick Response Product Line Development: 1990 Task Group Report of the Apparel Research Committee of the American Apparel Manufacturers Association. Arlington, VA: The American Apparel Manufacturers Association.

Bao, Mingxin. 1998. *Zhongguo Qipao* (Chinese Qipao). Shanghai: Shanghai Cultural Press.

Bao, Mingxin. 1999. *Jiedu Shizhuang*. Shanghai: Xuelin Press.

Bao, Xiaolan. 2001. *Holding Up More Than Half the Sky: Chinese Women Garment Workers in New York City, 1948–92.* Chicago: University of Illinois Press.

Barboza, David, and Elizabeth Becker. 2005. "Free of Quota, China Textiles Flood the U.S." *The New York Times* (March 10).

Barme, Geremie. 1999. *In the Red: On Contemporary Chinese Culture*. New York: Columbia University Press.

Barthes, Roland. 1982. "Authors and Writers." In *A Barthes Reader,* ed. S. Sontag, 185–193. New York: Hill and Wang.

Beijing qingnianbao. 2001. "Shanqian jizhe yunji shanghai meiti jiujiao APEC," October 15, 2001.

Beijing qingnianbiao. 2002. "Manyan 'tangzhuang' fei 'tangzhuang,'" February, 10, 2002.

Bestor, Theodore. 2001. "Supply-Side Sushi: Commodity, Market, and the Global City." *American Anthropologist* 103(1): 76–95.

Bian, Yanjie. 1994. *Work and Inequality in Urban China.* Albany: State University of New York Press.

Bian, Yanjie. 1996. "Chinese Occupational Prestige: A Comparative Analysis." *International Sociology* 11(2): 161–186.

Blair, Jennifer, and Gary Gereffi. 2003. "Upgrading, uneven development, and jobs in the North American apparel industry." *Global Networks* 3(2): 143–169.

Bonacich, Edna, et al., eds. 1994. *Global Production: The Apparel Industry in the Pacific Rim*. Philadelphia: Temple University Press.

Bonacich, E, and David V Waller. 1994. "The Role of U.S. Apparel Manufactures in the Globalization of the Industry in the Pacific Rim." In *Global Production: The Apparel Industry in the Pacific Rim*, ed. E. Bonacich, et al., 21–41. Philadelphia: Temple University Press.

Bourdieu, Pierre. 1986. "The Forms of Capital." In *Handbook of Theory and Research for the Sociology of Education,* ed. J. Richardson, 241–258. New York: Greenwood.

Bourdieu, Pierre. 1993. *The Field of Cultural Production*, ed. R. Johnson. New York: Columbia University Press.

Breslin, Shaun. 2004. *Capitalism with Chinese Characteristics: The Public, the Private, and the International.* Asia Research Center, Murdoch University Australia.

Breward, Christopher. 1998. "Cultures, Identities, Histories: Fashioning a Cultural Approach to Dress." *Fashion Theory: The Journal of Dress, Body, and Culture* 2(4): 301–314.

Breward, Christopher. 2003. *Fashion*. Oxford: Oxford University Press.

Brownell, Susan. 1995. *Training the Body for China: Sports in the Moral Order of the People's Republic.* Chicago: The University of Chicago Press.

Brownell, Susan. 2001. "Making Dream Bodies in Beijing: Athletes, Fashion Models, and Urban Mystique in China." In *China Urban: Ethnographies of Contemporary China*, ed. N. Chen. Durham: Duke University Press.

Cannon, Aubrey. 1998. "The Cultural and Historical Contexts of Fashion." In *Consuming Fashion: Adorning the Transnational Body*, ed. Anne Brydon and Sandra Niessen, 23–38. New York: Berg.

Cao, Yingwang. 2006. *Zhongguo de zhong guanjia: Zhou Enlai*. Shanghai: Shanghai Renmin Press.

Chiemi, Yamanouchi. 2001. *20 shiji hanzu fushi wenhua yanjiu* (A Cultural Study of the 20th Century Ethnic Chinese Clothing). Xi'an: Xibei University Press.

The China Daily. 2001. "Zhang Qiyue: Lingdaoren fuzhuang biaoda zhongguo renmin dui APEC de qiwang." October 21, 2001.

China Fashion Association (CFA). *http://www.e-vogue.com.cn*, accessed on March 5, 2004.

China National Textile Industry Council (CNTIC). 2000–2010. *China Textile Industry Development Report* (CTIDR). Beijing: China Textile Press.

Chua, Beng-huat. 2000. "Postcolonial sites, global flows and fashion codes: a case study of power cheongsams and other clothing styles in modern Singapore." *Postcolonial Studies* 3(3): 279–292.

Clark, Hazel. 1999. "The Cheung Sam: Issues of Fashion and Cultural Identity." In *China Chic: East Meets West*, ed. V. Steele and J. S. Major. New Haven & London: Yale University Press.

Collins, Jane L. 2003. *Threads: Gender, Labor, and Power in the Global Apparel Industry*. Chicago: University of Chicago Press.

Comaroff, Jean. 1997. "The Empire's Old Clothes". In *Situated Lives: Gender and Culture in Everyday Life,* ed. L. Lamphere et al.. New York & London: Routledge.

Constable, Nicole. 2006. "Nostalgia, Memory and Modernity: Bridal Portraits in Contemporary Beijing." *Visual Anthropology* 19(1): 39–55.

Davis, Deborah. 2000. *The Consumer Revolution in Urban China*. Berkeley: University of California Press.

Dickerson, Kitty G. 2003. *Inside the Fashion Business*. 7th edition. Upper Saddle River, NJ: Pearson Education, Inc.

Ding, Xiqiang, et al. 2002. *Xintangzhuang*. Shanghai: Shanghai Science and Technology Press.

Ding, Zhen. 2003. "Sanwen shizhuang xiu." *Fuzhuang* 119(13).

Dirks, Nicholas B. 1990. "History as a Sign of the Modern." *Public Culture* 2: 25–32.

du Gay, Paul. 1997. *Production of Culture/Cultures of Production*. London: Sage Publications.

Du, Yuzhou. 2004. Ushering the New Era for the Development of the World's Textile Industry. Proceedings of the Textile Institute 83rd World Conference, Shanghai, pp. i-ix. The Textile Institute and Donghua University.

Editorial Board of the Almanac of China's Textile Industry. 1981–1999. *Almanac of China's Textile Industry* (ACTI). Beijing: China Textile Press.

Editorial Board of the Yearbook of Shanghai Clothing. 1985. *Shanghai fuzhuang nianjian* (Yearbook of Shanghai Clothing). Shanghai: Shanghai fuznuang nianjian Press.

Eicher, Joanne, and Mary E Roach-Higgins. 1997. "Definition and Classification of Dress: Implications for Analysis of Gender Roles." In *Dress and Gender: Making and Meaning,* ed. R. Barnes and J. Eicher, 8–28. New York: Berg.

El Guindi, Fadwa. 1999. *Veil: Modesty, Privacy, and Resistance*. New York: Berg.

Entwistle, Joanne. 2000. *The Fashioned Body: Fashion, Dress and the Modern Social Theory*. Cambridge: Polity Press.

Entwistle, Joanne, and Agnes Rocamora. 2006. "The Field of Fashion Materialized: A Study of London Fashion Week." *Sociology* 40(4): 735–751.

Fabian, Johannes. 1983. *Time and the Other: How Anthropology Makes its Object*. New York: Columbia University Press.

Fennell, Vera L. 2001. "Just a Stitch in the Political Fabric: Gender, Labor, and Clothes in Reform-era China." PhD diss. The University of Chicago.

Finnane, Antonia. 1996. "What Should Chinese Women Wear? A National Problem." *Modern China* 22(2): 99–131.

Finnane, Antonia. 2008. *Changing Clothes in China: Fashion, History, Nation.* New York: Columbia University Press.

Foster, Robert J. 2002. *Materializing the Nation: Commodities, Consumption, and Media in Papua New Guinea.* Bloomington and Indianapolis: Indiana University Press.

Foucault, Michel. 1979. "What is an Author?" In *Textual Strategies: Perspectives in Post-Structuralist Criticism,* ed. J. Harari. Ithaca: Cornell University Press.

Friedman, Thomas. 2005. *The World Is Flat: A Brief History of the Twenty-first Century.* New York: Farrar, Straus and Giroux.

Frings, Gini S. 2005. *Fashion: From Concept to Consumer.* 8th Edition. Upper Saddle River, NJ: Pearson Education, Inc.

Gao, Shunwen. 2005. "Woguo zhiye shengwang yanjiu ershinian shupin." *South-Central University of Technology Journal* (Social Sciences Edition) 4: 40–45.

Garrett, Valery M. 1994. *Chinese Clothing.* New York: Oxford University Press.

Geertz, Clifford. 1973a. "Deep Play: Notes on the Balinese Cockfight." In *The Interpretation of Cultures,* ed. C. Geertz, 412–453. New York: Basic Books.

Geertz, Clifford. 1973b. "Thick Description: Toward an Interpretive Theory of Culture." In *The Interpretation of Cultures,* 3–30. New York: Basic Books.

Geertz, Clifford. 1983. *Local Knowledge: Further Essays in Interpretive Anthropology.* New York: Basic Books.

Geertz, Clifford. 1988. *Works and Lives: The Anthropologist as Author.* Stanford: Stanford University Press.

Gereffi, Gary, and Miguel Korzeniewicz, eds. 1994. *Commodity Chains and Global Capitalism.* Westport: Greenwood Press.

Gerth, Karl. 2003. *China Made: Consumer culture and the creation of the nation.* Cambridge: Harvard University Press.

Goodman, David S. G. 1999. "The New Middle Class." In *The Paradox of China's Post-Mao Reforms*, ed. M. Goldman and R. MacFarquhar, 241–261. Cambridge: Harvard University Press.

Guang, Lei. 2003. "Rural Taste, Urban Fashions: The Cultural Politics of Rural/Urban Difference in Contemporary China." *Positions: East Asia Cultures Critique* 11(3): 613–646.

Hannerz, Ulf. 1992. "The Global Ecumene as a Network of Networks." In *Conceptualizing Society*, ed. A. Kuper, 34–56. New York: Routledge.

Harvey, David. 1989. *The Condition of Post-modernity: An Inquiry into the Origins of Culture Change.* Cambridge: Blackwell.

Hobsbawm, Eric, and Terence Ranger. 1983. *The Invention of Tradition.* Cambridge: Cambridge University Press.

Hopkins, Terence, and Immanuel Wallerstein. 1986. "Commodity Chains in the World-Economy Prior to 1800." *Review* 10(1): 157–170.

Huang, Nengfu, and Chen Juanjuan. 1995. *Zhongguo fuzhuang shi*. Beijing: Chinese Tourist Press.

Huang, Shilong. 1994. *Zhongguo fushi shilue* (Brief History of Chinese Clothing and Accessories). Shanghai: Shanghai Culture Press.

Huang, Yasheng. 2008. *Capitalism with Chinese Characteristics: Entrepreneurship and the State*. Cambridge: Cambridge University Press.

Inda, J X, and R Rosaldo, eds. 2002. *The Anthropology of Globalization: A Reader*. Malden, MA: Blackwell Publishing.

Inda, J X, and R Rosaldo. 2002. "Introduction: A World in Motion." In *The Anthropology of Globalization: A Reader,* ed. J. X. Inda and R. Rosaldo. Malden, MA: Blackwell Publishing.

Jiefang ribao. 2001. "APEC lingdaoren fuzhuang." October 22, 2001.

Jiefang ribao. 2001. "Youguan renyuan zaijei APEC zhongzhuang beihou xianweirenzhi de mimi." November 06, 2001.

Johnson, Randal. 1993. "Editor's Introduction: Pierre Bourdieu on Art, Literature and Culture." In *The Field of Cultural Production*, ed. R. Johnson, 1–25. New York: Columbia University Press.

Kawamura, Yuniya. 2005. *Fashion-ology: An Introduction to Fashion Studies*. New York: Berg.

Kilduff, Peter. 2005. "Patterns of Strategic Adjustment in the U.S. Textile and Apparel Industries since 1979." *Journal of Fashion Marketing and Management* 9(2): 180–194.

Ko, Dorothy. 1997. "The Body as Attire: The Shifting Meanings of Foot-binding in Seventeenth-Century China." *Journal of Women's History* 8(4): 8–27.

Kondo, Dorinne. 1997. *About Face: Performing Race in Fashion and Theater*. New York: Routledge.

Kopytoff, Igor. 1986. "The Cultural Biography of Things: Commercialization as Process." In *The Social Life of Things*, ed. A. Appadurai, 64–91. Cambridge: Cambridge University Press.

Kroeber, Alfred. 1919. "On the Principle of Order in Civilization as Exemplified by Changes of Fashion." *American Anthropologist* 21(3): 235–263.

Kroeber, Alfred. 1957. *Style and Civilizations*. Ithaca: Cornell University Press.

Kroeber, Alfred. 1963. *An Anthropologist Looks at History*. Berkeley: University of California Press.

Kunz, Jean L. 1996. "From Maoism to ELLE: The Impact of Political Ideology on Fashion Trends in China." *International Sociology* 11(3): 317–335.

Lewellen, Ted. 2002. *The Anthropology of Globalization: Cultural Anthropology Enters the 21st Century*. London: Bergin & Garvey.

Li, Peilin. 2002. "Introduction: Changes in Social Stratification in China since the Reform." *Social Sciences in China* (Spring): 42–47.

Lin, Boyu, et al. 2000. *Zhongguo shao shu minzu fushi*. Taibei: National Museum of History.

Liu, Toming Jun. 2001. "Restless Chinese Nationalist Currents in the 1980s and the 1990s: A comparative reading of River Elegy and China Can Say No." In *Chinese Nationalism in Perspective*, ed. C.X.G. Wei and T. J. Liu, 205–231. Westport: Greenwood Press.

Lowe, John, and E Lowe. 1982. "Cultural Pattern and Process: A Study of Stylistic Change in Women's Dress." *American Anthropologist* 84(3): 521–544.

Marcus, George. 1995. "Ethnography in/of the World System: The Emergence of Multi-Sited Ethnography." *Annual Review of Anthropology* 24: 95–117.

Marcus, George, and Michael J Fischer. 1986. *Anthropology as Cultural Critique: An Experimental Moment in the Human Sciences*. Chicago: The University of Chicago Press.

Milberg, William. 2005. *Labor and the Globalization of Production: Causes and Consequences of Industrial Upgrading*. New York: Palgrave Macmillan.

Miller, Daniel. 1998. "Coke: A Black Sweet Drink from Trinidad." In *Material Cultures: Why Some Things Matter*, ed. D. Miller, 169–187. Chicago: Chicago University Press.

Nanfang ribao. 2005. "Duimei chukou pei'e gao ji fangzhi qiye buling chengben baoji chuhuo." July 4, 2005.

New Strait Times-Management Times. 2001. "Tradition, bright colors prevail in this year's APEC fashion statement." October 21, 2001.

The New York Times. 2001. "Burgers and limos on a visit to Shanghai." October 21, 2001.

Niessen, S. 2003. "Re-Orienting Fashion Theory." In *Re-Orienting Fashion: The Globalization of Asian Dress*, ed. S. Niessen, M. Leshkowich, and C. Jones, 243–266. Oxford: Berg.

Ong, Aihwa, and Li Zhang. 2008. "Introduction: Privatizing China: Powers of the Self, Socialism from Afar." In *Privatizing China: Socialism from Afar*, ed. Li Zhang and Aihwa Ong, 1–20. Ithaca: Cornell University Press.

Pan, Kunrou. 2003. "Zhongguo mote chanye xingcheng 'xianzai jinxingshi.'" *Zhongguo fuzhuang* 111: 28–30.

Piore, Michael J., and Charles F. Sabel. 1984. *The Second Great Divide: Possibilities for Prosperity*. New York: Basic Books.

Phillips, Ruth, and C. B. Steiner. 1999. *Unpacking Culture: Art and Commodity in Colonial and Postcolonial Worlds*. Berkeley: University of California Press.

Phizacklea, Annie. 1990. *Unpacking the Fashion Industry: Gender, Racism and Class in Production*. London and New York: Routledge.

Reinach, Simona S. 2005. "China and Italy: Fast Fashion versus Prêt à Porter. Towards a New Culture of Fashion." *Fashion Theory* 9(1): 1–12.

Ren, Bingwu. 1998. *Zhongguo you ge yage'r*. Beijing: People's Literature Press.

Richardson, J, and Alfred Kroeber. 1940. "Three Centuries of Women's Dress Fashions: A Quantitative Analysis." *Anthropological Records* 5(2): 111–153.

Ritzer, George. 2000. *The McDonaldization of Society: An Investigation into the Changing Character of Contemporary Social Life*. Thousand Oaks, CA: Pine Forge Press.

Rivoli, Pietra. 2005. *The Travels of a T-Shirt in the Global Economy: An Economist Examines the Markets, Power, and Politics of World Trade*. Hoboken, New Jersey: John Wiley and Sons Inc.

Roces, Mina, and Louise Edwards. 2008. "Transnational flows and the politics of dress in Asia." *ILAS Newsletter* 46(1): 3.

Rofel, Lisa. 1999. *Other Modernities: Gendered Yearnings in China after Socialism*. Berkeley: University of California Press.

Roseberry, William. 1988. "Political Economy." *Annual Review of Anthropology* 26: 25–46.

Roseberry, William 1997. "Marx and Anthropology." *Annual Review of Anthropology* 17: 161–85.

Rostow, Walt W. 1960. *The Stages of Economic Growth: A Non-Communist Manifesto*. Cambridge: Cambridge University Press.

Schlosser, Eric. 2001. *Fast Food Nation: The Dark Side of the All-American Meal*. New York: Houghton Mifflin Co.

Schneider, Jane. 1994. "In and Out of Polyester: Desire, and Disdain and Global Fiber Competitions." *Anthropology Today* 10(4): 2–10.

Scott, A. C. 1958. *Chinese Costume in Transition*. Singapore: Donald Moore.

Scott, Robert. 1998. "U.S. Trade Policies for the Textile and Apparel Industries: The Political Economy of the Post-MFA Environment." In *Constituent Interests and U.S. Trade Policies*, ed. A. Deardorff and R. Stern, 145–160. Ann Arbor: University of Michigan Press.

Shaw, C. H., K. C. Jackson, and P.D.F. Kilduff. 1994a. "Growth and Maturity in the Taiwanese Cotton Textile Industry." *Journal of the Textile Institute* 85(2): 255–268.

Shaw, C. H., K. C. Jackson, and P.D.F. Kilduff. 1994b. "Prospects for Upgrading in the Taiwanese Cotton Textile Industry." *Journal of the Textile Institute* 85(2): 270–281.

Shen, Congwen. 1997. *Zhongguo gudai fushi yanju*. Shanghai: Shanghai Bookstore Press.

Spence, Jonathan. 1990. *The Search for Modern China*. New York: Norton.

Steele, V., and J. S. Major. 1999. *China Chic: East Meets West*. New Haven & London: Yale University Press.

Tang, Xianbing. 2002. *Liti yu pingmian: Zhongxi fushi wenhua bijiao* (Three-dimensional vs. Two-dimensional: Comparison of Western and Chinese Clothing Cultures). Beijing: China Textile Press.

Thaxton, Ralph A., Jr. 2008. *Catastrophe and Contention in Rural China*. Cambridge: Cambridge University Press.

Tipps, Dean C. 1973. "Modernization Theory and the Comparative Study of Societies: A Critical Perspective." *Comparative Studies in Society and History* 15(2): 199–226.

Trevor-Roper, Hugh. 1983. "The Invention of Tradition: The Highland Tradition of Scotland." In *The Invention of Tradition*, ed. E. Hobsbawm and T. Ranger, 15–41. Cambridge: Cambridge University Press.

Troy, Nancy. 2003. *Couture Cultures: A Study in Modern Art and Fashion*. Cambridge, MA: MIT Press.

Tsai, Kellee. 2002. *Back-Alley Banking: Private Entrepreneurs in China*. Ithaca: Cornell University Press.

Tsui, Christine. 2010. *China Fashion: Conversations with Designers*. Oxford: Berg.

Turner, Victor. 1969. *The Ritual Process*. Chicago: Aldine.

U.S. Government Accountability Office (GAO). 2005. "U.S.-China Trade: Textile Safeguard Procedures Should Be Improved." Report to Congressional Committees.

U.S. International Trade Commission (USITC). 2004. *Textile and Apparel: Assessment of the Competitiveness of Certain Foreign Suppliers to the U.S. Market*, Vol. 1. Washington, DC: U.S. International Trade Commission.

The Wall Street Journal. 2011. "Rei Kawakubo." August 25, 2011.

Wang, Dongxia, ed. 2003. *Cong changpao magua dao xizhuang gelü* (From Cheongsam to Western Suits and Leather Shoes). Chengdu: Sichuan Renmin Press.

Wang, Zhao. 1999. "Qianyan (Preface)." In *Zhongguo xiandai fuzhuangshi*, eds, Yuying An and Genrong Jin, 1–2. Beijing: China Light Industry Press.

Watson, James, ed. 1997. *Golden Arches East: McDonald's in East Asia*. Stanford: Stanford University Press.

Wilson, Verity. 1999. "Dress and the Cultural Revolution." In *China Chic: East Meets West*, ed. V. Steele and J. S. Major, 167–186. New Haven and London: Yale University Press.

Wolf, Eric. 1982. *Europe and the People without History*. Berkeley: University of California Press.

Woodmansee, Martha. 1994. *The Author, Art, and the Market: Reading the History of Aesthetics*. New York: Columbia University Press.

World Trade Organization. 2009. International Trade Statistics (2009). http://www.wto.org/english/res_e/statis_e/statis_e.htm, last accessed September 25, 2010.

Wu, Juanjuan. 2009. *Chinese Fashion: From Mao to Now*. Oxford: Berg.

Wu, Renxu. 2005. *Sheci de nüren*. Taipei: Sanmin Press.

Xinhuawang. 2001. "Lingdaoren shenzhou zhongguo minzu teshefuzhuang banliang APEC." October 21, 2001. http://www.xinhua.org/news, accessed August 30, 2002.

Xinhuawang. 2002. "Yiyezhijian quanminjie "tang" tangzhuangre jihuo chuantong fuzhuangye." February 12, 2002. http://www.xinhua.org/news, accessed August 30, 2002.

Xinmin zhoukan. 2001. "Tuxian zhongguo minzu teshe." October 30, 2001.

Xu, Kunyuan. 2004. "Zhongguo fangzhigongye fazhan xianzhuang yu qushi." In *China Textile Industry Development Report 2003/2004*, 172–177. Beijing: China Textile Press.

Yang, Yuan. 1999. *Zhongguo minzu fushi wenhua tudian*. Chongqing: Public Culture Press.

Yang, Yuan, ed. 2003. *Zhongguo fushi, bainian shishang*. Huhuhaote: Yuangfang Press.

Yuan, Jieyin. 1994. *Zhongguo lidai fushi shi*. Beijing: Higher Education Press.

Zhang, Li, and Aihwa Ong. 2008. *Privatizing China: Socialism from Afar*. Ithaca: Cornell University Press.

Zhang, Wanli. 2002. "Twenty Years of Research on Stratified Social Structure in Contemporary China." *Social Sciences in China* (Spring): 48–58.

Zhang, Yingchun. 2001. *Zhongxifang nüzhuang zhaoxin bijiao* (Comparison of forms in Chinese and western women's dress). Beijing: China Light Industry Press.

Zhao, Jianhua. 2004. "Social Life of the Qipao: Clothing and Gender Politics in Contemporary China." Proceedings of the Textile Institute 83rd World Conference, 1592–1598.

Zhonghuawang. 2001. "APEC texie." October 21, 2001. http://news.sohu.com/53/20/news146972053.shtml, accessed August 30, 2002.

Zhongxinshe. 2002. "Shencheng fengjingxian: Shanghai danshengle tangzhuang yitiaojie." January 31, 2002. http://www.chinanews.com/, accessed August 30, 2002.

Zhou, Xun, and Gao Chunmin. 1984. *Zhongguo fushi wuqiannian*. Shanghai: Xuelin Press.

Index

Note: Chinese names are indexed as they are used in China; that is, the surname is followed by the first name, such as Wu Bangguo. Authors with Chinese names follow the English convention; that is, the surname is followed by comma and then the first name, such as Wu, Juanjuan. Page numbers in italics indicate illustrations.